F O R E S T S

ROBERT POGUE HARRISON

FORESTS

THE SHADOW OF CIVILIZATION

THE UNIVERSITY OF CHICAGO PRESS
Chicago & London

The University of Chicago Press, Chicago 60637
The University of Chicago Press, Ltd., London
© 1992 by The University of Chicago
All rights reserved. Published 1992
Paperback edition 1993
Printed in the United States of America
15 14 13 12 11   8 9 10

ISBN: 0-226-31807-9 (paperback)

Library of Congress Cataloging-in-Publication Data

Harrison, Robert Pogue.
     Forests : the shadow of civilization / Robert Pogue Harrison.
         p.   cm.
     Includes bibliographical references and index.
         1. Forests and forestry in literature.   I. Title.
     PN56.F64H37   1992
     809'9336—dc20   91-29531
                                                              CIP

♾ The paper used in this publication meets the minimum requirements of the
American National Standard for Information Sciences—Permanence of Paper
for Printed Library Materials, ANSI Z39.48-1992.

FOR MICHEL SERRES

De la Judée à Tunis, au Maroc, et d'autre part d'Athènes à Gênes, toutes ces cimes chauves qui regardent d'en haut la Méditerranée ont perdue leur couronne de culture, de forêts. Et reviendra-t-elle? Jamais. Si les antiques dieux, les races actives et fortes, sous qui fleurissaient ces rivages, sortaient aujourd'hui du tombeau, ils diraient: "Tristes *peuples du Livre,* de grammaire et de mots, de subtilités vaines, qu'avez-vous fait de la Nature?"

Jules Michelet, *La Bible de l'Humanité* 2:9

[C O N T E N T S]

[PREFACE]

WHEN THE ARCTIC FREEZE BEGAN TO SPREAD SOUTHWARD during the onslaught of the last ice age, the forests that had once covered much of the northern hemisphere disappeared under the advancing sheets of ice like algae under the roll of a long and luminous ocean wave. As global warming trends caused the glaciers to retreat many millennia later, the forests cropped up again as if they had merely weathered the season in hibernation: a spontaneous generation of arboreal, floral, and cryptogamal life.

Ice ages have come and gone, come again and gone again; and each time the glaciers pulled back—most recently, some ten to fifteen thousand years ago—the forests returned to recolonize the land. In short, most of the places of human habitation in the West were at some time in the past more or less densely forested. However broadly or narrowly one wishes to define it, Western civilization literally cleared its space in the midst of forests. A sylvan fringe of darkness defined the limits of its cultivation, the margins of its cities, the boundaries of its institutional domain; but also the extravagance of its imagination. For reasons this book explores, the governing institutions of the West— religion, law, family, city—originally established themselves in opposition to the forests, which in this respect have been, from the beginning, the first and last victims of civic expansion. The following study, however, does not recount a merely empirical history about how civilization has encroached upon the forests, exploited them, cultivated them, managed them, or simply devastated them. It tells the more elusive story of the role forests have played in the cultural imagination of the West.

The story is full of enigmas and paradoxes. If forests appear in our religions as places of profanity, they also appear as sacred. If they have typically been considered places of lawlessness, they have also provided havens for those who took up the cause of justice and fought the law's corruption. If they evoke associations of danger and abandon in our minds, they also evoke scenes of enchantment. In other words, in the religions, mythologies, and literatures of the West, the forest appears as a place where the logic of distinction goes astray. Or where our subjective categories are confounded. Or where perceptions become promiscuous with one another, disclosing latent dimensions of time and consciousness. In the forest the inanimate may suddenly become animate, the god turns into a beast, the outlaw stands for justice, Rosalind appears as a boy, the virtuous knight degenerates into a wild man, the straight line forms a circle, the ordinary gives way to the fabulous. In what follows I not only trace these paths of error in the Western imagination but also account for them in terms of specific historical frameworks.

I had originally noticed the consistency of such patterns in medieval and Renaissance literature, but I soon discovered that, just as forests were once everywhere in the geographical sense, so too they were everywhere in the fossil record of cultural memory. Given that no one, as far as I can tell, has ever treated the subject as a whole, I decided to undertake the labor of writing a comprehensive, though selective, history of forests in the Western imagination. By comprehensive I mean that the book begins with antiquity and ends in our own time, following the conventional epochal divisions of cultural history (there are, however, significant deviations from the line of chronology). By selective I mean that I was obliged to limit radically the forest scenes I chose to discuss. I wanted to avoid at all costs a mere encyclopedic catalog of the forest theme and to offer the reader a more intriguing, thought-provoking essay. Hence there are many forests I was forced to leave out of the book, and I have no doubts that there are many more of which I am simply unaware. I have written *a* history, not *the* history, of the topic. I feel reassured by the fact that countless other versions, quite different from my own, are possible here. If I have learned anything during the course of my work it is that the forest is uncircumscribable. To traverse it means also to shun vast areas of it.

I do not presume to defend my principle of selection on strictly objective grounds. It is neither wholly objective nor wholly subjective, but both. I have relied on intuition, to be sure, but also on the demands of narrative viability in the midst of a rather unviable matter. My hope is that the book will help disclose a hitherto unthematized dimension of cultural and literary history and that it will encourage others to pursue the forest theme in areas untouched by my investigation.

It is hard to believe that just six years ago, when the idea for such a book first came to me, there was very little talk about forests in the news. Since then the fate of the remaining forests on earth has become a major worldwide issue. In what follows I do not rehearse the well-known problems associated with planetary deforestation—the loss of wildlife habitat, of biodiversity, of climate regulation, and so forth; rather, I take them for granted. What I hope to show is how many untold memories, ancient fears and dreams, popular traditions, and more recent myths and symbols are going up in the fires of deforestation which we hear so much about today and which trouble us for reasons we often do not fully understand rationally but which we respond to on some other level of cultural memory. In the history of Western civilization forests represent an outlying realm of opacity which has allowed that civilization to estrange itself, enchant itself, terrify itself, ironize itself, in short to project into the forest's shadows its secret and innermost anxieties. In this respect the loss of forests entails more than merely the loss of ecosystems. (The fifth and final chapter of the book summarizes my vision of what is at stake for Western *culture,* if not nature, in current ecological debates about forests.)

Since I began working on this topic I have been asked on several occasions how the idea for it came to me. In fact I cannot remember exactly when or where the idea originated. What I do remember, however, is a trip to the provinces of the Veneto, in Italy, to visit the great Italian poet Andrea Zanzotto. In particular I remember an excursion to the Montello mountain, where Zanzotto walked us through remnants of the vast *selva antica,* or ancient forest, which had stood there for millennia but which has all but disappeared now. There and then I perhaps realized that the forest, in its enduring antiquity, was the correlate of the poet's memory, and that once its remnants were gone, the poet would fall into oblivion.

Robert Pogue Harrison
Stanford, 1991

This book does not contain numbered footnotes or endnotes. Notes and references have been consigned to the sections entitled "Notes and Bibliography" and "Works Cited."

[ACKNOWLEDGMENTS]

THIS BOOK IS DEDICATED TO MICHEL SERRES BUT ITS REAL-
ization owes a great deal to several people. Above all to Tyrus Miller,
whose help was invaluable during the revision process and whose
many creative suggestions made it a better book. Thomas Sheehan
was of significant help, both critically and morally, during the earlier
and later stages of composition. Likewise Pierre Saint-Amand's reading of almost the entire manuscript at various stages was a generous
source of inspiration and encouragement. I am grateful to Peter Pierson for our several forest conversations at the MacArthur Park restau-
rant in Palo Alto and, more specifically, for his critical reading of the
first two chapters. Seth Lerer's suggestions for the second chapter were
especially welcome. My sister Sandra Harrison served as my ideal
reader throughout the writing process. My brother Thomas Harrison
provided decisive critical advice. I remain indebted to Giuseppe Mazzotta for his formative influence on my intellectual work in general.

My sincere thanks go also to the following people for their direct
or indirect support: A. R. Ammons, Daniel Herwitz, Arnold David-
son, Stanley Cavell, Stefano Velotti, Rachel Jacoff, René Girard, Jeffrey
Schnapp, Jean-Marie Apostolides, James Winchell, Andrea Nightin-
gale, and Katie Gibson. Special thanks also to Alan Thomas of the
University of Chicago Press for his enthusiasm about my project and
his excellent job as editor.

I am grateful to Stanford University for its continuing generosity
and to the Stanford Humanities Center for my year there as a fellow in
1990–91, during which I was able to finish the book.

Heartfelt thanks to Molly and Stewart Agras for being such pleasant neighbors and for providing me with an ideal working environment next door to them. My deepest thanks, finally, go to Antonia,
without whose companionship I could not have written this book.

This was the order of human institutions: first the forests, after that the huts, then the villages, next the cities, and finally the academies.

Giambattista Vico, *The New Science*, §239

Giambattista Vico, *New
Science* (frontispiece)

FIRST *THE* FORESTS

IT IS NOT ONLY IN THE MODERN IMAGINATION THAT FOR-
ests cast their shadow of primeval antiquity; from the beginning they
appeared to our ancestors as archaic, as antecedent to the human
world. We gather from mythology that their vast and somber wilderness was there before, like a precondition or matrix of civilization, or
that—as the epigraph to this book suggests—the forests were *first*.
Such myths, which everywhere look back to a forested earth, no
doubt recall the prehistoric landscape of the West, yet this by itself does
not explain why human societies, once they emerged from the gloom
of origins, preserved such fabulous recollections of the forests' antecedence. Why, for example, should the founding legends of the
greatest of ancient cities declare that Rome had a sylvan origin? When
Aeneas travels up the Tiber and comes to the site of the future imperial
city, he finds himself in a wondrous forest. His host, Evander, explains
to him:

> These woodland places
> Once were homes of local fauns and nymphs
> Together with a race of men that came
> From tree trunks, from hard oak: they had no way
> Of settled life, no arts of life, no skill
> At yoking oxen, gathering provisions,
> Practising husbandry, but got their food
> From oaken bough and wild game hunted down.
> In that first time, out of Olympian heaven,
> Saturn came here in flight from Jove in arms,

I

An exile from a kingdom lost; he brought
These unschooled men together from the hills
Where they were scattered, gave them laws, and chose
The name of Latium, from his latency
Or safe concealment in this countryside. (*Aeneid* 8.415–29)

Virgil's Roman contemporaries might have read such a passage more naively than we do. They might have recalled how the hills of the imperial city were not so long ago still forested, and in their minds two images—forest and city—might have fused together to create an uncanny psychological effect. Evander's description of an Arcadian-like forest, where aboriginal men were born from the oaks, would have helped them not only to imagine a forest in their minds but also to feel in their veins, as it were, a genealogical affiliation with the wooded world of nature. They would have felt the affiliation as something lost or ruptured, to be sure, but to liberate such feelings of loss is the peculiar function of myths of origin, which so invariably speak to our nostalgias.

We will have more to say about the sylvan prehistory of Rome later in this chapter, as well as the paradoxical attitude of reverence and hostility toward origins which characterizes not only the founding legends of Rome but so many of the myths that look back to the forests. For however implicated they may be in civilization's prehistory, the mythic forests of antiquity stand opposed to the city in some fundamental way. We will find that Rome can become Rome only by overcoming, or effacing, the forests of its origins. Yet in the long run the city is overcome in turn by what it subdued: in the forests to the north Rome's doom awaited its time. Tacitus saw prefigurations of it in the German forests whose hardy tribes offered a contrast to Rome's moral and civic decadence. Likewise when Dionysos appears at the city of Thebes and leads the maddened citizens into the forests of the Cithaeron mountain, the king who opposes Dionysos in the name of civic law brings about the downfall of the house of Cadmus.

What is that antagonism, however imaginary, all about? Why does the law of civilization define itself from the outset over against the forests? For what obscure religious reasons is our humanity, in its traditional alienation from the animal kingdom, incompatible with that aboriginal environment? How is it that forests represent an abomination? These are questions that ask about the psychic origins of antiquity's founding institutions. They ask about the most archaic religious conceptions that first traumatized the relation between humanity and nature, indeed, that established the relation *as* a trauma. Questions such as these cannot be pursued merely empirically but rather by way of a genetic psychology of the earliest myths and fables, which preserve in their figures the hieroglyphs of that enigmatic psychic history from which empirical history derives its inspiration.

We have a remarkable starting point from which to pursue a psychology of this sort. In the eighteenth century an Italian theorist from Naples, Giambattista Vico, set out to recover the earliest modes of thought of the "gentile peoples." In his *New Science* (1744) he applied to ancient myths a genetic psychology that led him deep into the forests of prehistory in search of the origins of what he called the three "universal institutions" of humanity—religion, matrimony, and burial of the dead. Like most theories that have aged, Vico's too becomes a fable in retrospect, but since psychic origins are in any case never factual but fabulous, the *New Science* offers the sort of imaginative insight that makes its theory irrevocable, even long after it has become a fable. Indeed, it is precisely as a fable that it provides its most essential insights, which is one of several reasons why the present chapter gets underway in Vico's landscape of origins.

With Vico we also are introduced to the logic of tragedy which the present chapter goes on to explore in the myths of antiquity relevant to our theme. Tragedy reveals itself in this context as a fatal collision between divergent laws. This extreme edge, where opposing laws strive against one another and where the more primordial one wins out, is the boundary at which the city meets the forest. But again, what is this boundary all about? Where and when was it drawn?

VICO'S GIANTS

Dispersed throughout those primeval forests that spread across the earth after the flood, Noah's descendants gradually lost their humanity over the generations and became solitary, nefarious creatures living under the cover of branches and leaves. They became bestial "giants." Abandoned early on by their mothers, they grew up without families or consciousness, feeding on fruits and searching for water. They were shy, brutal, restless, incestuous, and lacked any notion of a higher law than their own instincts and desires. They copulated on sight, aggressively and shamelessly, exercising no restraint whatsoever over their bodily motions, and they roamed the forests incessantly. This is what Vico calls the giant's "bestial freedom"—a freedom from terror and authority, a freedom from fathers.

Wandering through forests grown extremely dense from the flood, the giants could not have suspected that beyond the canopies that shielded them there was such a thing as the sky. What is the sky, after all, if not the prodigious emptiness of an abstraction we have come to take for granted? But one day, some two centuries after Noah's time, the earth had dried up enough to send up exhalations or matter igniting in the air. On that occasion the sky burst with thunder and flashed with lightning for the first time since the great flood. Vico writes:

> Thereupon a few giants, who must have been the most ro-
> bust, and who were dispersed through the forests on the
> mountain heights where the strongest beasts have their dens,
> were frightened and astonished by the great effect whose
> cause they did not know, and raised their eyes and became
> aware of the sky. And because in such a case the nature of the
> human mind leads it to attribute its own nature to the effect,
> and because in that state their nature was that of men all ro-
> bust bodily strength, who expressed their very violent pas-
> sions by shouting and grumbling, they pictured the sky to
> themselves as a great animated body, which in that aspect
> they called Jove, the first god of the so-called greater gentes,
> who meant to tell them something by the hiss of his bolts
> and clap of his thunder. (*New Science,* §377)

Thunder rolls, lightning flashes, the giants, terrified, raise their eyes and become aware of the sky. But what did the giants see when they raised their eyes? What does one see vertically or laterally in a dense forest? The mute closure of foliage. The boundless oblivion of the dormant mind. What, then, did the giants see when they raised their eyes? They saw nothing: a sudden illumination of nothingness. They heard the "hiss of his bolts and clap of his thunder," but precisely because they saw nothing, or at least nothing definite, they had to "picture the sky to themselves" in the aspect of a huge animated body: a body not *seen* but *imagined* as there beyond the treetops.

This act of picturing an image within the mind marks, for Vico, the first humanizing event in prehistory. The giants produce an image in the empty space of their minds—a space as empty and abysmal as the sky itself. In this manner the first human idea was born: that of Jove, father of the world, hurling the lightning bolt from his abode in the sky. In the guise of Jupiter and Zeus, this deity will later reign supreme among the gods of antiquity.

To this first bolt of lightning Vico traces the primitive origins of the Age of Enlightenment, in which humanity comes to perfection. Awoken from its stupor by the lightning bolt, the human mind laboriously created the civic world and eventually attained its greatest achievements, namely science, metaphysics, and the institutions of human justice. When that first bolt struck over the heads of the giants, it announced an unearthly imperative beyond the closure of the forest. Only by the power of its terror could it ignite the first spark of human consciousness in the dull minds of the giants and thus force them to restrain their bestial urges.

From the moment the giants took cognizance of Jove's divine authority, the forests could no longer contain their consciousness, for the latter originated in its submission to something external—to a father who communicated by means of celestial signs. All of nature turned uncanny for the giants, for they now believed "that Jove commanded by signs, that such signs were real words, and that nature was the language of Jove" (§379). Thus at the origin of the first universal institution of humanity, that is, religion, was a disclosure of *logos,* or horizon of sense. The world suddenly became meaningful. It became phenomenal. It became, precisely, a *world*—and no longer a mere habitat.

The trauma of this awakening lies in the fact that Jove, at the very moment of his revelation, concealed himself. In his concealment he communicated his will through signs. Henceforth he would play a game of hide-and-seek with the disoriented giants, obliging them to scrutinize the auspices in order to divine his hidden intentions. Vico insists that the celestial auspices—signs in the sky, such as the lightning or the flight of birds—were the first of all languages, preceding even human phonetic language. The auspices were literally the language of god (*theo-logia*), and literacy in this divine language was later called "divination." Thus the first of all human ideas, the idea of divinity, implied an idea of providence: the intentional, meaningful, and nonrandom character of events.

Do we understand what this means? With the idea of a provident divinity in their minds, the giants were projected into the dreadful future of time. But what is the future? What is this dimension that is neither present nor absent? The future for the giants was an indefinite possibility that they sought to render definite by means of their divinatory theology. Divination was the science by which they hoped to secure signs of an insecure future. Jove, who opened time, also obscured its destiny—that was his ultimate power. To allay the anxieties of destiny the first giants provided for their families; that is to say, they "looked forward" (*pro-videre*) into the future by interpreting the auspices.

Given the supremacy of this law of the auspices, the forests became profane for a simple reason: they obstructed the communication of Jove's intentions. In other words, their canopies concealed an open view of the sky. We find here in Vico's text a fabulous insight, for the abomination of forests in Western history derives above all from the fact that, since Greek and Roman times at least, we have been a civilization of sky-worshippers, children of a celestial father. *Where divinity has been identified with the sky, or with the eternal geometry of the stars, or with cosmic infinity, or with "heaven," the forests become monstrous, for they hide the prospect of god.*

The second universal institution of humanity, matrimony, is also by nature hostile to the forest environment. Vico speculates that the first sign from Jove—the thunder and lightning—must have surprised some of the giants in the act of copulating. In their terror they took this sign as a command to eternalize the sexual union, or to become monogamous and so establish the institution of matrimony, with its linear family genealogy. But matrimony could not institute itself in the forests, for the forests encouraged dispersion, independence, lawlessness, polygamy, and even incest between father and daughter, mother and son. Folding time within its promiscuous matrix, the forests would have promptly disoriented the line of genealogical succession. In short, for the family to establish itself as a divine institution under the open sky, it had to clear a space for itself in the forest's midst. Only within the clearing could the family maintain its cohesion and guard its genealogy against the "infamous promiscuity" of the wilderness.

Or one could think of it in this way: where a primeval forest has already colonized the earth, the first human families had to clear the oak trees in order to plant another kind of tree: the genealogical tree. To burn out a clearing in the forest and to claim it as the sacred ground of the family—that, according to Vico, was the original deed of appropriation that first opened the space of civil society. It was the first decisive act, religiously motivated, which would lead to the founding of cities, nations, and empire.

Merely clearing the forest, however, was not in itself sufficient to ground the family in its clearing. In order to plant the genealogical tree and secure the place of residence under the auspices of god, burial ceremonies were necessary. Burial guaranteed the full appropriation of ground and its ultimate sacralization. Through burial of the dead the family defined the boundary of its place of belonging, rooting itself quite literally in the soil, or *humus,* where ancestral fathers lived underground. Humanity is bound to these funeral rites. The *humus* grounds the human. Burial preserves in its soil the essence of humanity. So while the universal institutions of humanity derive their law from the sky, they must ultimately take root in the ground. This is a paradox indeed, for by turning toward the openness of the sky humanity commits its essence to the enclosure of the earth.

By virtue of the burial of their dead, the giants could now claim that they belonged to a noble family "born of the earth," or born of ancestors lying in the ground. Vico writes:

> Thus by the graves of their buried dead the giants showed
> their dominion over their lands . . . With truth they could
> pronounce these heroic phrases: we are sons of this earth, we
> are born from these oaks. Indeed, the heads of families
> among the Latins called themselves *stirpes* and *stipites,* stems
> or stocks, and their progeny were called *propagines,* slips or
> shoots. In Italian such families were called *legnaggi,* lineages.
> And the most noble houses of Europe and almost all its
> reigning families take their names from the land over which
> they rule. (§531)

The giants in their respective clearings claim dominion over the land by demonstration: We are sons of *this* earth, we are born from *these* oaks. Which earth? Which oaks? They point: this earth *here,* where the wooden graveposts mark the presence of our ancestors in the ground. These posts are the oaks from which we are born. We belong to this place, for our tree has been planted here. These oaks, or these graveposts, have sprung up under the auspices of god. The family tree supplants the oak tree and thereby grounds the universal institutions of humanity: religion, matrimony, and burial of the dead.

We have here the fabulous origins of a phenomenon that we will encounter again and again throughout this study, namely the appropriation of the forest as a metaphor for human institutions. Human beings have by no means exploited the forest only materially; they have also plundered its trees in order to forge their fundamental etymologies, symbols, analogies, structures of thought, emblems of identity, concepts of continuity, and notions of system. *From the family tree to the tree of knowledge, from the tree of life to the tree of memory, forests have provided an indispensable resource of symbolization in the cultural evolution of humankind,* so much so that the rise of modern scientific thinking remains quite unthinkable apart from the prehistory of such metaphorical borrowings. Even the concept of the circle, we are told, comes from the internal concentric rings laid bare by the felling of trees (Bechmann, 258–63).

In such a manner, then, the three universal institutions instantiate the three temporal ecstasies which, properly speaking, define humanity's abode on the earth. Religion, matrimony, and burial of the dead embody the linear openness of time. Religion is born of the idea of providence. It implies an awareness of the future. Burial of the dead is grounded in reverence for the past, for the ancestral, in short for what we call tradition. Tradition comes to us from the domain of the dead. Both religion and burial, in turn, serve to consolidate the contract of matrimony, which maintains the genealogical line in the present.

This unearthly openness of linear time within nature's closed cycle of generation and decay is what underlies, at the deepest level, the enduring hostility between the institutional order and the forests that lie at its boundaries. Precisely because they lie beyond its horizon of linear time forests can easily confuse the psychology of human orientation. Later in this book we will see how often a protagonist wandering through a forest experiences a terrifying or enchanting loss of temporal boundaries, as if he or she had passed into a world of implications which renders our deepest structural categories superfluous or unreal. For as Vico's theory of the origins of human institutions suggests, we dwell in the disclosure of time. History pertains to clearings that correspond both literally and figuratively to the purely psychic reality of human consciousness.

One of Vico's lasting contributions is his creative archaeology of the metaphorical origins of human thought. He himself claimed that the breakthrough of his *New Science* was its recovery of what he called the "Poetic Wisdom" of the first ages. He argued that the primitive mind thought concretely, not abstractly, conceiving and signifying the world by means of "poetic characters" (*generi fantastici*). Poetic characters are imaginative personifications of generic concepts. In the minds of the giants every image or idea (they amounted to the same) was a poetic character, since, as Vico declares, "not being able to form intelligible class concepts, [the first men] had a natural need to create poetic characters; that is imaginative class concepts or universals, to which, as to certain models or ideal portraits, to reduce all the particular species which resembled them." (*New Science*, §209).

These poetic characters account for the genesis of the various deities of antiquity. Neptune, for example, originally figured as an imaginative universal by which the boundless extension of the sea was brought within the limits of an anthropomorphic image. Likewise all flowers in their particular diversities were gathered up in the image of Flora, an animate goddess; fruits in their multiple varieties were perceived in the character of Pomona, another goddess; and the earth as a whole was understood and signified in the character of the goddess Cybele (§402). Later in the mind's evolutionary cycle, when the capacity for synthetic thought became more developed, an abstraction like "courage" would be personified by the poetic character of Achilles, "shrewdness" by the character of Odysseus. In the *New Science* a number of the mythological as well as "historical" figures of antiquity turn out to be poetic characters. More than half a century before Friedrich August Wolf (1759–1824) put forward his revolutionary theories about the authorship of the *Iliad* and *Odyssey*, Vico had already claimed that Homer was not a historical individual at all but rather a poetic character for the popular wisdom of the Greek people as a whole. Likewise, well before Barthold Niebuhr (1776–1831) argued that the history of the foundation of Rome was essentially based on ancient myth, Vico had suggested that the legendary founder of Rome, Romulus, may originally have been a poetic character for the assembled family fathers who established the first Roman senate in prehistoric times (§414).

The case of Vulcan is particularly interesting, for it leads us back to the first family clearings in the forests. The most ancient myths indicate that this god, Vulcan, was related to the race of the Cyclops. Vico suggests that Vulcan and the Cyclops must originally have been two distinct, but related, poetic characters. The Cyclops were poetic characters for the pious, god-fearing giants in their respective clearings. Vulcan, on the other hand, was originally a poetic character for the otherwise abstract concept of "technical capacity" among these Cyclopean family fathers. In a remarkable passage of the *New Science* Vico explains:

> Every clearing was called a *lucus,* in the sense of an eye, as even today we call eyes the openings through which light en-

ters houses. The true heroic phrase that "every giant had his *lucus*" [clearing or eye] was altered and corrupted when its meaning was lost, and had already been falsified when it reached Homer, for it was then taken to mean that every giant had one eye in the middle of his forehead. With these giants came Vulcan to work in the first forges—that is, the forests to which Vulcan had set fire and where he had fashioned the first arms, which were the spears with burnt tips—and, by an extension of the idea of arms, to forge bolts for Jove. For Vulcan had set fire to the forests in order to observe in the open sky the direction from which Jove sent his bolts. (§564)

Lucus, clearing, eye. This is the eye, or burnt-out clearing, whose poetic character was already corrupted by the time it reached Homer. By a paradoxical reversal of poetic logic, Homer places this eye in the middle of the Cyclops's forehead and has Odysseus blind it with the burnt tip of an uprooted tree trunk, thus bringing the forest's darkness back upon the Cyclops's eye again.

The master of technical skill, Vulcan is the one who opens the eye. He sets fire to the forest in order to be able to see the direction of the lightning bolt, that is, to read the auspices. Fire itself came from this divine celestial source. Technology appropriated its uses for the purpose of deforestation. Hence technology too takes its origins from the sky. Vulcan forges the lightning bolt for Jove, fashions the giants' arms of war, and launches the missile through space by mastering the powers of the sacred fire.

But if fire was sacred in origin it was because it enabled the giants to open the eye through which god's intentions could be seen and scrutinized. As an obstacle to visibility, the forests also remained an obstacle to human knowledge and science. By burning out a clearing in the forest, Vulcan prepared the way for the future science of enlightened times:

> Thus in their science of augury the Romans used the verb *contemplari* for observing the parts of the sky whence the auguries came or the auspices were taken. These regions, marked out by the augurs with their wands, were called temples of the sky (*templa caeli*), whence must have come to the Greeks their first *theoremata* and *mathemata,* things divine

or sublime to contemplate, which eventuated in metaphysical and mathematical abstractions. (§391)

The *lucus,* then, was the original site of our theologies and cosmologies, our physics and metaphysics, in short, our "contemplations." The temples of the sky were the first tables of science. Science meanwhile has advanced a great deal since the time of its divinatory origins, but has it in any way altered its nature? For all its strides and breakthroughs in abstraction, science has never yet lost its initial vocation, nor has Vulcan ceased laboring to keep the eye of knowledge open. One way or another science preserves its allegiance to the sky. Space travel remains its ultimate ambition. It predicts the eclipse, contemplates the stars, observes the comet, telescopes the cosmic abyss. One way or another it continues to scrutinize the auspices, attending upon the celestial sign; and one way or another the vocation as well as criteria of science remain that of prediction.

As a humanist in the deepest traditional sense, Vico saw in the forests the place of humankind's perdition. His humanism, though, was in no way triumphalistic. Vico did his best to argue that the Christian God held sway over the "ideal eternal history" of humankind, yet despite its orthodox intentions the *New Science* ends up telling a disconsolate story about the order of institutions—a story that promises little or nothing in the way of salvation. Of the three universal institutions of humanity, burial remains the most primordial and irrevocable, for it grounds history in what history wants to overcome. What history opens up in the midst of the forests, the forests will once again draw back into its closure, for Vico's theory of the institutional order was that of a system governed by the law of entropy: "This was the order of human institutions: first the forests, after that the huts, then the villages, next the cities, and finally the academies" (§239). The order is systematic, progressive, and self-sustaining, but it comes to an end, haunted by finitude. An inner law of dissolution drives the system to disorder. This entropic drive becomes clear when we consider the correlates of Vico's axiom: "The nature of peoples is first crude, then severe, then benign, then delicate, finally dissolute" (§242). And in the same context: "Men first feel necessity, then look for utility, next attend to comfort, still later amuse themselves with pleasure, thence grow dissolute in luxury, and finally go mad and waste their substance" (§241). The drive toward greater and greater synthesis which sustains the order throughout the initial stages eventually takes a turn and gives way to analysis, and then to collapse. Why? What is it that leads to the system's undoing? Why do civilizations fall after the long labor of rising?

In a word, irony. In the trope of irony Vico saw the inertia of critical analysis. Irony, he remarks, is "fashioned of falsehood by dint of a reflection that wears the mask of truth" (§408). Vico reminds us that prior to its ability to think abstractly, the primitive mind was unable even to conceive of a distinction between truth and falsehood (so many centuries does it take even to become aware of such a dichotomy). But once the mind fully develops its powers of abstraction, critical reason becomes ironic. Reflecting on the pieties and customs of the past, irony discovers that they were based on errors and arbitrary beliefs. Thus a consciousness that has reached the stage of irony tends to repudiate the authority of tradition as lacking in either necessity or justification. An ever greater ironic distance from the past leads to skepticism about the institutions that had hitherto "preserved humanity" and prevented its fall back into bestiality. If such irony follows its course toward unrestrained cynicism, it can create the conditions for a new barbarism at the heart of the enlightened city of man. Vico calls it the "barbarism of reflection." In the final conclusion of the *New Science,* he observes:

> But if the peoples are rotting in that ultimate civil disease
> [skepticism] and cannot agree on a monarch from within,
> and are not conquered and preserved by better nations from
> without, then providence for their extreme ill has its extreme
> remedy at hand. For such peoples, like so many beasts, have
> fallen into the custom of each man thinking only of his own
> private interests and have reached the extreme of delicacy, or
> better of pride, in which like wild animals they bristle and
> lash out at the slightest displeasure. Thus no matter how
> great the throng and press of their bodies, they live like wild
> beasts in a deep solitude of spirit and will, scarcely any two
> being able to agree since each follows his own pleasure or ca-
> price. By reason of all this, providence decrees that, through
> obstinate factions and desperate civil wars, they shall turn
> their cities into forests and the forests into dens and lairs of
> men. In this way, through long centuries of barbarism, rust
> will consume the misbegotten subtleties of malicious wits
> that have turned them into beasts made more inhuman by the

barbarism of reflection than the first men had been made by
the barbarism of sense. (§1106)

Perhaps the *New Science,* in the final analysis, was an admonition
to the Age of Enlightenment about its principle virtue: critical reason.
Or perhaps Vico truly believed that the Christian era would break the
fatality of the *corsi* and *ricorsi* of history and perpetuate the "radiant
humanity" he saw flourishing under the benevolent monarchies of Europe during the early eighteenth century. One thing, in any case, is
certain: Vico had more than a figurative analogy in mind when he
spoke of cities becoming forests. The figurative and the literal in this
case overlap. At the end of the order of institutions cities become like
forests in the figurative sense—places of spiritual solitude where savagery lurks in the hearts of men and women—but this demoralization
merely prepares the way for a literal metamorphosis of the city itself.
As the city disintegrates from within, the forests encroach from without. The ancient city of Rome, whose destiny so preoccupied and fascinated Vico, was eventually reclaimed by the forests, first by analogy,
then in the form of forest-peoples from the north, and finally by the
vegetation belt itself. The Forum became wild pasture land for Dark
Age cattle. Wilderness overgrew the roads that led to Rome. The work
of history fell to the ground it had tried to surmount under the auspices of god. This is the ground, or *humus,* of the ancestors. As the
subterranean commandments of the dead cease to persuade the ironic
generations, the forests gradually overtake the clearings and close the
lids of the *lucus.*

THE DEMON OF GILGAMESH

Vico's imaginative reconstruction of the beginnings of things human
tells the story of a fundamental hostility, religious in origin, between
the institutions of humanity and the outlying forests. Humanity in its
very essence is a historical, that is, extraforestial, phenomenon for
Vico. To be human means to dwell in the openness of time, in defiance
of the oblivion of nature, and hence to be governed by memory, which
maintains the temporal coherence between past and future. By com-
mitting the dead to the ground, burial consigns the ancestors to the
past and ceremoniously assures that they will live on in the memory of
tradition, whose authority governs society and commands reverence
from the quick.

Memory in this primary sense, then, does not merely look backward to the has-been; it also preempts the future by virtue of its promise to save whatever exists in time from oblivion. The future too belongs to the monuments of memory, for *the drive to be remembered* looks forward to the memory of future generations. This drive to be remembered has motivated most of the deeds and achievements of history and is continuously forging the future—but a future that we experience in advance as past. Human beings, in other words, are always already dead. This proleptic knowledge of finitude predetermines their most creative as well as their most destructive dispositions.

Nowhere does this pitiless logic of transience become more pathetic than in the ancient epic of *Gilgamesh,* whose Sumerian version figures as the oldest literary work in history. Just as the Sumerians draw the boundary line between history and prehistory, thanks to their invention of the art of writing (which is memory par excellence), so Gilgamesh appears as the first great "hero" of civilization, in both the trivial and nontrivial senses of the term "first." Since historians refuse to speak of "civilization" prior to the invention of writing, but at most speak of "culture," Gilgamesh remains the first civic hero to be commemorated in a literary work; but beyond this he is "first" also as an enduring archetype—a sort of grand summary of the spiritual afflictions that arise from the inner, alienated core of civilization. The Sumerian hero's stern individualism; his obsession with death; his tragic and futile quest for personal immortality; his childlike rage against the absurd; his monumental will to power—this profound psychology of finitude which pervades the epic cycle, combined with its venerable antiquity, give *Gilgamesh* the dignity of a truly primary document.

What interests us about the epic above all is the fact that the first antagonist of Gilgamesh is the forest. In all the main versions of the story, the hero's major exploit figures as his long journey from Uruk to the Cedar Mountain to slay the forest's guardian, Huwawa. Why? What is it exactly that inspires Gilgamesh to undertake this journey and deforest the Cedar Mountain? This is our question in the present section. To answer it requires some preliminary background.

Gilgamesh was the legendary but real king of Uruk, a Sumerian city born under the auspices of Anu—god of the sky. He lived during the Early Dynastic II period, around 2700 B.C., some six hundred years before the composition of the first Sumerian epics that commemorate him. In the Sumerian and Babylonian literature Gilgamesh is commonly referred to as the "builder of the walls of Uruk." The epitaph effectively summarizes his civic heroism. Walls, no less than writing, define civilization. They are monuments of resistance against time, like writing itself, and Gilgamesh is remembered by them. Walls protect, divide, distinguish; above all, they *abstract*. The basic activities that sustain life—agriculture and stock breeding, for instance—take place beyond the walls. Within the walls one is within an emporium; one is within the jurisdiction of a bureaucracy; one is within the abstract identity of race, city, and institutionalized religion; in short, one is within the lonely enclosure of history. Gilgamesh is the builder of such walls that divide history from prehistory, culture from nature, sky from earth, life from death, memory from oblivion.

But the same walls that individuate the city, as well its hero, are precisely what oppress Gilgamesh, at least insofar as the epic cycle portrays him. Within his walls Gilgamesh finds himself exposed to insidious reminders of the fatality of personal death—the linear finality of human existence. It is in direct response to his aggravated sense of transience that Gilgamesh decides to undertake his forest journey. In the following passage from Samuel Noah Kramer's translation of "Gilgamesh and the Land of the Living," we hear Gilgamesh declaring to his friend Enkidu that he would perform some glorious deed by which he may inscribe himself within the annals of historical memory:

> O Enkidu, not (*yet*) *have brick and stamp* brought forth *the
>   fated end,*
> I would enter the "land," I would set up my name,
> In its places where the names have been raised up, I would
>   raise up my name,
> In its places where the names have not been raised up,
>   I would raise up the names of the gods. (4–7)

The "land" where Gilgamesh would go and set up his name is the forested Cedar Mountain. Because he has not yet achieved a lasting fame, because he has not yet *stamped his name in brick* (or in the tablets of the scribes), Gilgamesh must go to the "land" and slay the forest demon, Huwawa. This is the deed that will monumentalize him in stone or brick—preserve his memory after death.

But again, why precisely a forest journey? Before we can answer the question we should listen to Gilgamesh's plea to Utu, the Sumerian Sun god. Utu is the god who must grant Gilgamesh the permission to undertake the journey, for the land is in Utu's charge. The god does not understand Gilgamesh's irrational desire to go to the land, nor does he initially approve of the idea. Huwawa, whom Gilgamesh would slay, is after all a sacred forest demon. Utu does not understand why Gilgamesh wishes to challenge the demon. To convince the god of his desperate need to undertake the journey, Gilgamesh offers a pathetic confession:

> "O Utu, I would enter the 'land,' be thou my ally,
> I would enter the land *of the cut-down* cedar, be thou my ally."
> Utu of heaven answers him:
> ". . . verily thou art, but what art thou to the 'land'?"
> "O Utu, a word I would speak to thee, to my word thy ear,
> *I would have it reach thee,* give ear to it.
> In my city man dies, oppressed is the heart,
> Man perishes, heavy is the heart,
> I *peered over* the wall,
> Saw the dead bodies . . . *floating on* the river;
> As for me, I too will be served thus; verily 'tis so.
> Man, the tallest, cannot stretch to heaven,
> Man the widest, cannot *cover* the earth.
> Not (*yet*) *have brick and stamp* brought forth *the fated end,*
> I would enter the 'land,' I would set up my name." (17–31)

In ancient Sumerian funeral rites, the bodies of the dead were floated down the river in ceremonious processions. Gilgamesh has peered over the walls of his city and has seen the bodies floating on the river. In other words he has seen beyond life to the inanimate corpse—the mere object drifting toward decomposition and reintegration with the earth. He has peered over the wall of history and seen the remorseless transcendence of nature. With despair in his heart he has looked at the outlying earth: dumb, inert, insurmountable, revolving her relentless cycles, turning kings into cadavers, waiting impassively to draw all things into her oblivion. Is this not intolerable for someone who is a builder of walls, someone who is devoted to the memorial transcendence of history? Must Gilgamesh not react to the scene of dead bodies floating on the river by challenging such oblivion with the might of memory?

We come closer to accounting psychologically for Gilgamesh's desire to undertake the forest journey. He wants the glory of his deed to spare him from such oblivion. But what glory is there in slaying the forest demon? When Gilgamesh obtains the necessary permission from Utu for his journey, he arrives at the sacred cedar forests and engages Huwawa in battle, cutting off the demon's head. The cutting off of Huwawa's head represents, in its poetic image, the cutting down of the cedar forest. The "glory" of this exploit can be understood only against the historical background. We know from the written records that certain Sumerian individuals actually achieved considerable fame by undertaking expeditions to the cedar forests and seizing huge quantities of timber. Timber was a precious commodity for the Sumerians, since the alluvial plains of Mesopotamia were by that time devoid of forests. In the Early Dynastic periods the Sumerians apparently got their timber from the east, in nearby Elam, but after the deforestation of these regions they had to travel much further to the Amanus mountains in the north. To obtain wood they had to undertake dangerous expeditions to the mountains, cut down the cedars and pines, and ferry the logs back to the cities down the rivers. Such exploits were fraught with peril, especially since the forests were often defended by fierce forest tribes, but a leader could derive considerable fame from a successful expedition.

We can understand, therefore, why Gilgamesh's desire for monumental fame might lead him to conceive of a forest expedition. But the epic probes the hero's psychological motivations much deeper than this. There is more to Gilgamesh's inspiration than mere childish heroism and desire for fame through adventure. If Gilgamesh resolves to kill the forest demon, or to deforest the Cedar Mountain, it is because forests represent the quintessence of what lies beyond the walls of the city, namely the earth in its enduring transcendence. Forests embody another, more ancient law than the law of civilization. When Gilgamesh declares to Utu, "Man, the tallest, cannot stretch to heaven," he avows that human beings, however great, cannot become gods, or attain immortality. And when he declares: "Man the widest, cannot *cover the earth*," he avows that neither can they be like forests, which cover the earth and endure through the millennia according to their own self-regenerating cycles. Gilgamesh, in other words, is trapped within walls that close him off from two dimensions of transcendence, the one vertical and the other horizontal.

Gilgamesh journeys toward the forest as toward the veritable frontier of civilization. The forest is the counterpart of his city. He imagines perhaps that he could transcend the walls that enclose him through an act of massive deforestation. But to understand the hero's deeper psychological motivations we must try to imagine what really goes on in his mind when he peers over the walls of Uruk.

Gilgamesh peers over the walls and sees human bodies floating down the river in funeral processions. The sight of these bodies inspires in him the idea of a forest expedition. It is a visionary moment for Gilgamesh. In revolt against the scene of finitude, Gilgamesh has a vision: he will go to the forests, cut down the trees, and send the logs down the river to the city. In other words, he will make the trees share the fate of those who live within the walls. *Logs will become the cadavers.* The hero who dies within the city will project his own personal fate onto the forests. This is no doubt what Gilgamesh means when he says that he would enter the land and raise up his name. For if he is not wide enough to "cover the earth," yet may he still uncover it.

It is a sorry fact of history that human beings have never ceased reenacting the gesture of Gilgamesh. The destructive impulse with respect to nature all too often has psychological causes that go beyond the greed for material resource or the need to domesticate an environment. There is too often a deliberate rage and vengefulness at work in the assault on nature and its species, as if one would project onto the natural world the intolerable anxieties of finitude which hold humanity hostage to death. There is a kind of childish furor that needs to create victims without in order to exorcise the pathos of victimage within. The epic of *Gilgamesh* tells the story of such furor; but while Gilgamesh ends up as the ultimate victim of his own despair, the logs meanwhile float down the river like bodies of the dead.

From the epic cycle as a whole in its Sumerian and Akkadian versions, we gather that Gilgamesh's expedition to the Cedar Mountain was in fact a vain attempt to overcome the source of his afflictions. To begin with, the slaying of Huwawa angers the gods. It was a sacrilege, for Huwawa had the dignity of a sacred being. In some versions of the story, Gilgamesh's beloved friend, Enkidu, must pay for the crime of killing Huwawa with his own life. Upon the death of his friend Gilgamesh falls into an exacerbated state of melancholy, consuming himself with thoughts about death. Fame and the monuments of memory no longer console him for the fact of dying. That is why Gilgamesh sets out on another journey, this time in search of everlasting life. Yet the long and desperate quest for personal immortality only leads him to the knowledge that death is the ineluctable and nonnegotiable condition of life—that the cadaverous logs he sent down to the city from the Cedar Mountain cannot spare him his last journey of all down the very same river. And this, at the dawn of civilization, is called "wisdom."

From the time of the Cro-Magnon through the end of the last ice age and into the Neolithic period—for over thirty thousand years of its prehistory—the human race was a child of the great Mother goddess. In her round biosphere, life, death, and rebirth recurred eternally, like the cycles of the moon or menstruation. She revolved the seasons and gave the grain, replenished the herds and took the dead back into the safekeeping of her cosmic matrix. She appears to us across the ages as the great lap of the world, the first of all royal thrones. Remarkable icons depict her as huge, swollen with abundance, generous. She is the Cybele of Asia Minor, the fat lady of Malta, the Venus of Laussel with the horn in her hand. There was much that was sacred to her: caves, groves, lakes, mountain peaks . . . The horned bull was especially sacred to her, as were the forests through which it roamed. Those forests were probably the first labyrinths surrounding the sacred caves in whose depths prehistoric artists would impregnate her womb with the forms of wild animals.

Vico had little to say about the prehistory of this goddess, for his *New Science* was seeking to reconstruct the origins of patriarchy, that is to say the religious traumas that led to the differentiations, oppositions, and hierarchies of the patriarchal institutions we discussed in the opening sections of this chapter. Under the goddess's reign, however, earth and sky were not opposed, nor were life and death, animal and human, male and female, inanimate and animate, matter and form, forest and clearing. These unconditional distinctions (which the forest forever confuses) lie at the basis of "civilization" as opposed to mere "culture." We already alluded to this conventional distinction among historians in our discussion of Gilgamesh. Civilization institutes and grounds itself on oppositions. The great Mother, on the other hand, enveloped them and drew them back into the primordial chaos and unity of origins.

In retrospect we could say that the goddess's demise as the dominant deity of antiquity probably represents the most momentous cultural revolution in our human past to date. It was the result, it seems, of her violent overthrow by the male sky gods that erupted on the scene with dreadful fury during the Bronze Age. The nomadic Hebrew tribes, following their sky-and-thunder god, Yahweh, waged a pitiless war against her. Nor was the sky-and-thunder god of the marauding Indo-Europeans less inimical toward the aboriginal earth religions of the settled, Neolithic peoples they encountered in their restless migrations. The Dorians in particular were fiercely intolerant of the goddess, destroying her temples wherever they went.

In Mesopotamian art works Gilgamesh is often depicted as a brawny man with a beard fighting horned bulls, inspired no doubt by the famous episode in the epic cycle which recounts how Gilgamesh slayed the sacred bull of Inanna. Inanna (Semitic Ishtar) was the Sumerian goddess of love. In the epic cycle she appears as a wanton seductress angered by Gilgamesh's presumption in repudiating her charms, but what we see in the figure of Inanna is a historically transformed and degraded version of the great Mother who had once reigned throughout Mesopotamia. As Rachel Levy showed so persuasively in her book *The Gate of Horn,* the bull's horns had been one of the most pervasive symbols of her fertility throughout prehistory. As the slayer of the sacred bull, Gilgamesh figures as a poetic character for the historic triumph of Sumerian patriarchy over the earlier matriarchal religions of Mesopotamia. He slays Inanna's bull and severs its horns as a trophy (a memory), thus severing a bond that had once affiliated the people to an antecedent religion.

Ancient Greece witnessed similar religious revolutions during its prehistory, but in Greece too this goddess lived on in various transfigured versions even after the Olympian gods emerged victorious over the Titans. Her name in Greek is Artemis. She is one of the oldest, most enigmatic of Greek deities. Her worship goes back to the Pre-Hellenic period, but even in historical times she was widely worshipped as a fertility goddess in Asia Minor, her cult being based at Ephesus. From that city there has come down to us the famous marble statue that depicts her standing upright with arms extending outward from the elbows. A congeries of wild animals stare out from her gown and headdress, while her front side is weighed down by multiple bulbs that suggest a proliferation of female breasts. For a long time no one thought to doubt that these bulbs were breasts symbolizing the goddess's superabundant fertility, but then someone looked closer and remarked on their strange lack of plastic realism. In short, a group of Austrian archaeologists recently confirmed that these protrusions do not represent breasts after all but rather the testicles of bulls. The fact is corroborated by evidence uncovered at Ephesus which indicates that on her festival days Artemis's priests would castrate several bulls, string the scrotums together, and then place the gruesome garlands around a wooden image of the goddess, which her votives would then follow in an ecstatic procession from her sacred altar to the center of the city. Such was the nature of the "virgin" goddess, Artemis.

In her city the Christian prelates convened in A.D. 431 to discuss the alarming cults of the Virgin Mary which had spread throughout the Christian communities. The Church at that time was decisively hostile toward Mary, her worship being dangerously reminiscent of paganism. But it was decided by the bishops in Ephesus that her following was too popular and that the Church would do best to canonize her. Mary was officially declared the mother of God, and Artemis's traditional festival day—August 15—was chosen as the holy day of Mary's "assumption" into heaven. Thus was the virgin goddess assimilated yet again into a new religious order.

This was only the most recent chapter in the story of her various accommodations to new religious institutions. Prior to the Christian revolution, the Olympian pantheon had also been obliged to make room for Artemis, for she was originally an outsider among the Olympians, so much that Hesiod had to invent a genealogy for her. Homer, the great champion of Olympianism, was not very fond of this goddess and conspicuously degraded her dignity in the *Iliad* by portraying her as an adolescent girl completely out of place in the war, contemptuously roughed up and chided by Hera (*Iliad* 21.470–514).

Nevertheless Artemis remained for the Greeks an awesome goddess. When she chides her in the *Iliad,* Hera declares: "A lion unto women Zeus made you—to kill any at your pleasure" (21.483). The reference is to Artemis's role as the goddess who presided over childbirth—one of her ancient fertility functions that she managed to preserve. In this capacity she was often identified with Eileithyia, the goddess of release who responds to the cries of pain and fear of pregnant women at the moment of delivery. In a similar vein Artemis also presided over the initiation rites of young girls. At her cult in Brauron, in Attica, for example, young girls were placed in her service for extended periods of time and were dressed ceremoniously in bear skins in symbolic atonement for a sacred bear killed by Attic youths in one of the goddess's groves.

The traditional cults and myths indicate that Artemis was also a goddess of sacrifice. When Agamemnon kills a stag in one of her sacred groves, she demands the sacrifice of his daughter Iphigenia. This darker, crueler side of Artemis is ever present, but the aspect by which she is usually portrayed, and which interests us the most, is that of the

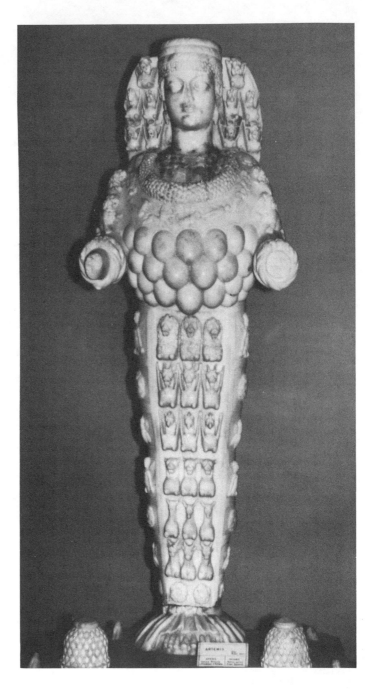

Artemis of Ephesus (ca. second century A.D.)

virgin huntress roaming the woodlands with her train of nymphs. If there is a deity of the wilderness in Greek antiquity, it is Artemis. Homer refers to her as "Mistress of the Hunt" and "Lady of the Wild Animals" (21.470); in Aeschylus's *Agamemnon* it is said that she is "gracious to the playful cubs of fierce lions and delights in the suckling young of every wild creature"(*Agamemnon* 141–43). We know from the myths that many groves were sacred to her, and that her chastity was inviolable. Her virginity referred, among other things, to the virgin forests beyond the bounds of the polis and cultivated fields. Her outlying domain may, in this sense, reflect her original status as an outsider among the Olympian gods.

For all their similarities, the Roman counterpart of Artemis, *Diana nemorensis,* or "Diana of the Woods," was not the same goddess, at least not in origin. It used to be assumed that the Romans merely adopted Artemis and gave her a Latin name, but Diana was in fact an aboriginal Latin deity whose worship also goes back to prehistoric times. The Latin myth of the Golden Bough, which provided the impulse for Frazer's monumental *The Golden Bough,* is one of the indications of her indigenous antiquity. Given this discrepancy between the two goddesses, then, we will leave *Diana nemorensis* to Sir James Frazer and focus here on Artemis of the virgin woodlands.

Her virginal aspect deserves greater emphasis, for in ancient times forests were by no means always virgin or beyond the bounds of human domestication. From the very beginning, it seems, the exploitation and harvesting of forests were an integral part of neolithic life. Silviculture is an ancient practice, but our goddess had nothing to do with it. She belonged to those dark and inaccessible regions where wild animals enjoyed sanctuary from all human disturbance except that of the most intrepid hunters. Like her domain, the goddess too was remote and inaccessible. She refused to be seen by man or woman. Even her most ardent priestesses and votives did not set eyes on her. The story of Hippolytus, son of Theseus, confirms this. So total was the youth's devotion to Artemis that he went so far as to spurn the power of Aphrodite, who in revenge devised a cruel fate for him at the hands of his stepmother Phaedra. In Euripides' *Hippolytus* the young hunter brings Artemis flowers from a wild meadow where no human being except himself could enter, and where he was granted the extraordinary privilege of hearing the goddess's voice. But even he could not set eyes on her. "True I may only hear," says Hippolytus, "I may not see God face to face" (*Hippolytus* 86–87). Likewise in *Iphigenia in*

Tauris, where Agamemnon's daughter appears as Artemis's priestess in the barbarous land of the Tauroi, it is said in reference to the goddess: "None of us ever sees Her in the dark or understands her cruel mysteries" (*Iphigenia* 476–77).

This, then, is how Artemis appears, or refuses to appear, in the mythologies: invisible, intangible, enigmatic, cruel, reigning over the nonhuman reaches of the wilderness. As virgin of the woodlands, she withdraws behind the forest's shadows into her noumenal realm where human beings cannot, or must not, have access. Her virginity does not suggest so much asexuality as the primordial chastity of this sylvan retreat. The Greek myth of Actaeon dramatizes in an unforgettable way this prohibitive, inviolable nature of Artemis. The myth is taken up by the Roman poet Ovid in his *Metamorphoses* (3.143–252) and elaborated in the following version.

Actaeon had been out hunting on the slopes of a mountain with his friends and hounds. As noon came around he told his companions that they had done well enough for the day, leaving them to gather up the nets and return home with the dogs. In a valley beneath the mountain there was a grove of pine and cypress trees, sacred to Artemis, where a waterfall poured into a pristine pool. Tired from hunting, Artemis would sometimes come here to bathe with her nymphs. On that particular day she had already disrobed, handed her weapons to her maidens and entered the pool, when Actaeon, wandering through unfamiliar woodlands, strayed into the grove by mistake. Seeing a man in their midst the nymphs began to beat their breasts and scream, gathering around the goddess to hide her nakedness. Artemis, however, being taller than them, remained exposed to the gaze of Actaeon. With no weapons handy, she gathered up a handful of water from the pool and flung it in Actaeon's face and hair. "Now you are free to tell that you have seen me all unrobed—if you can tell," she says to him (3. 192–93).

Actaeon will be incapable of telling any such thing, for he loses the capacity of human speech altogether. Horns begin to sprout from his forehead, his arms become legs; his hands become feet, his skin becomes a hide. Transformed into a stag, he takes flight through the forest. The only thing left to him of his former self is his personal awareness of himself. As he dashes through the forest he hears his bloodthirsty hounds in the distance rushing after him. The pursuer becomes the pursued. As the pack bears down on him Actaeon wants to call out to his hounds and say: "I am Actaeon! Recognize your own master!" But the hounds recognize only a deer and assault him with remorseless ferocity. His companions urge on the pack and wonder what has become of Actaeon, disappointed that he is not with them to join in the chase. As his dogs lacerate and tear him apart, Actaeon's life expires, and so was "the wrath of the quiver-bearing goddess appeased."

When it came to discerning and transcribing the meaningful core of classical myths, Ovid was an incomparable master, and his account of the Actaeon story contains several insights into the *dea silvarum*, as he calls her. To begin with, what is it exactly that leaves the forest goddess naked in this story? The answer lies in a subtle hint in Ovid's opening description: the high noon had "shortened every object's shade, and the sun was at equal distance from either goal" (*iamque dies medius rerum contraxerat umbras / et sol ex aequo meta distabat utraque;* 3.143–44). If Artemis became visible to human eyes on this occasion, it was due to the momentary loss of her natural cover at that critical time of day when the forest's shade is at its minimum. Her habitat proper is the dark side of the visible world. Her robe is none other than the forest's *umbrae,* its protective shadows.

Ovid's version emphasizes the sinister dialectic of the classical myth. On the most obvious plane, the veiled becomes unveiled, the hunter becomes the hunted, and the master becomes the victim of his own hounds; but the logic of reversal and retribution goes beyond this. In a moment of indiscretion, Actaeon actually partakes of the sort of vision that is forbidden to mortals. Human vision is privative in nature; it does not see directly into the nature of things but sees only the outward surface of phenomenal appearances. Actaeon transgresses these limits. He sees the goddess in a moment of noumenal, as opposed to mere phenomenal, vision. In retribution for his having violated the realm that lies behind the world of appearances, Artemis brings about Actaeon's change of appearance, while leaving his human essence intact. He retains his inner mind (*mens tantum pristina mansit;* 3.203) but is transfigured outwardly into a stag. In the process of external metamorphosis he comes to realize that his own inner identity is superfluous in a realm governed by appearances. Actaeon's dogs know nothing of the inner identity of Actaeon; nor do his companions. They fail to recognize him and respond solely to the outer phenomenon. In her ingenious retribution, the naked goddess who could not hide herself beneath her veils hides Actaeon beneath a strange new form, thus punishing his transgression by linking his fate to the transformed appearance that veils his identity. In this way she restores with a vengeance the cloak of discretion which Actaeon had violated.

The *Metamorphoses* in general, and this story in particular, use the trope of metamorphosis to express a materialist philosophy of reality, which holds that all embodied substances partake of the same primal matter. In Ovid's mythic world, all living species preserve an intimate affiliation with one another by virtue of their emergence from a mutual womb of creation. The possibility of one creature's metamorphosis into another points to the underlying material nature they share in common. Metamorphosis itself (from the Greek words *meta* and *morphé,* meaning change of form) is a kind of birth, or rebirth, as one material form returns to its matrix in order to assume a new form. This preformal kinship of all creation, which enables human beings to be transformed into animals, trees, flowers, and other forest phenomena, is the recurring materialist theme of the *Metamorphoses.*

In the Actaeon story Artemis is the agent both of metamorphosis and the guardian of nature's mysterious matrix of forms. By transforming the predator into the prey, she reveals to Actaeon in his person the true nature of what he has laid eyes upon: the preformal kinship of all creation. The story has an unmistakable psychological effect upon the reader, for while Actaeon is literally de-anthropomorphized, the stag that he turns into becomes humanized. Now that Actaeon has become a stag we are able to suffer its fate as if it were a human being. The distinctions collapse. The world reveals its deceptions, its *irrevocable* deceptions. Like Actaeon, we are made to see that the forms of the world are transient, illusory, and reversible. All things, whatever their formal natures, arise from a more primordial unity. This is the terrifying insight enjoyed by Actaeon that day in the forest, where he had the dubious privilege of seeing the *dea silvarum* naked.

There are important reasons why this materialist doctrine is expressed mythologically, through the trope of metamorphosis, rather than logically, but to understand them we must follow a detour that takes us back to the beginnings of Western philosophy, when *mythos,* or myth, presumably gave way to *logos,* or logical reason. These beginnings were dominated by a simple question: what is the essence of all that is? The early Greek "nature philosophers" looked to one or more of the elements for an answer—water, fire, earth, air, or a combination of these. Regardless of their local disagreements about elemental primacies, the materialist philosophers generally agreed that all things come into being—assume form and appearance—from out of the womb of some primordial, undifferentiated matter. While forms are forever changing and passing away, the matter of which they are composed remains eternal. In the most extreme versions of pre-Socratic materialism, the mere fact of coming into being, or assuming form, entails a tragic estrangement from the source of being. The oldest fragment of Western philosophy, attributed to Anaximander, expresses the doctrine in a wondrous sentence: "Whence things have their origin, there they must also pass away according to the order of necessity; for they must pay penalty and be judged for their injustice, according to the ordinance of time."

We call the early philosophers "pre-Socratic" because, with the new sort of thinking that Socrates and Plato brought to philosophy, the essence of phenomena got redefined in terms of form or outward appearance (*eidos*), and no longer in terms of elemental matter. Aristotle especially argued the case for form in a way that became decisive for Western philosophy as a whole. Aristotle revised the very agenda of philosophy by introducing a series of logical distinctions between the ways in which "we speak" about abstract things—being, change, cause, motion, substance, matter, nature, etc. The distinction he drew between form and matter—*morphé* and *hyle,* as he called it—was typical of his grammarian revolution in philosophy. He pointed out that the distinction is a logical, not ontological, one. Neither matter nor form has an independent existence of its own. We cannot, for example, separate the bronze from the statue and still have pure matter on one side and pure form on the other. No, matter and form are merely unavoidable categories by which we distinguish conceptually between the "stuff" and its "structure."

In the *Physics* Aristotle argues that, insofar as we separate them logically, form is more important than matter in defining the "nature" (*physis*) of substances. He cites the ingenious argument of the materialist Antiphon, which works by analogy. If a man were to bury a bedstead in the ground, and if the rotting wood were to take root and throw out a shoot, wood, and not a bedstead, would continue to exist. The form, then, may undergo external transformations, but the matter endures as the intrinsic "nature" of the thing. By extending the analogy to natural substances in general, Antiphon concludes that since what endures throughout the many transformations undergone by substances in their elemental matter, *physis* is the matter and not the form of substances.

Aristotle refutes this argument delicately. He does not deny the possibility of some ultimate underlying matter but emphasizes that when we speak of the "nature" of something, we mean its formal properties rather than its preformed matter. Even Antiphon's analogy unwittingly confirms this. If the inability to reproduce itself is what distinguishes the formal artifact from the matter of which it is composed, then the "nature" of natural (as opposed to artificial) substances must reside in their form, for *substances reproduce their forms.* Men beget men, not elephants, and elephants beget elephants, not men. Form is the *telos,* or goal, which governs the *physis* of natural substances. *Physis* is nothing other than the movement of things into their natural forms.

As for matter, we cannot speak about it in any logical fashion. There are neither words, images, or categories for undifferentiated matter, since form is the condition of our logical access to reality. (Even Antiphon's "wood" has formal properties by which we identify it as a substance.) Yet there is one word that Aristotle could not avoid using when he spoke about the unspeakable—*hyle.* He is the first to give the word its philosophical meaning of "matter." But *hyle* in Greek does not originally mean matter, it means forest. Let us repeat that: *hyle* is the Greek word for forest. The cognate of *hyle* in Latin is *silva.* The archaic Latin word was *sylua,* phonetically close to *hyle.* It is strange that the Romans should have translated the Aristotelian *hyle* with the word *materia* when the Latin language possessed such a cognate. But even the word *materia* did not stray very far from the forests. *Materia* means wood—the usable wood of a tree as opposed to its bark, fruit, sap, etc. And *materia* has the same root—yes, root—as the word *mater,* or mother.

The analogy of motherhood, or embryonic genesis, in fact pervades Aristotle's discussion. He compares *hyle* to embryonic tissue that merely has the potential for assuming specific form, but which has not yet assumed the determinate properties by which it can be categorized as this or that entity. The following passage from the *Physics* concludes Aristotle's argument in favor of the logical primacy of form over matter: "What is potentially flesh or bone has not yet its own nature, and does not exist by nature, until it receives the form specified in the definition, which we name in defining what flesh or bone is" (*Physics* 2.193b). Until a substance emerges into the *telos* of its form we simply cannot talk about it. *Logos* begins with the phenomenon.

Yet the fact that we cannot speak logically about matter does not mean that it loses its primacy as the genetic matrix. The matter and the matrix are one, but Aristotle takes the words away. Dylan

Thomas, the Welsh poet, cannot find those words anymore, hence he must speak about the logical impossibility of speaking about the immediate kinship he feels with creation:

> The force that through the green fuse drives the flower
> Drives my green age; that blasts the roots of trees
> Is my destroyer.
> And I am dumb to tell the crooked rose
> My youth is bent by the same wintry fever.

This preverbal kinship that the poet cannot communicate to the crooked rose finds expression in *mythos,* if not in *logos.* It is expressed by Ovid in stories of human beings turning into faun, flora, trees, and other forest phenomena. The trope of metamorphosis dramatizes the ultimately insubstantial nature of the forms of creation, and in so doing it points to the affiliations that link all things together by virtue of their common genesis. Actaeon will never be able to speak about what he saw, for his insight is prelogical and lies beyond the possibility of speech. "Now you are free to tell that you have seen me all unrobed—if you can tell," says Artemis, but she knows that Actaeon has already lost his capacity for speech. For Actaeon there is no choice but to undergo a material metamorphosis. He has seen into the goddess's nature and must be reborn. In his rebirth as a stag he will promptly be lacerated by his dogs and returned once again to the universal matrix of all things, for "Whence things have their origin, there they must also pass away according to the order of necessity."

Along this circuitous route that led from the ancient Artemis through Ovid's version of the Actaeon story to the materialist doctrine refuted by Aristotle, we arrived unexpectedly at a point of convergence where the various paradoxical characteristics of the *dea silvarum* reveal their covert interrelationships. She is the huntress and protectress of wild animals, but also the goddess of childbirth. She was worshipped during antiquity as the great womb of the world, yet she also haunted the outlying forests beyond the bounds of human dwelling. She is invisible and unapproachable, the guardian of cruel mysteries. She is the mother who "delights in the suckling young of every wild creature," yet she hunts them down and takes their lives. She is the matrix, the matter, and the forest in one.

We may go further: she is the noumenal spirit of the forests which gives birth to a multiplicity of species (forms) that preserve their originary kinship within the forests' network of material interdepen-

dence. In her wild woodlands there are no irreducible distinctions—
no noise that does not sound like a response to some other noise, no
tree that does not fuse into the arboreal confusion. The diversity of
species in the forest belongs to the same phylogeny, so much so that in
heightened moments of perception they appear as mere versions of
each other—the fern a version of the dragonfly, the robin a version of
its supporting branch, the reptile's rustle a version of the rivulet's
trickle, the wildflower a version of the ray of light that reaches it
through the canopy. Symbolist poets of the nineteenth century will
speak of the forest as the place of ancient "correspondences"—the mutual implication of the species and sense perception. Artemis reigns
over this inconceivable implication. In her forests the hunter and the
hunted become one, just as Artemis is both huntress and protectress
of the beasts. But Artemis is even more than that, as she demonstrates
so persuasively to Actaeon through his metamorphosis. By transforming him into a stag, she presides over his initiation into the genetic
mysteries of her nature—a nature imponderable, unspeakable, yet primordial enough to give new meaning to the phrase, "first the forests."

DIONYSOS

If Artemis is the goddess who never appears but who withdraws into
the wilder woodlands beyond the polis, Dionysos is her emissary in
the human world. This "god who comes," to adopt the phrase
of Walter Otto, reaches the city from afar. He arrives from foreign
Artemisian regions dressed in animal skins and crowned with ivy
wreaths. He is dissolute, wanton, and orgiastic, yet these characteristics that seem to oppose him to the chaste goddess arise from a more
originary source of kinship. In his dramatic epiphanies among men
and women we can see in Dionysos the *mask* of Artemis.

Consider, for example, the blithe image of Dionysos that comes
to us from a Homeric hymn, which assigns the god to the forest's
domain:

> I begin to sing of the boisterous Dionysos of the ivy-
>   wreathed head,
> the noble son of Zeus and glorious Semele.
> The lovely-haired nymphs nurtured him and from his
>   lordly father
> took him to their bosoms to cuddle and nurse
> in the dells of Nysa. He grew up by his father's will

inside a sweet-smelling cave as one of the immortals.
But after the goddesses brought him up with many songs,
covered with ivy and laurel he started
haunting the wooded glens. The nymphs followed him
and he led the way as the boundless forest resounded with
    din.
And so hail to you, Dionysos, with your many grapes!
Grant that we joyously reach this season again
and then after this season many more years.
(*Homeric Hymns,* "Hymn to Dionysos" no. 26)

The portrait of Dionysos roaming the woodlands with a train of
nymphs recalls traditional images of the huntress and her *thiasos,* or
retinue of dancing nymphs. This is only one of many characteristics
which links the two deities together. Walter Burkert, one of the
world's authorities on Greek religion, informs us of others:

> Artemis and Dionysos seem opposed to each other as the
> freshness of the morning to the sultriness of the evening, but
> their cults have many parallels. They, and they alone, have a
> *thiasos,* a retinue of animated dancers, though the maenads of
> Dionysos are mature women and the nymphs of Artemis are
> young virgins; masks and even phallic costumes are found in
> dances for Artemis as well as in dances for Dionysos. A pro-
> test was raised, however, when a song by Timotheus ad-
> dressed Artemis herself as a "frenzied Thyiad." Nevertheless,
> the things of Artemis can easily turn into the things of Dio-
> nysos. There is a story attached to the sanctuary of Artemis
> at Karyai which tells of the arrival of Dionysos and how he
> seduces a maiden. At Patrai the festivals of Artemis and Dio-
> nysos are intertwined: the central temple of the three prov-
> inces is dedicated to Artemis *Triklaria.* Young boys go down
> to the sanctuary by the river Melichos wearing garlands of
> corn-ears on their heads; they lay down the garlands by the
> goddess, wash themselves in the river, put on fresh garlands
> of ivy, and thus adorned they go to meet Dionysos Aisym-
> netes. . . . The myth tells how, after a young couple dese-
> crated her temple by making love there, Artemis had de-
> manded the sacrifice of a youth and a virgin until the arrival
> of Aisymnetes put an end to the practise. Virginal cruelty is
> resolved in nocturnal frenzy. Conversely, the licentious mad-

ness which overtook the daughters of King Proitos was brought to an end by the Dionysos priest Melampus in the temple of Artemis at Lousoi, at the place of the washing." (*Greek Religion*, 222–23)

To Burkert's remarks we may add those of Walter Otto, who emphasizes the degree to which Dionysos, like Artemis, is portrayed in the myths as an accomplished hunter. Referring to the maenads in Euripides' *The Bacchae*, who in a moment of frenzy become predators and assault a herd of cattle, Otto writes:

> The true victims of their gruesome hunt, however, are the animals of the forest, the very ones they have mothered [i.e., gazelle and wolves]. . . . Thus the madness of these bloodthirsty huntresses has evolved from the magic of a motherliness which has no bounds. The revel rout, however, is only following the example of its divine leader. Dionysos, himself, is a hunter. "Like a hare" (Aeschylus *Eumenides* 26), he hunted down Pentheus, a victim who is torn to pieces in a horrible manner. Agave in Euripides calls him "an experienced hunter" . . . and the chorus answers, "Yes, our king is a hunter!" (*Dionysus: Myth and Cult*, 108–9)

Just as Artemis both hunts and protects the wild animals, so Dionysos's relation to various animals is not simply one of predation but also one of guardianship and even identification. Dionysos is the animal god who is forever transforming himself—into a lion, a boar, a panther, a snake, a bull, a dragon. In this sense he is the god of metamorphosis par excellence. It is interesting to note in this context that Friedrich Nietzsche argued that metamorphosis is the very essence of the psychic ecstasy that overtakes the initiates of the Dionysian mystery cults, who during their dances believed themselves transformed into satyrs, or creatures of the forest:

> This process of the tragic chorus is the *dramatic* protophenomenon: to see oneself transformed before one's own eyes and to begin to act as if one had actually entered into another body, another character. This process stands at the beginning of the origin of drama. . . . Here we have a surrender of individuality and a way of entering another character. . . . Such magic transformation is the presupposition of all dramatic art. In this magic transformation the Dionysian

reveler sees himself as satyr [man of the woods], *and as a satyr, in turn, he sees the god,* which means that in his metamorphosis he beholds another vision outside himself, as the Apollinian complement of his own state. With this new vision the drama is complete. (*The Birth of Tragedy,* 64)

Here too metamorphosis is bound to the forest, which, as we remarked in the last section, preserves the original affiliations that enable individual forms to give way to one another in a promiscuous confusion of identities. Actaeon's transformation into a stag figures as the Dionysian state of ecstasy in its quintessential version—the state in which a man *sees* himself enter "into another body, another character." It is this visionary moment of seeing, even more than metamorphosis, which characterizes Dionysian ecstasy. In other words, Actaeon's having set eyes upon the naked Artemis represents the visionary moment of Dionysian insight as such. Such insight is perhaps prohibitive, unspeakable, abominable—but the tragic wisdom of the Greeks is bound up with it.

This brings us to the most compelling hint of kinship between Artemis and Dionysos, namely the consanguinity of their two most famous victims: Actaeon and Pentheus. These two Theban characters were first cousins. Both were the grandsons of Cadmus and both met their tragic deaths in the same forest on the Cithaeron mountain outside of Thebes. Their strangely parallel fates suggest underlying, subterranean connections between Artemis and Dionysos which go beyond the hard evidence of philology. We have already discussed the fate of Actaeon. In what follows we will look at the fate of Pentheus as dramatized by Euripides in *The Bacchae.*

One day the god appears, no one knows from where, but from afar, and the city loses its mind. Piety, laws, and the civic order break down before his epiphany. Thrown into a state of agitation by the presence of the god, the women rush from their homes and make their way in swarms to the mountains. Out of their houses, out of their city, out of their minds—they go into the forests.

Here they wear ivy or oak wreaths on their heads and dress in fawnskins. Snakes, coiled around the fur, lick their cheeks. Like Artemis who "delights in the suckling young of every wild creature," they hold young gazelle or wolf cubs in their arms, suckling them with overflowing breasts. Then the revelry begins. The maenads gather together and chant for Dionysos to appear. With their wands—the phallic *thyrsos*—they invoke the god and start to dance. The whole mountain, and all the creatures of the woods, sway to the rhythms of their drunken song.

At this point the maenads spot some herdsmen nearby and succumb to a wild paranoia. They realize they are being hunted out by envoys of the city. In a furious rage the hunted become the huntresses. They rush after their persecutors, who, seeing the swarm come after them with murderous intent, flee for their lives. Possessed by Dionysos, the women attack a herd of cattle with their bare hands and rip the cows apart, limb from limb. Even the proud bull they wrestle to the ground and tear to pieces. The maenads had called for the god to appear, and now whatever they assault is the god himself, for at the moment of his revelation Dionysos is everything and everywhere. He is the ancient, primordial matter behind the phenomena of the world. By dismembering their victims in a moment of ecstatic vision, the maenads merely destroy the illusions of formal integrity. All becomes indefinite in the Dionysian frenzy, for Dionysos, like Artemis, liquidates the boundaries of form.

Forms maintain themselves in the world through a kind of restraint. Restraint is active resistance against the amorphous chaos of matter, which forever wants to draw phenomena back into the matrix of life. The hero of such resistance in *The Bacchae* is Pentheus, king of Thebes. As a champion of the social order, he cannot tolerate the mad upheavals caused by the arrival of an effeminate foreigner who claims to be the son of Zeus. Hence Pentheus resists Dionysos, denies his divinity. But he will pay for his denial, for like Actaeon he will be made to undergo a Dionysian dissolution in his person.

This comes about as Dionysos lures the naive king to the scene of the orgies on the mountain. Disguised as a votary to spy on the women, Pentheus climbs high into a pine tree in order to get a better view of the proceedings. Once in the tree the god's resounding voice tells the maenads to behold the man who denied their god and mocked their rites, and commands them to punish this intruder. The god's voice sends the women into a trance. Spotting Pentheus in the tree, they become possessed, believing him to be a mountain lion. Led by Agave, Pentheus's mother, they swam around the tree, uproot it with their hands, and fall upon Pentheus with fury. Like Actaeon who tried to get his hounds to recognize their master, Pentheus removes his headband so that his mother might recognize her son, but to no avail. He is ripped apart from the limbs, first by his mother, then by the entire maniacal horde. Out of her senses, his mother spikes his head on her *thyrsos,* thinking it the head of a lion, and dances triumphantly around the countryside.

Pentheus thereby becomes the god's victim, no doubt, but the true victim of the Dionysian disaster is the social order he represents. Pentheus's dismemberment figures poetically as the destruction of the law that brings civilization into being—the law of binding. By killing her son Agave destroys a fundamental institutional bond, but the nature of Pentheus's murder points beyond the abomination of filicide to an even more sinister undoing of the "law of humanity," as Vico calls it. Vico defines this law in terms of synthesis. Civil society comes into being through the activity of gathering. Arguing that the meanings of our most common words change according to the order of institutions ("First the forests, after that the huts . . . ," etc.), Vico gives the example of the Latin word *lex.* The word *lex* means "law," but Vico writes:

> First it must have meant a collection of acorns. Thence we believe is derived *ilex,* as it were *illex,* the oak (as certainly *aquilex* means collector of waters); for the oak produces the acorns by which the swine are drawn together. *Lex* was next a collection of vegetables, from which the latter were called *legumina.* Later on, at a time when vulgar letters had not yet been invented for writing down the laws, *lex* by a necessity of civil nature must have meant a collection of citizens, or the public parliament, so that the presence of the people was the *lex,* or "law." . . . Finally, collecting letters, and making, as it were, a sheaf of them for each word, was called *legere,* reading. (*New Science,* §240)

Although the concrete referent of the word changes according to the stage of social evolution, the law of humanity remains constant insofar as it represents the law of gathering, collecting, binding. The word for Vico's *lex* in Greek is *logos,* from *legein,* which has the ancient meaning of "gathering," or "relating." Through this law of the *lex* or *logos,* civil society comes into being as a gathering—not an orgiastic gathering in the sense of communal Dionysian ecstasy but rather a gathering bound by limits, identity, form, and restraint.

The first human gathering was, for Vico, the family. The family institution binds its members together, defines their relations, and preserves the genealogical line. One could say in general that Greek tragedy, which had its origins in the Dionysian mystery cults, represents with obsessive repetition the disasters that befall the family institution, be it the stories of Oedipus, Agamemnon, Orestes, Antigone, or even Pentheus. *The Bacchae,* however, holds a special place among Greek tragedies to the degree that it deals with the god who brought the tragic art into being, namely Dionysos. In this sense *The Bacchae* gives us a reflective summary of the essence of tragedy as Euripides conceived it (perhaps such a summary was possible not only at the end of the great tradition of Greek tragedy but also at the end of Euripides's career, which *The Bacchae* concludes).

Dionysos appears in this play as the god who comes deliberately to unbind all that civic law binds together. He comes in effect to preside over the law's dispersion. In Pentheus's dismemberment we see the *lex* allegorically scattered throughout the "nefarious forests" where, according to Vico, the first human gathering took place.

This becomes dramatically obvious when we consider Euripides' tragic portrait of Cadmus, founder of the city of Thebes, who figures as the ultimate victim of Dionysos in the play. Vico saw in this legendary hero a poetic character for the law of synthesis by which civil society comes into being from out of the forests. Vico did not have Euripides' *The Bacchae* in mind, to be sure, but the Greek drama lends credence to such an allegorical interpretation of Cadmus as a poetic character. Toward the end of the play Cadmus enters the stage with attendants bearing the body of Pentheus, or what remains of it. Cadmus speaks:

> Come this way, please. . . .
> Put the dreadful burden which was Pentheus here, before the
>   palace.
> I've brought the body back: I searched forever.
> It was in the folds of Cithaeron, torn to shreds,
> scattered through the impenetrable forest,
> no two parts of him in any single spot.
> (*The Bacchae,* 1115–2120)

This is a quintessential tragic portrait: the founder of Thebes wandering through the forest to gather together the remnants of what Dionysos had scattered—the body of Pentheus. It is more than merely the body of a grandson which Cadmus pieces together, it is the race of Cadmus itself, which henceforth will be dispersed across the earth in exile. In this sense we could say that Cadmus on the Cithaeron mountain enacts his last, sorry gesture as civilizer, gathering the broken remains of his house from the forests.

Meanwhile we know that Cadmus has not recovered Pentheus's body in its entirety, for at this moment in the play Agave dances onto the stage with Pentheus's head upon her *thyrsos,* waving it in front of her father and boasting of her prowess as a huntress. Still possessed, she persists in believing that it is a lion's head. She speaks:

> Would my son at least could be a happy hunter,
> like his mother, when he goes out on the chase
> with his young friends from Thebes.
> But all he does is struggle with the god.
> Father, he needs talking to, by you.
> Someone call him, let me see him.
> Let him see his mother, Agave the blessed. (1251–57)

Cadmus, full of pity, brings his daughter to her senses and gets her to perceive in her trophy the head of her son. She awakens to the reality and screams. Pressed by her questions, Cadmus recounts what has happened:

> *Cadmus:* You killed him. With your sisters.
> *Agave:* Where did it happen? At home? Where?
> *Cadmus:* Where Actaeon was dismembered by his hounds.
> *Agave:* On Cithaeron? Why was my poor Pentheus there?
> *Cadmus:* He went to mock the gods, and your rituals.
> *Agave:* But we, why were we there?
> *Cadmus:* You were mad. The city was possessed by
>   Dionysos.
> *Agave:* I see now. Dionysos has destroyed us.
> *Cadmus:* You enraged him. You denied he was god.
> *Agave:* My son's beloved body, where is it, Father?
> *Cadmus:* There he is, what I could find of him.
> *Agave:* Is he decently put back together? (1290–1301)

We will never know Cadmus's answer to that macabre question, for the next few lines of the text are missing, as if to suggest, through the historical irony of the text's fragmentation, that parts of Pentheus's body are still missing. But we do know that Cadmus, founder of the city destroyed by Dionysos, gathered together what he could of what the god committed to the forest's dispersion. We know furthermore that we have been in that forest before. It is the forest where Actaeon previously met his fate at the hands of Artemis. Artemis and Dionysos come together in the shadows of the Cithaeron forest, the abyss of precivic darkness from which civilization is merely a deviation, and a precarious one at that.

In *The Birth of Tragedy* Nietzsche claimed that Euripides spent his long career as a dramatist denying the traditional Dionysian element of tragedy (thus dealing tragedy its death blow) but that he finally came to acknowledge it in his old age, composing *The Bacchae,* one of his last plays, as a work of contrition or atonement. By then, however, it was too late, for Greek culture was already in "decline." Tragic wisdom had given way to the triumphalistic claims of Socratic philosophy—its love of an abstract, nontragic wisdom that looked to contemplation—not Dionysian suffering—for its fulfillment. Turning against the vegetative and animal origins of life, Socrates idealized and formalized the essence of truth.

The world's phenomenal appearances remained deceptive for the philosopher, but for different reasons than the ones we found in the case of Dionysian ecstasy or the metamorphosis of Actaeon. Whereas earthly forms had previously been seen to arise from the primordial, preformal matrix of nature, they now were seen to descend or derive from an ideal realm of disembodied form. This was the sort of idealism that turned Socrates into one of the greatest apologists of the city—its institutional abstraction from nature. For Socrates the city represented a triumphant clearing in whose sphere of enlightenment the shadows of the Dionysian menace were dissipated. By promoting the revolution of critical reason, philosophy and the city were married to one another irrevocably, and the city became, more than ever, an *academy* ("First the forests . . . and finally the academies").

Socrates was condemned to death by the city, to be sure, but this ironic conclusion of his career only reaffirms his allegiance to the city in its ideal conception. The death of Socrates was not tragic. It was not linked to Dionysian disaster, which annuls the very basis of law, for Socrates was "unjustly" condemned. By exposing the scandal of the law's corruption through his martyrdom, he effectively upheld the law's ideal of justice. A critic of the law's shortcomings is not the law's enemy but rather an apologist for its ideal integrity. Furthermore, death was no calamity in Socrates' eyes, it was rather the *happy ending* of philosophy itself. Philosophy has nothing to do with tragic downfalls (only the benighted fall); on the contrary, by showing us where true happiness, virtue, and beauty lie, it promises to spare us tragedy. Thus Socrates appeared on the stage of Greek culture as the invincible opponent of Dionysos—an opponent who did not merely deny the god (like Pentheus) but who in every respect *overcame* him.

We will never sufficiently appreciate the fact that the *Symposium* is essentially a drama about Socrates' triumph over Dionysos—the god of inebriation as well as tragedy. At the beginning of Plato's dialogue Socrates teases his friend and enemy Agathon, who has just won a prize for one of his tragedies. Agathon, who hosts the banquet, answers him: "Enough of your sarcasm, Socrates. We'll settle our respective claims to wisdom a little later on, and Dionysos, the god of wine, shall judge between us" (*Symposium*, 33). Later in the evening Dionysos in fact appears on the scene in the guise of Alcibiades, the young and dashing Athenian aristocrat who arrives boisterously, in a state of drunkenness, with an ivy wreath on his head and train of revelers in his wake.

As he enters the room Alcibiades is initially not aware of Socrates' presence, so he takes off his wreath and crowns Agathon; but when he notices Socrates he leaps to his feet in surprise and says: "Agathon, give me some of those ribands to make a wreath for his head too, for a truly wonderful head it is. Otherwise he might blame me for crowning you and leaving him uncrowned, whose words bring him victory over all men at all times, not merely on single occasions, like yours the day before yesterday" (98). Dionysos judges between them, just as Agathon had predicted. Agathon and Socrates share the crown.

But as the evening wears on, it becomes clear how ironic this equivocal judgment is, or to what extent Socrates lies beyond the reach of the one who has presumed to judge his claims to wisdom. Alcibiades relates the story of his unsuccessful attempts to seduce Socrates into an amorous relationship with him, portraying Socrates as almost superhuman in his indifference or invulnerability to the lures of the body. But more important, as the banquet gives way to raucous drinking and revelry, only Socrates remains sober, not because he abstains from the wine of Dionysos—he in fact drinks as much as his companions—but because of his exceptional resistance to its effects.

What is the deeper source of this resistance? Is it actually resistance or something else? In essence Socrates overcomes Dionysos not merely by resisting him but by elevating Dionysian inebriation to a higher, abstract level. Just as he does not deny *eros* at its corporeal level but seeks to raise it beyond the body toward the absolute beauty that is presumably the object of all desire, so Socrates does not merely disavow Dionysianism but seeks to idealize it. In his speech about the true nature of love earlier in the evening, Socrates made it clear that only by way of spiritual ecstasy can the divine soul reascend to the realm of the absolute beauty. The soul must be possessed, must go beyond itself, must free itself of all constraints. Only through a sort of visionary ecstasy, brought about by a series of inner conversions or transformations, may the soul behold the absolute beauty that is the true object of all desire. A strange complicity links Dionysos, the god of ecstasy, to the rapturous "Platonic love" described by Socrates. In short, the Socratic soul is not immune to the lure of drunkenness; it is *already drunk with philosophy*—intoxicated with idealism. Herein lies Socrates' power of resistance to Dionysos. Only a passion can effectively resist another passion. Only Dionysianism raised to a higher level can overcome Dionysos.

After everyone else has succumbed to sleep at the banquet, Socrates continues to engage Aristophanes and Agathon in a discussion about the comparative virtues of comedy and tragedy. Here too we find that Socrates does not simply engage in denial or repudiation; he merely compels his interlocutors to admit "that the man who knew how to write a comedy could also write a tragedy" (113). Agathon and Aristophanes are nodding with sleep. In their drowsiness they give way to his arguments. Once they have dozed off for good, Socrates makes ready to leave. Having confronted Dionysos with his invincible idealism, he rises from his seat and ventures forth into the dawning day—the light of Apollo.

For ten years on his solitary mountain, Zarathustra would exit from his cave and face the rising sun in a spirit of Platonic triumphalism. "You great star," he declares one morning, "what would your happiness be had you not those for whom you shine?" On that day Zarathustra decides to put an end to philosophy. He leaves his luminous mountaintop and descends into the forest on his way to the city.

Whether or not it is true, as some have claimed, that Nietzsche brought to an end the history of philosophy which began with Socrates and Plato, there is no doubt that he introduced a new word which is no longer Greek but Latin in origin: *amor fati*. *Philosophia*—a word coined by Plato meaning "love of wisdom"—becomes *amor fati*, or the love of fate. The idea of *amor fati* can be found already in the Stoics, but Nietzsche gives it a wholly new inflection. One could say that the so-called overturning of Platonism which we hear so much about with regard to Nietzsche takes place in the shadows of the obscure, almost imponderable distinction between *fatum* and *sophia*. In both cases we are left with love, but of a different nature. *Philosophia* is love in its most dynamic, projective, anticipatory state; *amor fati* is love deprived of its horizon of otherworldly expectation. *Philosophia* loves forward to a prospect of truth and beauty which lures the lover on with a promise of happiness; *amor fati* would seem to love backward, without prospect. It would seem to love backward, but to what? That is the question that recalls Dionysos at the end of the history of philosophy.

Let us follow Nietzsche's Zarathustra down the mountain. On his way toward the world of humanity Zarathustra enters a forest. There he meets a solitary saint who has made the forest his home. The saint remembers Zarathustra from ten years ago, when Zarathustra passed through that very forest on his way to the mountain. The saint now says to him: "You lived in your solitude as in a sea . . . alas, would you now climb ashore?" Zarathustra answers: "I love man." "Man is for me too imperfect a thing," says the saint, "Love of man would kill me." Zarathustra answers: "Did I speak of love? I bring men a gift." The saint becomes emphatic: "Do not go to man. Stay in the forest! Go rather even to the animals! Why do you not want to be as I am—a bear among bears, a bird among birds?" (*Zarathustra*, Prologue, 2).

The saint has a point. Zarathustra's love is at bottom a love of the earth and its species, but there is a problem. Detached from the events of history in his forest, the saint has not yet heard the news that "God is dead," or that the human age that murdered God is wreaking havoc with the earth, the animals, the species. The saint is unaware that history and nature now share a common destiny and that his forest will soon become a wasteland as humanity embarks upon a godless conquest of the earth. The death of God has left history in a state of reckless uncertainty. Zarathustra therefore cannot stay in the forest and be a bear among bears, a bird among birds, for he must go down into the city where the fate of the earth is being decided by men and women who dwell in oblivion.

Leaving the saint behind, Zarathustra arrives in a city at the edge of the forest and enters the marketplace (the entire modern city is now nothing but a marketplace). There he begins to preach to the people: "I beseech you, my brothers, remain faithful to the earth, and do not believe those who speak to you of otherworldly hopes. . . . To sin against the earth is now the most dreadful thing, and to esteem the entrails of the unknowable higher than the meaning of the earth." The meaning of the earth is the "gift" that Zarathustra brings to humankind from the mountains. "The overman is the meaning of the earth," he says, "Let your will say: the overman *shall be* the meaning of the earth." Thus spoke Zarathustra, but to no avail, for at that point his audience becomes distracted. A tightrope walker has begun his performance in the central square. "Man is a rope tied between beast and overman," says Zarathustra "man is a bridge and not an end." The people mock Zarathustra. The tightrope walker meanwhile falters and then plunges down to his death in the marketplace. Zarathustra will later bury him with his own hands in the forest (Prologue, 3–4).

At a later moment in the book, in fact right in its very middle, we find Zarathustra on a bridge—another tightrope, as it were—surrounded by cripples, blindmen, hunchbacks, and beggars. A hunchback asks him what redemption he can offer them for their suffering and deformities. But Zarathustra's idea of redemption has nothing to do with recompense. He turns to his disciples and says: "Verily, my friends, I walk among men as among the fragments and limbs of men. . . . The present and the past on earth—alas, my friends, that is what *I* find most unendurable; and I should not know how to live were I not also a seer of that which must come" (2, "On Redemption").

Zarathustra stands on the bridge of time stretching between past and future, between beast and overman. If there is to be any redemption at all, it must come from the future. But herein lies Zarathustra's dilemma on the bridge: redemption must somehow also redeem the past. "To redeem those who lived in the past," he says, "and to recreate all 'it was' into a 'thus I willed it'—that alone should I call redemption" (ibid.). But Zarathustra knows that such retroactive redemption remains impossible, for when it confronts the past the human will is impotent:

> Willing liberates, but what is it that puts even the liberator himself in fetters? "It was"—that is the name of the will's gnashing of teeth and most secret melancholy. Powerless against what has been done, he is an angry spectator of all that is past. The will cannot will backwards; and that he cannot break time and time's covetousness, that is the will's loneliest melancholy. . . . This, indeed, and this alone, is what revenge is: the will's ill-will against time and time's "it was." (ibid.)

But how can the will overcome its ill-will if it cannot will backward? How can it turn the "it was" into a "thus I willed it"?

The only way out of the dilemma is to will the past forward in repetition. In other words, one must will "the eternal return of the same." Zarathustra's famous doctrine of the eternal return bends the line of time into a circle. As time becomes a cycle of repetition, the will can will backward by willing forward.

The doctrine has frightening implications, however, for by willing the eternal return of the same, the will in effect renounces its willfulness. Rather than becoming empowered, it merely surrenders to the fateful dictates of things as they are. Is this the true meaning of *amor fati:* the willful annulment of the will itself, its shattering against the order of necessity? Is the shattering of the will against the dictates of fate what Nietzsche saw as the wisdom of Greek tragedy? Perhaps.

But surely the doctrine of the eternal return is more enigmatic than this. Zarathustra, after all, calls it a "riddle." In what sense is it a riddle? Let us see what happens to Zarathustra just after he proclaims the doctrine of the eternal return to a dwarf on a country path at the twilight hour:

> And this slow spider [he says to the dwarf], which crawls in the moonlight, and this moonlight itself, and I and you in the gateway, whispering together, whispering of eternal things— must not all of us have been there before? And return and walk in that other lane, out there, before us, in this long dreadful lane—must we not eternally return?
>
> Thus I spoke, more and more softly; for I was afraid of my own thoughts and the thoughts behind my thoughts. Then suddenly I heard a dog howl nearby. Had I ever heard a dog howl like this? My thoughts raced back. Yes, when I was a child, in the most distant childhood: then I heard a dog howl like this. And I saw him too, bristling, his head up, trembling, in the stillest midnight when even dogs believe in ghosts—and I took pity: for just then the full moon, silent as death, passed over the house. . . . that was why the dog was terrified, for dogs believe in thieves and ghosts. And when I heard such howling again I took pity again.
>
> Where was the dwarf gone now? And the gateway? And the spider? And all the whispering? Was I dreaming, then? Was I waking up?

Among the wild cliffs I stood suddenly alone, bleak, in the bleakest moonlight. *But there lay a man.* And there—the dog, jumping, bristling, whining—now he saw me coming; then he howled again, he *cried*. Had I ever heard a dog cry like this for help? And verily, what I saw—I had never seen the like. A young shepherd I saw, writhing, gagging, in spasms, his face distorted, and a heavy black snake hung out of his mouth. Had I ever seen so much nausea and pale dread on one face? He seemed to have been asleep when the snake crawled into his throat, and there bit itself fast. My hand tore at the snake and tore in vain; it did not tear the snake out of his throat. Then it cried out of me: "Bite! Bite its head off! Bite!" Thus it cried out of me—my dread, my hatred, my nausea, my pity, all that is good and wicked in me cried out of me with a single cry.

You bold ones surround me! You searchers and research-ers . . . guess me this riddle that I saw then, interpret me the vision of the loneliest. For it was a vision and a foresee-ing. . . .

The shepherd, however, bit as my cry counseled him; he bit with a good bite. Far away he spewed the head of the snake—and he jumped up. No longer shepherd, no longer human—one changed, radiant, *laughing!* Never yet on earth has a human being laughed as he laughed!

(3, "The Vision and the Riddle")

This vision is a riddle indeed. "Must not all of us have been there before?" Zarathustra asks the dwarf. Yes, for everything repeats itself. "Had I ever heard a dog howl like this?" he asks himself. Yes, in distant childhood. But when Zarathustra approaches this dog, the howling becomes singular and unprecedented: "Had I ever heard a dog cry like this for help?" he asks. The variant repetition of the question contains its own answer: No, never. Zarathustra then sees the shepherd and says: "what I saw—I had never seen the like."

The German word *Gleich,* or "the like," occurs in Nietzsche's phrase *die ewige Wiederkehr des Gleichen,* literally "The eternal return of the like." But Zarathustra says that he had never before seen the like of this. And after the shepherd stands up and laughs, Zarathustra de-clares: "Never yet on earth has a human being laughed as he laughed!" Never yet on earth . . . ? The eternal return of the same?

How can time become a circle and still retain its dimensions of the unprecedented? This is the riddle solved by the overman, whom Zarathustra calls "the meaning of the earth." In the overman Zarathustra envisions an evolutionary miracle of the will which enables it to will backward and forward at once, not in a literal sense but in the sense of its "return" to the earth as a place of origin. By remaining "faithful to the earth," the overman *wills the origins* of all that is and is thereby transformed, metamorphosed. Origins do not merely belong to the past; they do not merely pass away like an event in time; rather, they endure as the ongoing *fatum* of life. This is the *fatum* that contemporary humanity, which finds itself midway between beast and overman, abhors. For to be midway means to be nowhere on earth. The overman overcomes the midway state by way of a conversion, and in so doing comes full circle back to the earth and its species, bridging the chasm that separates humanity from the animal kingdom. The bridging is a metamorphosis, and it goes by the name of Dionysos, who is at once beast and god.

Zarathustra's message to the people in the marketplace—"Remain faithful to the earth"—is a profoundly conservative enjoinder. In it we hear a call to save the earth from those who have conquered it but who have not yet overcome their revulsion to it, like the shepherd in Zarathustra's vision. If Zarathustra does not stay in the saint's forest, it is not because he has no wish to be at one with the forest's animals. On the contrary, he goes down into the world because the shepherd's *dog* is crying for help. This dog, on which Zarathustra takes pity in his vision, stands for all the animal species of the earth. But to come to the aid of the dog Zarathustra must counsel the shepherd, who writhes on the ground with Gilgamesh's snake of nausea in his mouth, in the ways of self-transformation. Which is to say that by going down to the world of humanity Zarathustra in effect wills backward—backward along the evolutionary chain—in an effort to save the species of the earth from the rage of an incomplete humanity.

Who are the ones who truly understand Zarathustra? Not the saint in the forest, nor the people in the marketplace, nor even the "higher men" who become his disciples. Only the animals understand Zarathustra. Without his animals Zarathustra is nothing. "Do not go to man," says the saint, "go rather even to the animals." In his elliptical journey, that is precisely what Zarathustra does. After his long, futile odyssey among the contemporary race of human beings who have yet to overcome their half-way natures, Zarathustra returns to his mountain and says: "Only now do I know and feel how much I love you, my animals." The love of animals—their enduring, original nature in ourselves—is the *amor fati* that Nietzsche proposed at the end of philosophy.

Nietzsche once called himself a "destiny," but some hundred years later we still do not know what that statement could mean, or whether it means anything at all. All we know is that at the end of his active life Nietzsche saw a coachman flogging a horse in Turin. Overwhelmed by pity for the beast, he suffered a mental collapse from which he would not recover. We also know that at the time of his collapse he was working on his *Dionysian Dithyrambs*. Nietzsche's career as a whole, from *The Birth of Tragedy* to his last works, was essentially a long appeal to Dionysos, the mystery god of the earth. But Dionysos failed to appear, and we have by now forgotten what it means even to long for such an epiphany. Pentheus is our ruler, and the Cithaeron forest has disappeared. The city extends everywhere, while the Dionysian animals are either extinct or in hiding. It is an unlikely age for "the god who comes." But then again, one never knows in advance when or how the ancient *fatum* will happen, or who its victims will be.

THE SORROWS OF RHEA SILVIA

The hostile opposition between forest and civilization we have been tracing in this chapter is in many ways summarized by the legendary history of Rome, the so-called eternal city. Rome, more than any other city, has truly mythic origins. But by the same token it also has a truly mythic afterlife, for Rome's history has become a prodigious legend that still lives on. In this sense the myths of its foundation are irrevocable. An austere community of farmers and herdsmen does not come to conquer the world through mere diligence, prowess, or good fortune. Rome became Rome through the blessings of myth. Myths of origin—the Romans were obsessed with them—hold within their poetic logic a city's historical destiny, even after the city "falls."

Did Rome ever really fall? Its legend in any case lives on, spreading its shadow of empire across the earth still today. It suffices to scrutinize the American dollar bill—its Great American Seal that speaks in Latin mottoes (*annuit coeptis* [God blesses our beginnings] and *novus ordo seclorum* [a new order of the ages has arrived] from Virgil) and that features the emblem of the auspicious eagle, the bird of Jove—to realize that Rome remains eternal by virtue of the auspices of its beginnings. That is why it is so crucial to recall time and time again the story of this city's origins.

The traditional legends of Rome's foundation tell us, in their own way, that the city was born of the forests, but they also suggest that Rome had to turn against its matrix in order to fulfill its destiny. When Aeneas descends into the underworld in book 6 of the *Aeneid,* the shade of his dead father shows him the yet unborn generations of the family lineage—the illustrious individuals who will contribute to Rome's future greatness. The first in the series is a youth leaning on a headless spear. Anchises remarks:

> The youth
> you see there, leaning on his headless spear,
> by lot is nearest to the light; and he
> will be the first to reach the upper air
> and mingle with Italian blood; an Alban,
> his name is Silvius, your last-born son.
> For late in your old age Lavinia,
> your wife, will bear him for you in the forest;
> and he will be a king and father kings;
> through him our race will rule in Alba Longa. (6.1004–12)

We do not know very much about this character, Silvius, or what exactly it means that he was "born in the forest." It could mean that Rome's mother city, Alba Longa, had a sylvan origin. Furthermore there is some confusion about Silvius's place in the genealogy, for while Virgil identifies him as the son of Aeneas, Livy claims that he was the grandson. But Livy too remarks that Silvius was born in the forests (*casu quodam in silvis natus* [Livy 1.3.7]), and that all the subsequent kings of Alba Longa kept the last name *Silvius,* which means literally "of the forests."

This Sylvian family, as Livy calls it, leads from generation to generation in a genealogical line down to Romulus, the legendary founder of Rome. When Anchises points Romulus out to Aeneas in the underworld, he remarks that Romulus is destined to become a god, and that

> it is benath his auspices
> that famous Rome will make her boundaries
> as broad as earth itself, will make her spirit
> the equal of Olympus, and enclose
> her seven hills within a single wall,
> rejoicing in her race of men;

just as the Berecynthian mother, tower-crowned,
when, through the Phrygian cities, she rides on
her chariot, glad her sons are gods, embraces
a hundred sons of sons, and every one
a heaven-dweller with his home on high. (6.1033–43)

The great Romulus, who will exalt the Sylvian lineage to heaven and
enclose the seven hills of Rome within a single wall, also leads back
into the woods. Not only does he belong to the Sylvian family, but he
too, in his own way, is born of the forests. Let us follow the story.

Rhea Silvia was the daughter of Numitor, king of Alba Longa.
When his brother, Amulius, deprived Numitor of his throne and murdered his male children, he arranged for Rhea Silvia to become a vestal, ensuring thereby that she would remain childless. But as a virgin
guardian of the sacred fire, Rhea Silvia was raped by Mars on her altar
and gave birth to twin boys, Romulus and Remus. Amulius, horrified
for both religious and political reasons, ordered the infants to be
drowned in the Tiber, proclaiming them monsters. The twins, however, were carelessly abandoned in a basket near the river at high tide.
Livy reminds us that in those days the country was completely "wild
and uncultivated." A she-wolf, coming down from the hills to drink at
the river, heard the infants crying and, becoming mother to them, began to suckle them. When the boys were discovered by the herdsman
Faustulus, the she-wolf was affectionately licking them with her
tongue. Faustulus proceeded to take them into his care, and the two
brothers grew up as brigands in the forests of Latium.

Romulus, then, was born of the forests in more ways than one. He
was born of Rhea Silvia and belongs to the Sylvian family line; as an
infant he is mothered by the forest's mythic figure, the she-wolf; and
as a child he grows up in the forests. This same Romulus, after attain-
ing manhood and helping his grandfather win back the kingship from
Amulius, will go on to found Rome on the Palatine, "the scene of his
own upbringing" (Livy 1.7). Livy reports that in order to increase the
scant population of his new city, Romulus opened an asylum in a clearing on the Capitoline hill (1.8). Into this asylum he received forest
vagabonds—homeless unfortunates—who had been living in the wilderness outside the bonds of domestic religion and civil society. Thus
the refugees received by Romulus into Rome's civic asylum were also
"born of the forests."

But the myths of Rome's genesis also tell us that the city was fated to define itself antagonistically with regard to its matrix. To begin with we have the sinister story of Rome's relation to its mother city, Alba Longa. For the legendary history of Rome effectively begins with the destruction of Alba Longa. Livy makes it clear that nothing could have averted the war against Alba Longa. Some inevitable logic dictated it. To recast a famous historical saying: *Alba Longa delenda est*. Violated on the vestal altar by the true god of Rome—the god of war—Rhea Silvia did indeed give birth to a monster.

Furthermore, a paradoxical irony pervades the very concept of Rome as an *asylum*. During their youth Romulus and Remus enjoyed asylum in the forests of Latium, but when Romulus founds his city at the "scene of his own upbringing," he opens an asylum in a clearing. Those who entered the civic boundaries took refuge there from the forests, which became a frontier or margin against which the civic, strictly institutional space was defined. The god of sacred boundaries in Roman religion was *Silvanus*, deity of the outlying wilderness, and historically the natural boundaries of the Roman *res publica* were drawn by the margins of the undomesticated forests, which in ancient Roman law had the status of *res nullius* (belonging to no one). The public Roman domain—the domain of its civic jurisdiction—included the sacred city as well as the patricians' rural estates, but it did not extend past the edge of the forests. The forests were in fact commonly referred to as the *locus neminis*, or "place of no one" (it is probable that even the Latin word *nemus*, or woodlands, comes from *nemo*, meaning "no one").

City and forest were thus rigorously set off from one another. In the forests one was no one—*nemo*. The *res nullius* stood over against the *res publica* in such a way that a sylvan fringe gave the civic space its natural boundaries.

But the irony of the concept of asylum does not end here. In the preamble to this chapter we cited a passage from book 8 of the *Aeneid* which describes the precivic landscape of Rome beheld by Aeneas during his visit to Evander, the mythical king who established a colony at Pallenteum after his exile from Arcadia. Virgil calls Evander "founder unaware / of Rome's great citadel" (Virgil 8.413–14). Evander earns this venerable epithet not only because he helps Aeneas overcome his enemies on the Italian mainland, but because he was the first to establish a citadel at the site where Rome would eventually rise. Let us recall

what Evander tells Aeneas about the forests in whose midst he established his "poor and meager" citadel:

> These woodland places
> Once were homes of local fauns and nymphs
> Together with a race of men that came
> From tree trunks, from hard oak: they had no way
> Of settled life, no arts of life, no skill
> At yoking oxen, gathering provisions,
> Practising husbandry, but got their food
> From oaken boughs and wild game hunted down.
> In that first time, out of Olympian heaven,
> Saturn came here in flight from Jove in arms,
> An exile from a kingdom lost; he brought
> These unschooled men together from the hills
> Where they were scattered, gave them laws, and chose
> The name of Latium, from his latency
> Or safe concealment in this countryside.
> In his reign were the golden centuries
> Men tell of still, so peacefully he ruled,
> Till gradually a meaner, tarnished age
> Came on with fever of war and lust of gain. (8.415–33)

Virgil here recast the myth of Arcadia, Evander's original homeland in
the Peloponnesus, and makes of Rome's site an Arcadian forest whose
woodlands offered cover and shelter to Saturn after Jove had replaced
him as leader of the gods. Virgil links the word *Latium* to the word
latebra, or hiding place, to suggest that the word derives from the "latency" or concealment that Saturn found from Jove in the forests (*La-
tiumque vocari/maluit, his quoniam latuisset tutus in oris* [and chose /
the name of Latium, from his latency / or safe concealment in this coun-
tryside]). The theme of exile and asylum prevails in this crucial scene
of the *Aeneid.* The precivic forests of Rome not only offered asylum to
Saturn, persecuted by Jove, but also to Evander, who wandered in exile from his Arcadia. Nor can we forget that Aeneas too is an exile in
search of a new homeland. Saturn, Evander, and Aeneas converge in
this place as refugees, and the refuge is none other than Latium itself—
its latent forests of asylum.

Virgil of course knew that, just as Saturn's golden age gave way to
"a meaner, tarnished age," so too those forests around Pallanteum
gradually disappeared to make room for the great metropolis. Evan-

der's small citadel, he says, is "built heavenward by Roman power now," as if to suggest that Saturn would no longer find much refuge from Jove in this vicinity. There is in Virgil's scene a troubling awareness that Aeneas's arrival in Italy and Rome's ordained destiny as the greatest and most belligerent city on the face of the earth meant the end of the more authentic prehistory of Latium. For all its glory, civilization cannot console us for the loss of what it destroys. It destroys the matrix of its greatness, severing its ancient bonds with the land on which the citizens build their monuments to power and civic heroism.

To these remarks about Rome's legendary history we may add the following about its actual history: that as Rome turned against its matrix and went on to conquer the world, its civic administration also went on to triumph over the great forest mass of the ancient world. The forests were literally everywhere: Italy, Gaul, Spain, Britain, the ancient Mediterranean basin as a whole. The prohibitive density of these forests had once safeguarded the relative autonomy and diversity of the family- and city-states of antiquity, precisely because they offered a margin of cultural privacy, as it were. One could say that they actually fostered cultural diversities by providing the necessary "latency" for self-generating identity in language, customs, deities, traditions, styles, etc. The forests were obstacles—to conquest, hegemony, homogenization. They were, in a word, asylums of cultural independence. By virtue of their buffers, they enabled communities to develop indigenously; hence they served to localize the spirit of place. This is confirmed by the fact that in their woodlands lived spirits and deities, fauns and nymphs, local to *this* place and no other. Through these local inhabitants the forests preserved the spirit of difference between the here and the there, between this place and that place.

In the drive to universalize their empire, the Romans found ways either to denude or traverse this latent sylvan mass. They were not merely invaders who sacked and plundered and then moved on; they were builders of roads, imperial highways, institutions, a broad integrated network of "telecommunications." It was through their administration that they assimilated their nearby and far-flung colonies into the sovereign order of their institutions. It suffices to observe how the Roman architectural style took over the world. Traveling around Gaul, the Near East, or North Africa, we can still see the astonishing uniformity of the Roman towns, each built according to a standard prototype, with the same structural principles and the same cuts of stone, so much so that what you see in the valleys of Gaul is what you get on the headlands of Asia Minor. Empire erased untold variations of local culture: a diversity fostered and preserved by the latency of locale.

Legend and history are distinct from one another, no doubt, yet Rome reveals to what extent their relation remains indeterminate. For what is Rome if not a legendary historical phenomenon? Scholars, historians, and archaeologists will continue to uncover the empirical facts of its early history, but if we want to account for Rome's *destiny,* as opposed to its history, we must wander through the forests of its fabulous origins, the way Aeneas wandered through the Avernus wood in search of the golden bough that would permit him to descend into the underworld.

That underworld was protected from the outside world by the Stygian forest. You could enter it easily enough, but without the golden bough you could not find your way out of it. We too need a golden bough of sorts when dealing with the story of Rome's past, if only to find our way back to the present and future, where its legend lives on. Aeneas, after all, descends into the underworld not merely to visit the past but above all to consult the oracle of the future—which speaks from the past. Likewise we who wish to interrogate the mythology of Rome's origins must look both backward and forward, and in both directions we see the shadows of myth.

One of the myths which persists about Rome is that its history follows a pattern of rise, decline, and fall. There are as many ironies in this story as in the ones about Rome's foundations. According to tradition the founding of Rome was from the start predicated upon the fall of Troy. But is it not the case that, precisely in its "fall," Rome, like Troy, succeeded in gaining a new life and continuity in history? Its universalism was merely taken up in new versions of the same story. By falling the eternal city perpetuated its legend; and still today we can say that its conquest of the world will not come to an end until all cultural diversities will have been reduced to sameness by new forms of empire for which Rome remains forever the model.

FROM MYTHIC ORIGINS TO DEFORESTATION

We often hear the phrase "Greek and Roman" used in reference to a constellation of events we think of, vaguely enough, as our "antiquity," ignoring the various distinctions and oppositions that lurk in the modest conjunction "and." Among present-day Greeks and Italians there exists an expression that goes back to the Second World War, when these Mediterranean neighbors unwillingly became enemies for a while: *una faccia, una razza.* Or, as the Greek adapted it, *mia faccia, mia razza.* It so happens that the rhyme which phonetically reinforces this proverbial identity between the two peoples can also be rendered in English: "one face, one race." It may be that over the centuries these faces and races have come to appear as one, the way the faces of husband, wife, and domestic dog turn strangely similar after numerous years of conjugality. In the past, however, a veritable "sea" of differences separated the Greek and Roman peoples, in face and race as well as temperament.

Already by Homer's time the Greeks were looking to the "winedark" expanse of the open sea as a horizon of destiny. Their love of its dangerous extravagance was wary yet profound. The Roman hatred of the sea, on the other hand, had tenacious roots in the unprivileged but reliable soil of Latium, where a rustic people emerging from the forests cleared the land for cultivation and loved above all the prosaic results of their labor. The Roman dread of the sea finds expression not only in the first half of Virgil's *Aeneid* but also in the very site of Rome, upstream at a safe remove from the mouth of the Tiber. Rome remains an enigma. Having deliberately refused the destiny of a great port city, it sought the shelter of the land; but by thus turning its back on the world it conquered the world all the more inexorably. Its vast crown eventually stretched out everywhere, but its trunk was rooted in a single place—the *lucus* of Latium itself.

Yet in retrospect we could say that the Greeks and Romans were of the same "face and race" at least as far as the demise of their civilizations is concerned. This demise is what is implied in the notion of "antiquity." It is an unusual notion, if one thinks about it. It implies a bygone epoch of cultural flourishing followed by a decline into barbarism and a subsequent revival of the past. Where does this peculiar notion come from? Why does Western culture have an antiquity in the first place? Where and when did this cyclical view of civilization, so wholly embraced by Vico, originate?

It did not originate in the Renaissance, that much is certain. We have just seen that Rome's foundation was mythologically predicated upon the downfall of Troy. From the ashes of a fallen city another one is born. In this respect the Romans were similar to the Greeks, who also looked back to a lost antiquity in their myths of origins. In the case of the Greeks, however, the myths recalled a certifiable historic reality. The age of the Mycenean war heroes had long since passed by the time Homer sang its legendary splendor, and Homer had no doubts that he belonged to the darkness of its extinguished shadows. The great palaces of Mycenae fell before 1100 B.C. Economy and overseas trade collapsed. Written documents vanished altogether. Arthur Slavin, a historian, writes:

> For as certainly as the Greeks lost writing, the greatest monuments of its revival showed men conscious of their connection with a distant past, over an abyss of 500 years of silence. Homer claimed one dialect of the Greek language as a legacy. Through him, later Greeks claimed as their common legacy a historical tradition. And to it they traced the origins of their cities, families, gods, and heroes. Every Classical cult had at its center a god or hero familiar from myths, epics, and folktales of Mycenaean origin. (*The Way of the West*, 1:121)

In other words, what we consider Greek antiquity began with an even earlier, lost antiquity. We are often not impressed enough by the fact that the first epic of Western literature, the *Iliad*, tells a story of the destruction, not the foundation, of a great city. Troy falls to the Achaeans. Historically, however—and Homer seemed to know this— the destruction of Troy and the downfall of the civilization that destroyed it were simultaneous events. Thucydides puts it mildly when he states: "The return of the Greeks from Troy . . . witnessed many changes; revolutions and factions disrupted the cities" (*History* 1.12). When Agamemnon returns from the war, he is murdered in his own bath by his wife and her lover. When Odysseus returns home, after twenty years abroad, he finds his kingdom in turmoil—not because of war or invasion but because of domestic anarchy.

These stories have an undeniable element of historical truth in them, suggesting that Homer was somehow aware of the fact that while the warlords of Mycenae were storming the walls of Troy, the foundations of their own societies were crumbling. Troy was destroyed from without, but Mycenae fell from within. Is it not the case, then, that while the *Iliad* tells the story of a destruction, it veils the story of a decline? What is certain is that this "first" literary monument of Western culture speaks from the night after the decline, claiming for the Greeks an illustrious but also tragic antiquity—that of a society that could not save itself from self-ruin.

These reflections lead us back to Vico's theory of the law of entropy which supposedly holds sway over the order of institutions. But before we return to Vico to conclude this chapter, let us consider at least one other reason why Greeks and Romans deserve to be conjoined by that innocent "and," which is not so innocent after all. In their drives to promote their civilizations both the Greeks and the Romans also promoted a mindless deforestation of the Mediterranean. Already by the fourth century B.C. Plato recalls with nostalgia a time when forests still covered much of Attica. Speaking of the hills around Athens, Plato writes in the *Critias:*

> In comparison of what then was, there are remaining only the bones of the wasted body . . . all the richer and softer parts of the soil having fallen away, and the mere skeleton of the land being left. But in the primitive state of the country, its mountains were high hills covered with soil . . . and there was abundance of wood in the mountains. Of this last the traces still remain, for although some of the mountains now only afford sustenance to bees, not so very long ago there were still to be seen roofs of timber cut from trees growing there, which were of a size sufficient to cover the largest houses; and there were many other high trees, cultivated by man and bearing abundance of food for cattle. (*Critias* 3.75)

The deforestation Plato alludes to in this passage came about largely as a result of the Athenian navy's need for wood. Forests became fleets, sinking to the bottom of the wine-dark sea. Trees became masts, drifting among the waves of Poseidon. The temple to Poseidon at Cape Sounion, overlooking the waterway that leads into and out of the bay of Piraeus, is an inspiring monument still today, but the barren mountain on which it stands, as well as the entire surrounding landscape, now drenched with that brilliant Hellenic light, shows no traces of the forests that once covered them.

As for the agrarian Romans, the insatiable mouth of empire devoured the land, clearing it for agriculture and leading to irreversible erosion in regions that were once the most fertile in the world. It is hard to imagine that a civilization as brilliant as that of the Greeks, or an empire engineered and administered so efficiently as that of the Romans, could remain so blind in their practices as to bring about the ruin of the ground on which their survivals were based. In the following passage from *The First Eden: The Mediterranean World and Man* (117–18), David Attenborough describes the ecological legacy of our "antiquity":

To them [the Romans], it seemed that nature could be rav-
ished and plundered as men wished. They saw no reason
why men should not take what they wanted as often as they
wanted. The state gave legal title to undeveloped land to anyone who cleared it of forest. As the human population
around the Mediterranean grew, so more and more of the
forests that had once girdled it with green were destroyed. . . . When states went to war, entire forests were
devastated to provide the armies with vehicles and the navies
with ship. So, as the classical empires spread from east to
west along the Mediterranean and north into Europe, the forests were demolished.

The consequences were most severely felt on the south-
ern and eastern shores, where the rainfall was low. Here the
forests had been a key factor in maintaining the health of the
land. They absorbed the rain when it fell in winter, and retained it in the soil around their roots. In summer they re-
leased it slowly, so that the shaded land never dried out entirely, and springs flowed throughout the year. Their removal
was catastrophic. The provinces of North Africa were, originally, among the richest in all the Empire. Six hundred cities
flourished along the African shore between Egypt and Mo-
rocco . . . By the end of the first century A.D., North Africa
was producing half a million tons of grain every year and
supplying the huge city of Rome, which had outstripped its
own agricultural resources, with two-thirds of its wheat.

The end was not long in coming. There is still argument
as to how much a change in climate contributed to the final
collapse. The balance of opinion seems to be that, though
rainfall did diminish, the crucial blow was the stripping away
of trees and the relentless ploughing and reploughing to extract maximum tonnage of crops. Year after year the soil of
the fields was lost. In summer it was baked by the sun and
blown away by the hot winds. In the winter, rain storms
swilled it away and rivers carried it down to the coast and de-
posited it in their deltas . . .

All along the African coast, the land dried out. Wheat
could no longer be grown; olives, which had once been pro-
hibited by law lest they should displace the more highly val-
ued wheat, were the only crops that would grow. Then even

they began to fail. The human population dwindled. Sand blew through the stony fields and the grandiose buildings tumbled into ruins. Today, the harbor at Leptis, where once great ships came to fill their holds with grain, is buried beneath sand dunes.

The syndrome described by Attenborough is best summarized by the fate of Artemis, goddess of the forests and superabundant fertility. Her temple at Ephesus was one of the Seven Wonders of the World, but it lies in ruin now, as does her city, which two thousand years ago was one of the most prosperous of the ancient world. The ruin came about not as a result of wars or some violent calamity but by the steady degradation of its surrounding environment. Samples of the pollen grains in the sedimentary strata around Ephesus indicate that four thousand years ago, around the time of the first settlements, the hills were covered with forests of oak. A few centuries later the oak gave way to plantain weed, which typically colonizes land that has been cleared for animal grazing. By 100 B.C. it is wheat pollen that predominates in the samples, indicating that pasture had given way to intensive agriculture. Transformed from forests to pasture to cultivated fields, the land around Ephesus became more productive, to be sure, but the loss of the outlying forests eventually led to disaster. As the hills could no longer retain water, the runoff rushed down into the valley. With the ploughing of the land, soil erosion was exacerbated and led to a severe buildup of silt in the great harbor of Ephesus, so severe in fact that the city was eventually forced to relocate itself farther along the coast. At least four times the city's harbor silted up in this fashion, and by the ninth century A.D. it was too shallow to receive the Byzantine fleet. The city of Artemis declined into oblivion. Today it lies some three miles from the sea, prostrate under the rays of Apollo's glory.

And here we may finally return to Vico, whose speculations about civilization's emergence from out of the forests served to get us underway in this chapter. Vico believed that nature and history followed two fundamentally different laws. Civilizations rise according to the "ideal eternal history" of institutional evolution. They eventually fall by virtue of a law of entropy which brings about disorder in the system as a whole. Once the cities fall, the forests return and reclaim the ground on which they were founded. For Vico nature was a closed and stable system of self-regeneration. He never suspected that civilization's law of entropy could contaminate or compromise the domain of nature as a whole, nor was he in a position, historically speaking, to suspect such a thing.

Some two-and-a-half centuries later, we now know that what Vico says about the reforestation of the civic clearings is not only inaccurate but also ironic. While forests did indeed reclaim part of Rome's civic space during the early Middle Ages, the same is by no means true for most of the illustrious ancient cities that had their origins in the once densely forested environment of the Mediterranean. It suffices to travel around Asia Minor today and visit such cities—Ephesus, Miletus, Aphrodisias, Priene, Pergamum, Side, Kaunos, Halikarnasos, etc.—to see how nakedly they lie under the open sky. There is little in the vicinity to hide the celestial auspices now. The *lucus* long ago lost its limits, and from its wide-open eye one can see today not only the ruins of a great ancient city but also those of an even more ancient forest. One face, one race. So many deserts.

William Blake, *Dante and Virgil Penetrating the Forest*

SHADOWS OF LAW

DURING THE EARLY MIDDLE AGES THE NORTHERN FORESTS
of Europe were still vast, stretching across the continent like domes of
darkness and the indifference of time. Interspersed throughout them
were smaller or larger settlements lost in the shadows of antiquity's
decline. With respect to the medieval social order that was reorganiz-
ing itself on the basis of new feudal and religious institutions, the forests were *foris,* "outside." In them lived the outcasts, the mad, the lovers, brigands, hermits, saints, lepers, the *maquis,* fugitives, misfits, the
persecuted, the wild men. Where else could they go? Outside of the
law and human society one was in the forest. But the forest's asylum
was unspeakable. One could not remain human in the forest; one
could only rise above or sink below the human level. *Renaud de Montaubon,* a medieval epic describing the privations suffered by a band of
robbers, moved its readers with pity for the forest outcasts, much the
way a television documentary about the homeless might move Americans today. The audience felt a certain shame, since the forests did
indeed harbor such misery.

The Christian Church that sought to unify Europe under the sign
of the cross was essentially hostile toward this impassive frontier of
unhumanized nature. Bestiality, fallenness, errancy, perdition—these
are the associations that accrued around forests in the Christian mythology. In theological terms forests represented the anarchy of matter
itself, with all the deprived darkness that went with this Neoplatonic
concept adopted early on by the Church fathers. As the underside of
the ordained world, forests represented for the Church the last strong-
holds of pagan worship. In the tenebrous Celtic forests reigned the

Druid priests; in the forests of Germany stood those sacred groves where unconverted barbarians engaged in heathen rituals; in the nocturnal forests at the edge of town sorcerers, alchemists, and all the tenacious survivors of paganism concocted their mischief.

The Church had good reasons to be suspicious of these havens. Age-old demons, fairies, and nature spirits continued to haunt the conservative woodlands, whose protective shadows allowed popular memory to preserve and perpetuate cultural continuities with the pagan past. If certain elements of pagan culture survived the Christian revolution in covert forms, leaving their legacy in popular legends, fairy tales, and traditional folklore, it was thanks in part to the fact that Christian imperialism did not take it upon itself to burn down the forests in a frenzy of religious fervor, despite the enjoinder of certain ambiguous passages from the Old Testament. In Deuteronomy, for example, Moses orders his people to destroy the sacred groves of the gentiles: "But thus shall ye deal with them: ye shall destroy their altars, and break down their images and cut down their groves, and burn their graven images with fire" (Deut. 7:5). "And ye shall overthrow their altars, and break their pillars, and burn their groves with fire. . . ." (12:3). "Thou shalt not plant thee a grove of trees near unto the altar of the Lord thy God. . . ." (16:21). Fortunately for the forests, and for the ancient folklore they fostered and perpetuated, the Christians did not organize crusades on the basis of such passages. All of which serves to remind us that, when forests are destroyed, it is not only an accumulated history of natural growth that vanishes. A preserve of cultural memory also disappears.

It should not surprise us by now that, here too, the paradoxes abound. We have already seen how forests have a way of destabilizing and even reversing the terms that would place them on either side of an imaginary dichotomy. While the Christian attitude toward forests was generally hostile, hagiography tells of many devout souls who took to the wilderness and lived as hermits far from the corruption of human society. There, in the forests' asylum, they lived in the intimate presence of their God. Their holy bewilderment helped them purge the soul of sin and make it saintly. The medieval epic of *Valentine and Orson,* for instance, tells of how Orson, a wild, subhuman man living in the forests, is captured by some hunters and brought back to human society. There he undergoes a complete education, learning the codes of civilization, the eloquence of speech, and the fundamental doctrines of Christianity. His natural prowess turns him into an exceptional knight, while his moral education directs that prowess toward worthy and virtuous deeds. After an illustrious career of chivalry, Orson chooses finally to reject human society and return to the forest in order to devote himself exclusively to God. He returns to the scene of his origins as a holy hermit. All is transfigured, yet all is the same, as the space of the profane and the sacred become one. The human world that Orson leaves behind lies between two extremes that intersect in the forest.

The story of Orson is merely a prelude to the intriguing patterns that we will see emerging throughout the present chapter, which explores the relation between forests and civilization during the Christian era. We will see how the law of identity and the principle of noncontradiction go astray in the forests, and how certain conventional distinctions collapse when the scene shifts from the ordinary world to the forests outside its domain. The profane suddenly becomes sacred. The outlaw becomes the guardian of higher justice. A virtuous knight turns into a wild man. The straight line becomes a circle. Or the law of gender is confused. Be it religious, political, psychological, or even logical law, the forests, it seems, unsettle its stability. Forests lie "beyond" the law, or better, they figure as places of outlaw.

It would be historically inaccurate to say that forests lay literally beyond the law during this period. An English outlaw who took refuge in the forest, for instance, violated the king's so-called Forest Law when he entered it (see sections two and three). Nevertheless, as an outlaw who sought the forest's asylum, he entered, as it were, the *shadow of the law.* The shadow of law—be it social, religious, or otherwise—is not a place of lawlessness; it lies beyond the law like a shadow that dissolves the substance of a body. The shadow of law is not opposed to law but follows it around like its other self, or its guilty conscience.

As Georg Lichtenberg once said about books: "A book is a mirror. When a monkey looks in, no apostle can look out" (Lichtenberg, 64). Likewise when we look into the forests—at what happens in them, at how they get represented, at their allegorical implications—we see a strange reflection of the order to which they remained external. From this external perspective the institutional world reveals it absurdity, or corruption, or contradictions, or arbitrariness, or even its virtues. But one way or another it reveals something essential about itself which often remains invisible or inaccessible to the internal perspective.

In our discussion of antiquity we were led to consider above all the logic of tragedy which haunted the relation between forests and civilization. In this chapter we will be led to consider the logic of *comedy*, understood in a broad sense of the "happy ending." The difference is as fundamental as the difference between paganism and Christianity. The sylvan world was no mere shadow of civilization for the ancients; it had for them a substantial reality of its own, at times more substantial than civilization itself. Tragedy, we suggested, was a reminder that every founding law is also a fatal transgression—a transgression of some other law. Such is the essence of polytheism: a plurality of laws laying equal claim to legitimacy, often in strife with each other. In the Judeo-Christian doctrine, however, the law of a single, universal God holds sway over the totality of creation. As a result this law has only its own shadow to fear. The Christian revolution in the West puts an end to tragedy as the highest form of wisdom, for Christianity (like Platonism) promises a happy ending. You have only to choose it, by turning to the light of God. In its insistence that the happy or sorrowful outcome (damnation or salvation) depends upon free will and no longer upon a fatal order of necessity (against which the tragic hero was powerless), Christianity effectively destroys the ideological basis of tragedy. This revolution is reflected everywhere in our theme, however indirectly or latently, even in spheres that do not necessarily have specific connections to Christian doctrine. A new "comedy" pervades the ideology of law in all its instantiations.

Even in secular domains the reigning law does not have another law as its antagonist; it has rather its own shadow of corruption, or bad faith, or imperfection. Nor can one say that divine law and secular law are fundamentally or ideologically opposed to one another during the Christian era; on the contrary, an opposition between them arises only when the latter falls short of its avowed vocation or oversteps its legitimate limits.

Christian theology accounts at least in part for the fact that forests during this period so often become the locus of comic inversions, errors, reversals, etc. If it is true that forests figure as places of the law's shadow during the Christian era, then it seems natural they should also appear as the locus of comedy, which is essentially ironic, dialectical, and critical. Comedy, in other words, *shadows its subject*. Understood in this broad sense, the comic is not necessarily funny; it can be harsh, bitter, ironic, or even desperate. But unlike tragedy, it serves to remind us that beyond the reigning law there is only the law's outcast shadow.

The literature and iconography of the Middle Ages inform us of the survival of an ancient figure whose genealogy goes back as far as the epic of *Gilgamesh*. This bestial creature lives in the forest alone, naked and hirsute, strong and aggressive, for the most part speechless, feeding on herbs or the raw flesh of venison, yet he is essentially human. He is known during the Middle Ages as *l'homme sauvage,* or the wild man. In literature we meet him for the first time in the figure of Enkidu, the trusted friend of Gilgamesh who grew up among wild beasts and who had literally to be seduced into human society by a harlot; we find him much later in the figure of Tarzan and, even more recently, Italo Calvino's Baron in the trees. Vico's giants belong to this species of creature as well.

The medieval imagination was fascinated by wild men, but the latter were by no means merely imaginary in status during the Middle Ages. Such men (and women as well) would every now and then be discovered in the forests—usually insane people who had taken to the woods to make their dwelling there. If hunters happened upon a wild man in the more remote recesses of the forest they would frequently try to capture him alive and bring him back to the community for people to marvel and wonder at. Given the Christian doctrine of species creation which excludes intermediary species between beast and human, the wild man was generally thought to be a human being who had either lost or never acquired the faculty of reason, thereby degenerating to the level of a beast.

In Chrétien de Troyes's romance, *Yvain,* the knight Calogrenant meets such a wild man in a clearing of the Broceliande forest. This "rustic boor," as he is called, tends a flock of wild bulls and is hideous beyond belief. Unlike most wild men, however, this one can speak. Questioned by Calogrenant about his nature, he declares that he is indeed a "man." It is then Calogrenant's turn to identify himself to this strange brother in kind. "I am, as thou seest," says Calogrenant to the wild man, "a knight seeking what I cannot find; I have long sought without success." The wild man asks: "And what is this thou fain wouldst find?" Calogrenant answers: "Some adventure whereby to test my prowess and bravery" (*Yvain,* 184).

Calogrenant identifies himself as a knight looking for *avanture,* adventure. The wild man does not understand the concept of adventure.

It is not, in fact, an easy concept to grasp. What, indeed, is the *avanture* that Arthurian knights go searching for in the forests? By Calogrenant's own admission, adventure figures as an occasion to test one's prowess and bravery beyond the walls of the court. If the wild man does not understand the concept, it is because he embodies, quite naturally, the very prowess and bravery that Calogrenant seeks to test in himself. Even the wild bulls fear this rustic boor, "[f]or when I can get a hold of one I give its two horns such a wrench with my hard, strong hands that the others tremble with fear, and gather at once round about me as if to ask for mercy" (ibid.). The prowess and bravery of the wild man are beyond dispute. He has no need to put to the test what belongs to him by nature. Only an alienated nature seeks adventure.

In the same romance, Yvain—one of the most illustrious of the Arthurian knights—goes off in search of adventure and meets the wild man whom he has heard about from his cousin Calogrenant. Master of the forest, the boor shows Yvain the way he must follow through the forest to reach the magic fountain. Yvain thanks him and takes his leave, "[b]ut more than a hundred times he crossed himself at the sight of the monster before him—how Nature had ever been able to form such a hideous, ugly creature" (190). Yvain takes his leave from the wild man in horror, but in truth he merely goes off in search of this monster within himself. For the wild man and the knight share, in effect, a common nature. What distinguishes Yvain from his natural counterpart is merely the law of the social contract, for the knights of medieval romance are at bottom wild men who have become heroes of the social order, yet who must periodically return to the forests in order to rediscover within themselves the alienated source of their prowess, the wild man's prowess. In short, the wild man defines the knight's own shadow—the shadow of his heroism, his prowess, his rage.

This is borne out in a dramatic way later in Chrétien's romance when Yvain goes completely mad in a fit of amorous grief and becomes a raving wild man. Repudiated by the woman he loves, he loses possession of his rational faculties and disappears into the wilderness. The following passage describes the knight's transfiguration:

> Such a storm broke loose in his brain that he loses his senses;
> he tears his flesh and, stripping off his clothes, he flees across
> the meadows and fields, leaving his men quite at a loss, and
> wondering what has become of him. They go in search of

him through all the country around—in the lodgings of the knights, by the hedgerows, and in the gardens—but they seek him where he is not to be found. (216–17).

Yvain's men will not find him where they seek him, for they search the medieval rural countryside. But Yvain has abandoned the lodgings, the hedgerows, and the gardens, in short, he has crossed the very boundary of the human world and taken to the nonhuman depths of the forest. There, in his dark and wild refuge, "he lies in wait for the beasts in the woods, killing them, and then eating the venison raw. Thus he dwelt in the forest like a madman or a savage" (217).

If Yvain were the only chivalric hero to become a wild man during the course of his *avanture* there would be no reason to insist on the critical episode of his metamorphosis in the forest, yet the fact is that most of the famous knights of medieval romance undergo similar degenerations, becoming wild men for shorter or longer periods. In all the main versions of the Tristan legend, Tristan becomes temporarily a wild man in the Forest of Morrois. The case of Lancelot is more extreme. Lancelot loses his sanity on four separate occasions, spending years in the woods as a savage. The case of Lancelot in particular dispels the superficial notion that such episodes of literal bewilderment served merely as conventional hyperboles for the representation of the knights' amorous devotion to their ladies, or their despair over being repudiated by them. Only in the case of the fourth and final recurrence of Lancelot's insanity is the degeneration brought on by love. These episodes, in other words, have an altogether sinister, more subterranean meaning that points beyond the topos of amorous devotion to a mysterious law of self-overcoming which underlies the law of medieval society itself. It is as if the chivalric champions of the social order must lose themselves without in order to find themselves within, thereby regenerating the forces that defend the social order.

In Yvain's case it is clear that his transformation into a wild man enables him to encounter the shadow of his own exalted knighthood. At the extremity of his degeneration he undergoes a regeneration, or better, a conversion. His bewilderment in the forest marks the turning point of his *avanture*. When he eventually recovers his sanity Yvain is both empowered and raised to a higher order of moral equilibrium. Having overcome himself, he is now more heroic and virtuous than ever. His subsequent deeds indicate as much. All the adventures that Yvain sets out to seek now come to meet him from every direction, giving him ample opportunities to turn his prowess against evil giants and fiendish oppressors of innocent people. Indeed, like the wild man who masters a flock of bulls, Yvain now becomes the lord of a staunch and grateful lion whose life he saved from a malicious serpent in the forest. The slaying of the serpent—one of his first exploits after recovering his sanity—is symbolic to an extreme degree. It indicates that Yvain's lion, which henceforth stays by his side during the subsequent adventures, is more than merely a beast of great prowess, like the wild man's bulls. The lion is a symbol of prowess married to virtue. In other words it is a sign that Yvain's metamorphosis in the forest has turned him into a *redeemed* version of the wild man who first showed him his way through the forest at the outset of his errantry.

The experience of bewilderment not only empowers Yvain but also enables him to realign his prowess and direct it against the inimical forces that threaten to pervert the social order. Such episodes provide insight into what knight-errantry is all about in the medieval imagination of those who served as an audience for these romances. It is about the realignment or social rehabilitation of the lawless nature against which the social order defines itself. The knight must descend into its shadows as a way of overcoming its menace. From this perspective we cannot say that knight-errantry merely represents an occasion for knights to "compensate themselves in the wilderness for the tension engendered by protracted confinement and enclosure within the peace of society," as Friedrich Nietzsche once wrote (*Genealogy of Morals,* 40). Such a theory of repression, which states that the "hidden core [of bestiality] needs to erupt from time to time, the animal has to get out again and go back to the wilderness," fails to account for the way in which the hero of medieval romance rediscovers his alienated nature only in order to reaffirm the law of its overcoming. The natural prowess of the wild man is the same *realigned* power that preserves a precarious social order against the dangers that threaten it both from within and without.

It is from the same perspective that we must understand the comic patterns that govern medieval romance. Comedy in this case means the renormalization of law and circumstance. Errancy through the forests is a comic adventure to the degree that it turns the world inside out, or upside down, only to reestablish the proper order. The romance typically ends with the knight's recognition by his lady and his repatriation within the system, but these are merely superficial aspects of the comic ending. The more essential ending lies in the knight's empowerment of the law that preserves his alienation from his own shadow. This law is forever threatened by the nature within and without, but the knight returns from his adventure as its self-surpassing defender.

FOREST LAW

Medieval chivalric romances tend to represent forests as lying beyond the confines of the civic world and its institutions of law. But early on in the Middle Ages many forests had already come under the jurisdiction of law. The word "forest" in fact originates as a juridical term. Along with its various cognates in European languages (*foresta, forêt, forst*, etc.), it derives from the Latin *foresta*. The Latin word does not come into existence until the Merovingian period. In Roman documents, as well as in the earlier acts of the Middle Ages, the standard word for woods and woodlands was *nemus*. The word *foresta* appears for the first time in the laws of the Longobards and the capitularies of Charlemagne, referring not to woodlands in general but only to the royal game preserves. The word has an uncertain provenance. The most likely origin is the Latin *foris,* meaning "outside." The obscure Latin verb *forestare* meant "to keep out, to place off limits, to exclude." In effect, during the Merovingian period in which the word *foresta* entered the lexicon, kings had taken it upon themselves to place public bans on vast tracts of woodlands in order to insure the survival of their wildlife, which in turn would insure the survival of a fundamental royal ritual—the hunt.

A "forest," then, was originally a juridical term referring to land that had been placed off limits by a royal decree. Once a region had been "afforested," or declared a forest, it could not be cultivated, exploited, or encroached upon. It lay outside the public domain, reserved for the king's pleasure and recreation. In England it also lay outside the common juridical sphere. Offenders were not punishable by the common law but rather by a set of very specific "forest laws." The royal forests lay "outside" in another sense as well, for the space enclosed by the walls of a royal garden was sometimes called *silva,* or wood. *Forestis silva* meant the unenclosed woods "outside" the walls.

Two further remarks about the origin of the word. First, the word itself speaks of the "outsideness" of forests with respect to the public domain. Second, an ecologist today cannot help but be a monarchist of sorts. Up until the decline of the great European monarchies, nothing was quite as offensive to peasants as the royal hunting privilege, for a number of good reasons. Nevertheless, these hunter-kings appear as the first public or institutional conservationists in history. If "forests" in the juridical sense had not been introduced during the Middle Ages, forests in the natural sense may well have begun to disappear from the face of civilized Europe long ago.

There exists a treatise on forest laws composed in 1592 by a man who lends credibility to Otto Rank's notion that people are destined to live out the meaning of their last names: *A Treatise of the Laws of the Forest, Shewing not only the Laws now in Force but also the Origin and Beginnings of Forests; and of what Forests are, and how they differ from Chases, Parks and Warrens; with all such things as are Incident to either, . . .* by John Manwood. The treatise deserves attention for its uniqueness as a historical document. As an admiring editor wrote in his preface to a later edition: " 'tis the only valuable book written on that subject . . . [it contains] many useful things, not to be found in any other Law Book whatsoever" (William Nelson, preface to the fourth ed., 1717). Two-and-a-half centuries later, that editor's fond remark still holds true.

Writing toward the end of the reign of Queen Elizabeth, at a time when the Forest Law was frequently abused and the forests of England were undergoing rapid degradation, John Manwood, who was a jurist, a gamekeeper of the Waltham Forest, and a judge at the New Forest, laid out in systematic fashion the ancient laws pertaining to the afforestation and preservation of the wilderness. He admitted that few of the ancient laws were still being enforced, and he lamented the widespread laxity regarding their enforcement. One could say that Manwood undertook to defend those laws not so much because he was a monarchist but because he was a naturalist. Only the monarch, he thought, could save the wilderness from the ravages of human exploitation.

Manwood's treatise is pervaded by nostalgia for bygone times when the king could afforest at will and when infractions of the forest laws were punished severely, sometimes to the extent of the enucleation or castration of the offender. In composing his treatise Manwood hoped not only to reinvigorate the Forest Law but also to define and formalize it in such a way as to vindicate its legitimacy. We cannot review here the wealth of fact and detail which fills this extraordinary work of love, but some of Manwood's remarks about the Forest Law should be brought forward for their historical as well as symbolic significance.

We may begin with Manwood's account of how the first forests, in the juridical sense, came into being. He writes:

> Before this nation was replenished with inhabitants, there were many great woods full of all sorts of wild beasts then known in England; and after the same came to be inhabited, the woods were, by degrees, destroyed, especially near the houses; and as the land increased in people, so the woods and coverts were daily destroyed, and, by that means, the wild beasts retired to those woods which were left standing, and which were remote from their habitations. (Manwood, 139)

Describing a state of affairs before the time of William the Conqueror, this initial account tells a universal story about humankind's consuming encroachment upon wild woodlands. One is forced to wonder how, after so many centuries of the same, there are any forests at all left to assault in Europe. What could preserve a remnant of woodlands and wildlife from the rapacious demands of an advancing humanity? In those times, only the king. Manwood continues:

> But there were still, and even in the Saxons time, many great woods which were not destroyed, and those were called Walds, that is, forests or woods where wolves and foxes did harbour; which being afterwards destroyed by Edgar, a Saxon king, *Anno* 959, and very few remaining, the Welshmen paid him a yearly tribute of wolves-skins; and those and such ravenous beasts being thus destroyed, the residue being beasts of pleasure, as well as delicate meat, the kings of this land began to be careful for the preservation of them, and in order thereto to privilege certain woods and places, so that no man may hurt or destroy them there; and thus the said places became forests. (139–40)

In other words, the "said places" were placed off-limits by royal decree. It is important to notice the logic here. According to Manwood's account, afforestation came about only after the extinction of England's "ravenous beasts," like the wolf. What remained were the "beasts of pleasure." These were the wild but nonravenous animals of the woods which, in Manwood's catalog, included the hart, hind, hare, buck, doe, fox, coney, pheasant, and partridge. Manwood goes on to offer a rigorous definition of what constitutes a forest. This is the definition that interests us, for it is at once legal, natural, and symbolic:

> A forest is a certain territory of woody grounds and fruitful pastures, privileged for wild beasts and fowls of forest, chase, and warren, to rest and abide there in the safe protection of the king, for his delight and pleasure; which territory of ground so privileged is meered and bounded with unremovable marks, meers and boundaries, either known by matter of record or by prescription; and also replenished with wild beasts of venery or chase, and with great coverts of vert, for the succour of the said beasts there to abide; for the preservation and continuance of which said place, together with the vert and venison, there are particular officers, laws, and privileges belonging to the same, requisite for that purpose, and proper only to a forest, and to no other place. . . . And therefore a forest doth chiefly consist of these four things: of vert and venison; of particular laws and proper officers. . . . All of which are appointed that the same may be better preserved for a place of recreation for kings and princes. (143)

This definition of what constitutes a forest is governed by the idea of privilege—the privilege granted by the king to his wildlife to live in freedom and safety within the afforested areas of his kingdom. Manwood repeatedly insists that such privilege is what distinguishes a forest from other places, "because many other places have woods, coverts, and fruitful pastures, yet are no forests; so that 'tis this privilege that distinguishes a forest from those places" (144). The forest should be replenished with venison, writes Manwood, "for otherwise 'tis no forest; and in such case men may fell their woods which they have in the forest, and destroy their coverts, because there are no beasts to take shelter there, and may also convert their pasture into arable" (ibid.).

The concept of a forest thus becomes more and more precise, and more and more precarious: a forest is no longer a forest the moment it loses the wildlife it is meant to protect. If the forest ceases to be a *sanctuary* for wildlife, it is no longer a forest.

Essential to the royal forests are the "particular laws" that enforce the preservation of the "vert and venison," the former indispensable to the survival and well-being of the latter. "And these laws of the forest," writes Manwood, "are called particular laws, not because they relate to one forest, and no more; for they are general to all forests alike; but because they are particular only, and proper to forests, and not to any other places" (146). As a place unto itself like no other place, a forest requires its own particular laws. The existence of such laws accounts for the difference between a forest and a "chase," for example, since offenders in the latter were punishable by the common law.

Given that a forest "comprehends" the wildlife specific to a chase, a park, and a warren (Manwood differentiates and taxonomizes the species), *all* such animals receive the king's protection once they cross the natural boundaries that define a forest: "and therefore, if any such beasts or fowls of chase, park or warren, are hunted or killed in a forest, 'tis a trespass of the forest, and to be punished by the laws thereof, and by no other law whatsoever" (148). Enforcement of the Forest Law is the responsibility of the king's especially appointed officers: game wardens, forest sheriffs, and so forth. These officers of law, moreover, have jurisdiction only over their appointed forests. Without this particularized legal bureaucracy, forests cannot exist.

Let us summarize. For Manwood a forest is a natural sanctuary. The royal forests granted wildlife the same sort of asylum that the Church granted criminals or fugitives who entered its precincts. Forests and churches thus become equivalent in their authority to offer asylum, one to men or outlaws and the other to beasts of pleasure. Manwood believed that the word itself—*forest*—contained in its etymons the notion of asylum. He remarks that the words *silva* and *saltus* are not proper Latin equivalents for a forest, since they refer only to a wood: "Though the word *sylva* is often taken and translated for a forest, and so is the word *saltus,* yet neither of them are proper words for a forest, but for a wood" (151). A forest, to be sure, is a "place full of woods. . . . But it doth not follow from thence, that every wood is a forest, though there are deer and other wild beasts there, *unless the place is privileged by the king for the quiet and protection of the wild beasts there*" (ibid.).

Adopting phrases from Budaeus's *Liber de Philologia,* Manwood states that the proper Latin equivalent for a forest would be *sylva sacrosancta* or *Saltus sacrosanctus*—a sacrosanct wood. He goes on to claim that Latinists compounded the word *foresta* from the words *fera* and *statio,* "i.e., a safe abode for wild beasts." He then goes on to suggest that the English word "forest" is compounded of the words *for* and *rest,* "the name being derived from the nature of the place which is privileged by the king for the rest and abode of the wild beasts" (151–52). An ancient philology comes to the aid of an ancient corpus of forest laws.

It is natural law itself, claims Manwood, that gives the king the right to afforest *ubicumque eam habere voluit,* wherever he so pleases (140). His status as the transcendent sovereign of the land invests the monarch with responsibility for the natural world on which his kingdom is founded. Implicit throughout Manwood's treatise, though never declared outright, is an unconditional imperative behind the monarch's divine right and responsibilities: thou shalt save the wilderness from utter destruction. By privileging certain places as forests the king declares them off-limits to the encroachments of history. The very space of history must be contained, restricted, held in check, and the voracious world of social humanity must be prevented from assimilating the land entirely to its own ends. Sanctuaries of original nature must continue to exist. The sovereign therefore inherits a dual responsibility along with his crown and privileges: he must govern the domestic world of his kingdom, but he must also delimit its boundaries and preserve a margin of wilderness.

What we sometimes fail to understand, and what critics of the royal hunting privilege refused to accept, is that an essential dimension of the king's personhood belonged to the forest. The wilderness beyond the walls of his court belonged every bit as much to his nature as the civilized world within those same walls. In that wilderness the king avidly pursues the fugitive deer in a chase that takes on the character of a sacred ritual. The hunt ritualizes and reaffirms the king's ancient nature as civilizer and conqueror of the land. His forests are sanctuaries where the royal chase may reenact, in a purely symbolic way, the historical conquest of the wilderness. The king cannot be deprived of this symbolism for it belongs to his nature as well as his sovereignty. The king embodies and represents in his person the civilizing force of history, but by the same token he harbors in his sovereignty a savagery that is greater and more powerful than the wilderness itself. Had he not this more primordial nature he could be neither the protector nor the ruler of his kingdom. As sovereign of the land, the king overcomes the wilderness because he is the wildest of all by nature. A double nature, therefore, links the king to the forest no less than to the court.

So who is Manwood's king ultimately? He is the savior of the forests' beasts of pleasure, but he is also their persecutor. The "ravenous beasts" of England had been destroyed by the end of the first millennium by Edgar, "a Saxon king, *Anno 959*." After such extinction came conservation, but under a wholly new regime of law. In the royal forests there is now only one ravenous beast left: the king himself. All the other wolves are gone. The surviving beasts of pleasure, once hunted by other ravenous beasts, are now hunted solely by the lupine monarch within the protected confines of his forests. Thus does the king's sovereign nature belong to nature, and thus does it return every so often to the sanctuaries to ritualize the law of its overcoming. Forests lie beyond the royal walls as the court's shadow. Like the chivalric knight of medieval romance the king too errs through his forests, but in his case the comedy takes the form of a long and eager chase full of reversals and peripeties, full of sound and fury, which ends with the death of a beast of pleasure.

OUTLAWS

The Forest Law discussed by Manwood was introduced into England in a rigorous way by William the Conqueror, who fell upon the Saxons in the eleventh century like a cataclysm. The Norman invader laid such waste to the island that twenty years after his arrival, the *Domesday Book* reported that many villages still lay in ruins and that in some regions of the country it was impossible to determine whether anyone at all had survived. Most of the English nobles had either been killed, imprisoned, dispossessed of their land, or driven into exile. New masters took the place of old ones, and servitude became the lot of many of the free sokemen of the Danelaw. The Normans brought with them their foreign language, imposed their laws and customs on the English with harsh intolerance, and generally made themselves hated. The hatred gradually gave way to resentment, but it would last for a long time to come.

William's passion for conquest was surpassed only by his passion for the hunt. "He loved the stags as much / as if he were their father," we read in a poem from the *Peterborough Chronicle*. William's passion was such that he afforested vast regions of the country *ubicumque eam habere voluit,* wherever he so pleased. Entire villages were demolished and their inhabitants driven off the land when William decided to afforest the region that came to be known as the New Forest. Its name has since become ironic, for it remains to this day the oldest forest of England; yet it was appropriately named at the time, since much of it was not even wooded then.

The Norman's Forest Law was as harsh as it was inviolable. Infractions were dealt with ruthlessly, offenders being punishable by enucleation or castration. In the entries on the death of William the Conqueror in the *Peterborough Chronicle* (1087), the poem now referred to as "The Rhyme of King William" (written in Old English), alludes to the inordinate measures taken by this legendary hero of conservation, William the Conqueror, father of the stags. The "Rhyme" deserves to be cited in its entirety:

> He caused castles to be built
> And poor men to be greatly oppressed.
> The king was very severe
> And took from his subjects many a mark
> Of gold and more hundreds of pounds of silver.
> He took this weight and with great injustice
> From his people, for little need.
> He fell into covetousness,
> And he loved greediness very much.
> He set up many deer preserves and also enacted laws
> That whoever killed a hart or hind
> Should be blinded.
> He placed a ban on harts, also on boars.
> He loved the stags as much
> As if he were their father.
> He also made laws concerning hares that they should run
> free.
> His great men complained of it and the poor men bewailed
> it,
> But he [was] so stern that he did not care for all their hate.
> But they had to follow the king's will
> If they wanted to live or hold land,
> Land or property, or particularly his favor.
> Alas! that any man should be so proud,
> Should raise himself up and account himself above all men.
> May almighty God show mercy to his soul
> And grant him forgiveness of his sins. (Rositzke, 121)

Ironically, the forests that William's laws placed beyond the reach of human interference did not thereby become asylums for William's beloved stags alone, but also for English noblemen dispossessed of their lands and ancient rights. Many who could not accept subjugation or work the land as laborers, and who were too proud to beg, took to the forests and lived there as they could, hunting animals and harassing the Normans. From their lairs in the forests they continued to resist the invaders through fierce guerrilla warfare, setting traps and ambushes for their enemies. These bands of English exiles placed themselves outside of the law—a law whose legitimacy they repudiated. Their hatred of the Normans was widely shared by the native population, and some of the more daring outlaws gained considerable fame throughout the land. Their reckless raids and reprisals against officers of law became the matter of legends and popular ballads, giving birth in England to a fabulous figure who would continue to fascinate the popular imagination for centuries to come: that of the heroic outlaw fighting the forces of injustice from his lair in the forest.

Herewald, Fulk Fritzwarin, Eustace the Monk—these are historical characters who achieved legendary fame as outlaws. The latter two belong to the reign of King John, but Herewald fought against William himself. Along with the Danes he sacked the monastery of Peterborough and carried off its treasures. The island of Ely in the fenlands became his base. A century and a half later, the baron Fulk Fritzwarin took to the forests to wage a guerrilla war against King John, who had done him injustice, and he too achieved widespread notoriety through his exploits. By that time the Norman conquest had become only a distant memory in the lore of the outlaw, and by the time the tales of Gamelyn, Robin Hood, and Adam Bell began to appear (the earliest ballads were written down in the fourteenth and fifteenth centuries, although an oral tradition presumably existed since much earlier times), the Norman invasion no longer played a part in the outlaw legends, nor were the outlaws historical characters as such. But like their historical predecessors, these outlaws of folklore were neither mere criminals nor enemies of justice. They appear in the legends as rebels challenging a law that had perpetrated injustices against them, hence as enemies not of the law but rather of its degradation. In their forests they haunt the law's shadow, but in so doing they confuse the conventional dichotomy between light and shadow. By placing themselves outside an arbitrary or corrupt law, they appear as the true champions of natural justice, while institutional law appears as the mere shadow of its resplendent ideal.

To understand the extent to which the British outlaw is anything but revolutionary in his ideology, let us dwell a moment on the rhetoric of a historical document that has come down to us from the fourteenth century. In 1336 Lionel, a real outlaw, sent the following letter to Richard de Snaweshill, who at that time was the chaplain of Huntington:

> Lionel, King of the rout of raveners salutes, but with little love, his false and disloyal Richard de Snaweshill. We command you, on pain to lose all that can stand forfeit against our laws, that you immediately remove from his office him whom you maintain in the vicarage of Burton Agnes; and that you suffer that the Abbot of St. Mary's have his rights in this matter and that the election of the man whom he has chosen, who is more worthy of advancement than you or any of your lineage, be upheld. And if you do not do this, we make our avow, first to God and then to the King of England and to our own crown that you shall have such treatment at our hands as the Bishop of Exeter had in Cheep; and we shall hunt you down, even if we have to come to Coney Street in York to do it. And show this letter to your lord, and bid him to cease from false compacts and confederacies, and to suffer right to be done to him whom the Abbot has presented; else he shall have a thousand pounds worth of damage by us and our men. And if you do not take cognizance of our orders, we have bidden our lieutenant in the North to levy such great distraint upon you as is spoken of above. Given at our Castle of the North Wind, in the Green Tower, in the first year of our reign. (Cited by Keen, 200)

This is not the voice of someone who would overthrow the established order, or who challenges it at its basis. It is the voice of an outlaw who swears to God and to the King of England that he will take matters into his own hands and harass those who abuse the law by "false compacts and confederacies." Lionel speaks of "disloyalty," of "laws," of "rights," and of "worthiness." He refers to himself as a "king" who routs the profane and "ravenous" beasts of lawlessness. He will "hunt down" Richard de Snaweshill—a wolf in the chambers of the institutions. As king of the rout of raveners, Lionel is the hound of justice in a world that perverts its principles and turns them inside out.

We are dealing here with the logic of comedy at its most rudimentary level, namely that of the absurd. Comedy does not always entail cynicism—Lionel as well as the legendary British outlaws are the very opposite of cynics in their moralistic faith in justice—but it always entails absurdity. Absurdity is based on the fact that something appears as other than what it intends or pretends to be. Such absurdity can become comic when there is an *unmasking* of the deceptive appearance. In the case of heroic outlawry, it is the outlaw himself who unmasks the institutions that conceal behind the cloak of legitimacy their perversion of the law. Lionel the outlaw will not let stand the false compacts and confederacies of those raveners who dress up their profanity in the apparels of legitimacy.

Given this logic of the absurd, whereby appearances mask a contrary reality and the outlaw becomes the law's apologist, it is not surprising that British outlaw stories are pervaded by a motif typical of comedy in the usual sense, namely the motif of *disguise*. In the legends of Herewald we find that the outlaw disguises himself as a potter and enters the king's camp near the Isle of Ely. Robin Hood and his band are forever disguising themselves to trick the sheriff or carry out some fabulous exploit. In the *Littel Geste of Robyn Hood and his Meiny,* one of the oldest surviving ballads of Robin Hood, it is King Edward himself who disguises himself as a monk in order to penetrate Robin Hood's hideout in the forest. The motif of disguise creates a number of comic effects, to be sure, but thematically it runs much deeper in these stories than would appear at first glance. The guile, tricks, and disguises, in short, the various ruses of *deception* that characterize the outlaw's strategies, all seem to point to the same fundamental or underlying absurdity, namely the travesty of the law by its presumed custodians. Corrupt sheriffs, bribed judges, arbitrary decrees of law—these are common stock in stories that evoke a world where the apparels of justice all too often merely disguise its opposite. Disguise, then, is first and foremost the scandal of the legal system. Once the scandal becomes apparent the outlaw assumes his own disguise in order to answer the system, reflecting through his ruses its own insidious deception. In short, he shadows the system.

The phenomenon of disguise appears in the very name of "Robin Hood," which most certainly derives from it. The *hood* is that which *hides,* providing a protective cover for the outlaw's head. The name "Robin," in turn, derives from the French *robe,* the garment that cloaks the body. We could say, then, that from head to foot Robin Hood exists under cover, in the shadow of the law. But the first and most essential cover of all for the outlaw is none other than the forest itself. The forest represents his locus of concealment. Its canopy is his hood, and its foliage his robe. In its shadows the outlaw finds safe haven from the established order and can harass his enemies like an invisible presence that every now and then reveals itself, suddenly and unexpectedly, only to withdraw again under the forest's cover. Robin Hood wears the forest's protection wherever he goes.

By the same token the forest is more than merely a strategic hiding place in the outlaw lore; it is the place of cover which symbolically governs the comic absurdity that defines the relation between reality and appearance, or the institutional order and its own shadow. Forests represent an *inverted* world, or the shadow of irony itself. The ruses of deception adopted by outlaws in their guerrilla tactics arise as a response to an already existing deception. In the logic of these stories, then, deception serves ultimately to unmask the deceptive veneers of the ordinary, legitimate world. Such paradoxical logic no doubt helps explain why forests typically become the locus of comic inversions and disguises in the literature of this period. Nor are they restricted merely to this period. In comedies of the Elizabethan period, forests also provide the scene for disguise, tricks, gender reversals, confusions of identity, and so forth, becoming the site where conventional reality loses its persuasion and gets masked or unmasked in a drama of errors and confusion. If one of the main functions of comedy is to dramatize the instability or absurdity of the world as human beings define it, forests represent a natural scene for the enactment of its ironic logic, thanks to their shadows of exteriority with regard to society.

Medieval outlaw legends belong to the comic mode in more ways than their ironic inversion of the world's appearances. Just as comedy turns a situation upside down in order eventually to set it right again, so too the outlaw stories that unmask the travesty of justice typically end with reconciliations that vindicate the outlaws' faith in justice. The worthy cause, which momentarily puts itself outside of the law, eventually makes peace with the law as justice comes to prevail. Almost all the medieval outlaw stories possess a happy ending that reveals to what extent they in fact reaffirm the founding principles of the social order. Like Yvain and the medieval knights who eventually recover their reason after bewildering themselves in the forest, the outlaw is sooner or later repatriated within the system whose corruption he descried. In the *Gesta Herewaldi,* Herewald is pardoned by the king and restored to his former dignity. Likewise Fritzwarin, Gamelyn, and Robin Hood, after challenging the arbitrariness of the law, are rewarded for their efforts by ceremonious reconciliations with the king. The king, whose very person embodies the legitimacy of the law, typically grants them pardon, allowing them to reenter human society and repossess their full rights.

These happy endings imply that heroic outlawry represents an attack on the system of law from *within*—but from within its own shadow. The shadow of the law is not in this case some other law, as in the tragic myths of antiquity. Dionysos does not belong to the shadow of Thebes's law; he unleashes an anarchy fundamentally opposed to the one that founds civil society. The forest outlaw has a wholly different vocation. He challenges the law on its own terms, exposing its inherent contradictions, shortcomings, ironies; in short, the failures of its pretensions to correspond to its reality. His vocation represents a practical critique. As a guardian of the law's ideal justice, he takes to the forest to wage his war, but his happy ending lies in vindication—his repatriation within the system. Tragic wisdom gives way to comic heroism. Once absolved, the outlaw leaves the forest behind and steps into the light of salvation.

<h2 style="text-align:center">DANTE'S LINE OF ERROR</h2>

The forests of comedy take on a new dimension of meaning in Dante's *Divine Comedy,* but one that is not incongruous with what we have seen so far. When Dante finds himself lost in a "dark forest" at the beginning of the *Inferno,* he too is in the law's shadow, only in this case it is not secular law but God's moral law. Here too the pilgrim is an outlaw of sorts, and the forest in which he errs is likewise an inverted world, but the difference is that Dante is not an "innocent." Unlike secular law, God's law is infallible. The "dark forest," then, is not a refuge from the law's injustice but an allegory for Christian guilt in general. The process of redemption, however, follows certain comic patterns already familiar to us.

Our hermeneutic approach to Dante's poem requires particular attentiveness and caution. When forests become allegorical they already become treacherous; but when the allegory is theological, as in Dante's case, they become even more so. There is no better example of this than the opening verses of the *Divine Comedy,* which are among the most famous in literary history:

> In the middle of our life's path
> I found myself in a dark forest,
> where the straight way was lost. (*Inferno* 1:1–3)

Sinfulness, error, errancy, alienation from God—these are the allegorical associations of Dante's *selva oscura,* or dark forest. The forest stands for the secular world as a whole deprived of God's light, or better, for the perdition of a soul cut off from God's saving grace. The protagonist finds himself disoriented and bewildered in the midst of his mortal life. The straight way is lost. The forest of moral confusion is deviant, pathless, issueless, terrifying. Leaving aside its allegorical import for a moment, we may remark that the opening of the *Divine Comedy* may well be the first occurrence in literature of a motif that will later become archetypical: fear of the forest. In earlier medieval literature we encounter protagonists who fear wild animals or malicious brigands in the forest, but Dante's fear in the "Prologue Scene," as it is sometimes called, has no specific object. It is a vague and indefinite fear verging on existential anxiety. In effect it is the forest's alienation itself that terrifies him:

> Ah, how hard to describe it,
> this savage forest, so dense and rugged,
> which even in memory renews my fear! (1:4–6)

The Prologue Scene of Dante's *Inferno* has been commented on and analyzed endlessly by scholars over the centuries, yet a number of basic questions, amazingly enough, remain either unasked or unanswered. This is because one merely takes for granted that the *selva oscura* represents a place of confusion where the pilgrim goes astray, or deviates from the straight path of moral rectitude. And why, after all, should one not take such a thing for granted? Is the forest not typically the place where one gets disoriented, where the straight path is lost? Such self-evident assumptions make it easy to overlook the fact that the allegorical logic in the first canto of the *Inferno* does not quite support them.

One of the questions that goes unasked concerns precisely the status of the straight line. The first verses allude to "life's path" as well as to the "straight way." We naturally assume that mortal life is being compared here to a linear path that loses its way in the forest. But perhaps that is not the case at all. The "middle of our life's way" is not a midpoint on a linear trajectory; it is rather a turning point that calls for conversion, or turning around, in the Christian sense. At this midpoint one can no longer proceed in a straight line, or if one does one goes astray. *It is precisely because Dante is moving in a straight line that he loses himself in the "selva oscura".*

This becomes evident when we raise another question about the Prologue Scene, passed over by scholars, which is as simple as it is crucial: How does Dante get out of the *selva oscura?* We do not know. The poem does not tell us. All we know is that he finds himself immediately in another kind of landscape—the deserted slope of a mountain whose summit shines with the light of transcendence. The scene changes abruptly. Dante is all of a sudden on a *piaggia diserta,* a desert beach. The forest gives way inexplicably to the desert. How does Dante get from the closed density of the forest to the open vacancy of a desert? Why this inversion of landscape? And what does this inversion have to do with Christian conversion?

If what we claimed is true—that by following a straight path Dante goes astray—then this inversion of landscape makes perfect sense. As Dante finds himself no longer in a forest but on a desert slope, he is now free to walk in a straight line up the mountain. In fact he proceeds to do so. The path, however, becomes promptly unviable as our pilgrim encounters three beasts that block his way—a leopard, a lion, and a she-wolf (allegories for the three major categories of sin: fraud, violence, and incontinence). Dante is not out of the forest after all, for these beasts belong to its wilderness. We could say, therefore, that the landscape changes to a desert while remaining essentially a forest. By inverting the topography of the scene without changing its nature, Dante is able to dramatize for the reader that the straight line, the *diritta via,* is the line of error.

Dante's solitary attempt to climb the mountain has been appropriately interpreted by some critics as a misguided attempt at *direct* intellectual transcendence of the material world, in the Neoplatonic vein. The flight of the soul toward its spiritual origin on a straight ascending axis turns out to be a false promise for Dante, for it fails to bring the *will* into alignment with the *intellect.* In Christian doctrine the will bears the burden of sin, for it bears the weight of the body itself. While the faculty of reason may understand the good, the will must find a way to overcome the gravity of the material world. It can do so only by means of a moral conversion—by turning to God in faith and humility—and not merely through intellectual enlightenment alone. In the Prologue Scene Dante *sees* the light of transcendence at the top of the mountain, yet he cannot proceed toward it insofar as his will suffers impediments. The *selva oscura,* then, figures as the scene of the will's impotence or abandon.

We know from Dante's literary autobiographies that just prior to embarking upon the *Divine Comedy* he had in fact been following a strictly intellectual path. His earlier work, the *Convivio,* tells the story of his rapturous love affair with philosophy, which promised him transcendence through intellectual contemplation. That promise proved vain and insubstantial for Dante, so much so that we could say that the *diritta via* of his philosophical engagement is what leads him directly into the *selva oscura.* Indeed, in the general economy of Dante's career, the unfinished *Convivio* appears as what the Germans call a *Holswege:* a path through the forest that leads nowhere.

Thus the pilgrim cannot proceed in a straight line up the mountain of salvation. Three beasts block his way. He is rescued from his dilemma by Virgil, a figure of wisdom who arrives on the scene and informs him that the way up the mountain actually leads *downward* through the center of gravity—through the very heart of the material world. Following his guide, Dante will descend through the circles of Hell, pass through the center of the earth, and then reemerge on its other hemisphere, finding himself on the shores of the mountain of Purgatory. Strangely enough this is the *same* mountain that he had tried vainly to climb at the outset of his journey. Having taken the longer, more circuitous, descending route—the route of humility instead of arrogance—the pilgrim undergoes a miraculous conversion. The world is turned upside down, or right side up, and Dante is now finally in a position to find his way out of the *selva oscura.*

If the forest of the Prologue Scene represents a wilderness of sin and bestiality—the material world in all its fallenness—deforestation in the broad allegorical sense would seem to be the essence of the purgatorial process that leads Dante up the mountain of Purgatory. But this is a strange kind of deforestation indeed, for at the top of the mountain Dante in effect finds himself once again in a forest. It is no longer the *selva oscura* but rather the *selva antica,* or ancient forest, of the earthly paradise. Something uncanny haunts the poem here. The forest is not only a place of departure but also a place of arrival, so much so that a series of striking verbal parallels recalls the Prologue Scene here in the earthly paradise. The intersections between the two scenes suggests that the *selva antica* is a redeemed, or prelapsarian, *selva oscura.* This redeemed forest no longer inspires fear but enchantment. The purgatorial process has made Dante's will "free and straight," as Virgil tells him (*Purgatorio* 27:130–31), but "straight" is an ironic adjective in this particular context. It cannot be understood in a rectilinear sense. On the contrary, what Virgil suggests to Dante at the top of the mountain is that he is now free to *wander aimlessly* throughout the beautiful woodlands, without error or terror. He has freed himself from the *diritta via*—the line of error.

In fact the first thing Dante does after he has been left alone in the ancient forest is to wander about this way and that:

> Already desiring to explore inside and out
> the divine forest, so dense and alive,
> which tempered the new day before my eyes,
> without delay I left the bank,
> proceeding slowly slowly through the country
> whose ground exuded fragrance everywhere. (28:1–6)

The word *vago* that opens the canto means "desirous" (hence it recalls the faculty of will), but *vagare* in Italian also means "to wander." Dante's will has now become free to wander, to stray, in a word, to *divagate*. The will's freedom, and even its straightness, takes the form of divagation. In other words, by the time Dante arrives at the earthly paradise he has learned to *master the ways of the forest*. He has become a forester. When he meets Beatrice in this same forest, she will reaffirm this explicitly:

> Here you will be for a short while a *forester;*
> and with me you will be forever a citizen
> of that Rome whereof Christ is a Roman. (32:100–102)

The next question we must ask at this point is why Dante's earthly paradise appears as an ancient forest? What before was profane has now become sacred, to be sure, but this redeemed forest nevertheless remains an enigma. What is it that distinguishes it from the dark forest of the Prologue Scene? In what sense is it "redeemed"? And what does such redemption have to do with the redemption of the human will? We cannot hold back in our interpretation here but must go to the heart of the matter.

The crucial difference between the redeemed and unredeemed forest is the following: Dante's *selva antica* is merely a denatured *selva oscura*. Only because it is thus denatured can the pilgrim wander around the ancient forest at will, freely. The *selva antica* is the *selva oscura* deprived of its dangers, its savagery, in short, of its wildlife. Here there are no more lions, no more leopards, no more she-wolves. Thanks to the purgatorial process, this forest has ceased to be a wilderness and has become a municipal park under the jurisdiction of the City of God.

In Christianity's vision of redemption, the entire earth and all of its nature become precisely such a park, or artificial garden.

The beasts in Dante's Prologue Scene are allegorical, to be sure, but in their allegorical status they retain some literal link to the earth's wildlife, for the *selva oscura* refers ultimately to unhumanized nature. In Christian doctrine the redemption of nature—and this includes human nature in its fallenness—means its complete rehumanization, for God originally created Adam in His own image and gave him mastery over the beasts. To say that the human will has been redeemed means that it has triumphed over nature, mastered its wilderness (Dante the forester). The overcoming of nature is God's will and therefore His law, which works itself out through human history. Whether we call it redemption or mastery, this law guarantees the happy ending of the comedy as a whole. The comedy in this case is "salvation history." Its law declares that the wildly diversified freedom of nature shall be overcome and that only the human will shall remain "free," in accordance with God's law. The triumph of the will over its shadow—its own impotence—is what sustains the allegory of the *Divine Comedy*.

What remains enigmatic about Dante's scheme of redemption, however, is its need to posit a denatured forest at the top of the mountain of Purgatory. Given the Christian humanism that sustains the poem, it would seem more fitting to find a city rather than a forest at this end point of the purgatorial journey. Saint John seems more consistent than Dante when he envisions a geometrically designed "new Jerusalem" at the end of his Book of Revelation. Such a city which "lieth foursquare," and where "the length and the breadth and the height of it are equal"—such a city, "according to the measure of a man," seems altogether more appropriate as the allegorical counterpart to Dante's *selva oscura*. Instead, at the other extremity of the dark forest we have another forest, or the same denatured forest, where Dante may wander about freely and become a forester.

Dante's journey of course does not end in the earthly paradise but takes him beyond, toward "that Rome whereof Christ is a Roman," namely paradise itself. From the *selva oscura* he comes to the *selva antica,* after which he ascends the spheres of heaven and finally arrives at the great "celestial rose" of paradise, where the glorified souls have their seats. This celestial rose appears as the final metamorphosis of the forest that so terrified Dante in the Prologue Scene. From forest to garden to celestial rose, the earth loses its gravity. The rarefied image of the rose brings to its comic conclusion the Christian dream of levitation. But there is more to that dream than the fantasy of levitation. Levitation means that nature has been overcome, not merely left behind, and that its wilderness has been brought under the governance of law. In a word, remastered.

We claimed at the outset that when forests become allegorical they become treacherous, for allegory easily obscures the links between forests in the figurative and literal senses. The *Divine Comedy* deploys a daunting machine of allegory indeed, but we who approach a new millennium at the speed of light are in a historical position to approach the poem from a certain distance, as it were, from which perspective it reveals itself as an allegory of will—the will of civilization to overcome nature and achieve unconditional human mastery over the earth, in the name of God's law. Call it redemption or call it salvation, this will is the will to power.

By the same token we are in a position to see precisely the sense in which the *selva oscura* represents the shadow of law in Dante's Prologue Scene. If the law means the will's absolute empowerment, its shadow figures as the will's impotence—its failure to empower itself. This impotence is the terror of Dante's *selva oscura*. But Dante must pass through its shadow to overcome its darkness, for according to Christian doctrine the process of redemption involves the redemption of the earth as a whole, not merely its transcendence. What this means is that nature too must be drawn into the comedy. If the Neoplatonists were happy to rise above the material world, or leave it behind through intellectual enlightenment alone (the *diritta via*), Christianity insists on descending to the center of nature's gravity and mastering it through the force of will. Dante therefore cannot simply climb up the mountain in a straight line when he finds himself lost in the *selva oscura,* for the earth as a whole must become the legitimate inheritance of humankind.

SHADOWS OF LOVE

In literary history forests begin to appear early on as the scene for what later comes to be known as the "unconscious." A story from Boccaccio's *Decameron* will serve as our example. The *Decameron* has been called a "human comedy," as opposed to the "divine comedy" of Boccaccio's predecessor, and with certain qualifications the characterization is apt enough. The story that interests us is particularly comic, for the theme for the entire Fifth Day of the *Decameron* (on which the novella is narrated) prescribes a happy ending: "Here begins the Fifth Day, wherein, under the rule of *Fiammetta,* are discussed the adventures of lovers who survived calamities or misfortunes and attained a state of happiness" (405).

The third story of the Fifth Day tells of two young lovers who run away from home and end up getting lost in a forest. Pietro Boccamazza belongs to an aristocratic Roman family. Agnolella is the daughter of a well-respected but bourgeois father. Pietro wants to marry Agnolella, but his family refuses consent, threatening to disown him and thereby forcing Agnolella's father to deny her hand in marriage. So one morning Pietro and Agnolella elope on horseback and head toward a town where Pietro has some friends. On their way they come across a nefarious band of soldiers. Agnolella takes flight into a "huge forest," but Pietro is seized. When Pietro promptly manages to escape from the rogues' clutches he too takes to the forest, but he cannot find his companion. Each is left alone, and each gets completely lost wandering through the pathless woods in search of one another.

After a day of desperate errancy, Agnolella happens upon a cottage and receives hospitality from an elderly couple. During the night, however, the house is raided by bandits. Agnolella hides herself in a haystack in the yard. One of the robbers, with nothing better to do, hurls his lance into the haystack unawares and almost kills her. The head of the lance tears through her clothes and grazes her left breast. She remains unharmed, but the bandits make off with her mare. Meanwhile Pietro has also spent the day erring miserably through the forest, "shouting and calling, sometimes going round in circles when he thought he was proceeding in a straight line." By nightfall he is exhausted, and he climbs into a tree to pass the night, fastening his mare to an oak. But during the night he is overcome by horror as he sees a pack of wolves approach his beloved mare, which, thrown into a panic, attempts in vain to escape. Pietro watches as the wolves close in. They bring the mare to the ground and tear it apart, gorging themselves on its innards.

The next day Agnolella is escorted to a nearby castle by the kind elderly couple, while Pietro comes across some shepherds who lead him to the same castle. The castle belongs to a family that has close ties with both the lovers' families. The noble lady, after hearing the lovers' stories and seeing how determined they still are to get married, arranges for a splendid wedding in her mountain retreat, "and it was there that they tasted the first exquisite fruits of love" (431). The same lady then intercedes with the kinsfolk on their behalf, and so Pietro and Agnolella go on to live to a ripe old age "in great peace and happiness."

This is hardly one of the more remarkable tales of the *Decameron*, but, like all of them, it reaches deep into the *selva oscura* of social law. Boccaccio never psychologizes his protagonists in the *Decameron*, yet he discloses through literary figures the obscure underworld of their passions. We must approach any novella of his with the assurance that it possesses an implicit but deliberate literary logic, for Boccaccio remains the greatest of literary storytellers. In the case of this novella, the happy ending seems predicated upon the experience of alienation which the two lovers undergo as they lose one another in the forest. Pietro and Agnolella are not merely united again after losing each other; rather, they find each other for the first time in this happy ending. When they set out on their elopement they knew neither themselves nor each other, for they were ignorant of the nature of the desire that was drawing them together. In short, they were both virgins— virgins in the literal as well as the psychological sense. With characteristic subtlety Boccaccio remarks that during their journey the two lovers did no more than exchange an occasional kiss: "Since they were afraid that they might be pursued," writes Boccaccio, "they had no time to stop and celebrate their nuptials, so they simply murmured sweet nothings to one another as they rode along, and exchanged an occasional kiss" (425). Later we learn that it was only after their marriage that they "tasted the first exquisite fruits of love."

The lovers' mutual estrangement in the forest, then, figures as their symbolic initiation into the mysteries of sexuality. At the outset they may have defied the authority of their families and overcome the obstacles that kept them apart, but they had yet to come to terms with the compulsive desire that urged them to matrimony. This desire is of a paradoxical nature, for just as surely as it draws the lovers together, so too does it drive them apart. It is as if this unifying desire must first withdraw back into itself—its primordial sources—before coming out of itself in the sexual encounter.

As the lovers go astray in the forest, then, they enter the shadow of the sexual impulse, where the benevolence of love gives way to dramas of violence. They are both in their own ways symbolically raped, Agnolella by the spear that tears her clothes and grazes her breast, and Pietro by the scene of wolves assaulting his defenceless mare. Earlier Pietro was actually seized by the band of soldiers and stripped of his clothes before he managed to escape. From this perspective the forest figures as the place of sexuality's deeper source in violence and bestiality. But these symbolic rapes represent more than an adolescent awakening to the darker side of sexual desire. They dramatize above all the singular state of *loneliness,* or of the one-against-many entailed in the scene of rape. Loneliness is the state that matrimony repairs by turning two into one, so to speak, yet before they can become one, Pietro and Agnolella must first become two, which is to say they must first estrange themselves in the forest.

What they discover in their estrangement is that loneliness exposes them to the threat of an overpowering multiplicity. The two lovers who have singled each other out through their passion are threatened throughout Boccaccio's story by figures of multiplicity. Their initial separation is caused by a band of a dozen inimical soldiers; Agnolella almost loses her life (and her virginity) to a group of prowling bandits; and Pietro's lonely mare is attacked by a pack of wolves. It seems that the lovers must confront in these experiences the contrary of what love ostensibly desires, namely the sole and legitimate possession of its object. The one-for-one equation of love gives way to a different equation: the one-against-many.

In other words, the violent seizure entailed in the act of rape or ravenous assault appears in this novella as the shadow of love—the shadow of love's impulse to appropriate its object. The difference lies essentially in the element of consent. Love, and this means above all the sexual encounter that consummates it, figures as self-expropriation according to the law of consent, but in love's shadow this element of consent is disregarded. In the forest Pietro and Agnolella witness how the object of desire is either seized arbitrarily by robbers (they steal her mare), or assaulted savagely by wolves.

This law of personal consent is precisely what Boccaccio's novella, in its deepest dimension, explores. Failing to obtain the legitimate consent of their families, Pietro and Agnolella elope in the name of a more authentic law—the mutual consent of love itself. Pietro belongs to an aristocratic family that refuses to expropriate him to a family of the middle class, considering him its own possession. Pietro rebels against the will of such institutional authority and violates it. Agnolella does likewise. In so doing the lovers act on the basis of their personal will, yet their choice to individuate themselves in such a radical manner means that they must discover for themselves the essential loneliness of the personal will. As they enter love's shadow they discover that love's law of consent is violable, that the will of others easily overpowers it, and that solitude means being vulnerable to the randomness of desire. In other words they discover in the forest the impersonal nature of desire itself.

The forest reveals that desire has no virginity. It does not belong to itself, it belongs to everything that shares in the life impulse itself. Desire is a promiscuous sort of will that appropriates its object and expropriates its subject. The contract of personal consent sublimates this desire as love, but it does not alter its nature.

If consent is the element that personalizes desire, matrimony is the institution that legitimates it. The two are initially opposed to one another, yet the story ends with their reconciliation. Such reconciliation can take place only after the lovers pass through the shadow of alienation, which in this case means that what belongs most intimately to the individual—his or her personal will—must first find itself expropriated by the acquisitive, impersonal compulsions of others. In other words it is in the forest that the lovers first lose their virginity, that is to say their self-possession; only after their devirgination do they become ready for the sexual consummation of love itself.

The consummation coincides with their marriage, or the social contract that stabilizes and institutionalizes sexuality, but we know from Boccaccio's *Decameron* as a whole that this happy ending is neither final nor absolute, for the shadow of love never goes away. It keeps returning to the world of legitimacy, throwing it into crisis. Just as Pietro and Agnolella challenged the will of their families, so too desire challenges any attempt to bring it under governance of a stable law, be it the law of consent or the law of matrimony. In the *Decameron* desire appears as the margin of exteriority within the system of social law, or as the self's measure of self-dispossession, or, quite simply, as the forest of alienation in which the lovers go astray.

THE HUMAN AGE

We could almost use the term "modernity" for the period in question, but the term "human age" seems more appropriate insofar as the concept of modernity refers strictly to cultural history. The term "human age" alludes, on the one hand, to Vico's "age of men" (which follows the so-called age of heroes) and on the other to the humanist revival of the Italian Renaissance which gave rise to the modern period as such. But beyond this it evokes the age of a species—of the triumph of a species. It is the age when Boccaccio's wolves literally begin to disappear as human beings become the sole inheritors of the earth.

We know, for example, that the fourteenth, fifteenth, and sixteenth centuries in Europe witnessed the widespread extermination of those species of wild animals which could neither be tamed nor utilized, and that deforestation took place on unprecedented scales around the Mediterranean and in England. The Italian peninsula had already undergone severe deforestation during the eleventh and twelfth centuries, but the emergence of Venice as a formidable sea power during the fifteenth century spelled disaster for many of the remaining woodlands. At that time forests still stretched from the edge of the Venetian lagoon to the foot of the Alps, and shipbuilders availed themselves indiscriminately of larch, spruce, fir, walnut, beech, and elm trees—each of which species was well suited for planking, masts, rudders, oars, and capstans, respectively. By the end of the century, as the timber supply began to vanish, the Republic adopted extreme measures to protect the remaining forests in their mainland territories, but the effort came too late. The Venetians were now obliged to obtain their ships from other shipbuilders in the Mediterranean. The war between the Christians and Turks during the sixteenth century sealed the fate of most of the remaining forests around the Mediterranean. By the end of the century the Mediterranean region could no longer sustain the shipbuilding industries, which subsequently moved north.

The story contains no surprises. In other parts of the world and at other times in history humankind had exterminated species and subjugated nature to its own ends, and systematically at that. What was unprecedented about the human age, however, was the humanist ideology that accompanied its empowerment of means and ambition. Never before had an ideology so thoroughly divorced the human from the animal species and considered the earth as a whole the former's natural inheritance.

Yet our story cannot be told merely by surveying the ways in which humanity encroached upon the wilderness, cleared the forests, assaulted the animal kingdom, and colonized new worlds across the oceans. Nor even by reviewing humanism's faith in self-governance and human *virtù*. In keeping with the spirit of Vico's *New Science,* our concern is to narrate a "poetic history" which has its basis in empirical and cultural history but which cannot be reduced to either. Thus we ask what these cultural as well as empirical transformations meant for forests in the Western imagination.

One sure sign of the advent of the human age is the transformation of forests into sites of lyric nostalgia. In one of Petrarch's most famous poems, "Chiare, fresche e dolci acque," the forest appears as a refuge from the boisterous world of human society where the poet withdraws to recollect himself with blissful self-affection. In this benign wood his solitude finds an intimate lyric correspondence with the animated landscape of trees, flowers, and running streams, so much so that the poet can declare rhetorically: "elsewhere I have no peace." Assuredly we are no longer in a *selva oscura*. There is no savagery left in Petrarch's wood, nor wild men or monsters, nor any error apart from the "lovely errancy" of imaginary leaves falling through the air and landing on the benevolent lap of Laura. Petrarch does not seek out his laurel forest to find adventure or rediscover his primordial nature; he withdraws there to engage in psychological introspection. Here too the forest figures as a haven—no longer for an outlaw, however, but for a worldly man suffering from the stress and excess of civilization.

We will return to Petrarch's forest of private lyricism further on, but first we will follow a circuitous route that leads through the forests of one of the great epics of the Italian Renaissance—Ariosto's *Orlando furioso*. The poem contains some of the most fabulous forests of literary history, full of magic, monsters, knights, and strange adventures. They are also utopic places, yet not in the same sense as Petrarch's. Taking up the tradition of medieval romance in an age when chivalry had become a fable of the past, Ariosto's poem is pervaded by a bitter comic irony with respect to the troubled geopolitics of the times. Apart from the menacing advance of the Turks on Europe, Italy was locked in a series of irrational peninsular wars whose protagonists were the major city-states of Italy, the Papacy, Louis XII of France, Ferdinand of Spain, and Swiss mercenary armies. Alliances were constantly shifting as circumstances changed, such that Ariosto's city of Ferrara found itself at one moment allied with Pope Julius II against the Venetians, and the next moment allied with the French against the acquisitive ambitions of Julius. The sole motivation for these wars seemed to be that of will to power and conflicting personal ambitions, and it was against this historical background that we must see the forests of Ariosto's epic, the first version of which was published in 1516.

The geopolitics of the age made a mockery of the humanistic rhetoric about *virtù* and self-governance. Politically speaking Italy was dominated by foreign powers, and the Italians conspired with the principle of their subjection. The unadulterated realism of Machiavelli's *The Prince* stands as a last desperate call for order, control, and self-reliance, in short, a last call for *virtù* in the traditional humanist sense. Ariosto did not share Machiavelli's earnestness. While Machiavelli dreamed of political redemption, Ariosto subjected the notion of *virtù* to irony, and it is precisely in the forests of the *Furioso* that such *virtù* goes astray in its own shadow.

This is clear at the outset of the poem, where we enter without delay the errant byways of the forest. The poem begins with Angelica's escape from captivity. She is the bewitching Saracen princess amorously pursued by several of Charlemagne's paladins, including the great Orlando himself. In the opening scene of the poem she is evading Rinaldo and Ferraù, two knights who follow separate paths through the woods in their pursuit of the princess. When we meet Rinaldo in the early octaves of the first canto, he is wandering aimlessly in search of his horse. This is the first of several occasions in the *Furioso* where formidable knights fall from their horses, or lose possession of them through theft or negligence. These horseless knights conjure up the famous Platonic analogy between virtue and competent horsemanship, which had become something of a commonplace by the time of the Renaissance. According to the analogy, the virtuous soul is like a charioteer who manages to keep his two steeds (will and intellect) on a straight path. The horses of Ariosto's *Furioso* are hardly kept in check in such a manner. Without virtue to keep them on a straight path, they dash off in random directions through the forest—the place of erotic errancy. The poet's irony with regard to *virtù* is already summarized, then, in the opening image of the heroic Rinaldo straying through the woods in search of his horse.

As for Ferraù, the other knight who is also pursuing Angelica through the forest, we meet him by the side of a stream, where he has stopped to quench his thirst. Bending down to drink, his helmet falls into the water. This helmet is the traditional emblem of virtuous reason. Orlando lost it, and now it drops from Ferraù's head into the stream: a symbolic announcement of things to come, namely Orlando's total loss of reason and degeneration into a raving wildman of the forests.

These two episodes signal from the start one of the main themes of the *Furioso,* namely the failure of the great paladins to exert control over desire. Most of the action in the poem takes place in the forests, which represent the scene of the wayward passions and impulses that forever seduce the paladins away from their more exalted mission (namely, defending Christendom from the invading heathens). Almost all of Ariosto's characters suffer the alienation of erotic desire—Angelica is the very figure for it—and the forests through which they roam (for the most part randomly, without ever arriving where they intend to go) are the places of their self-dispossession. They wander through the forests at the mercy of forces they do not control or direct, of which they are frequently unaware, and whose power of seduction arises from the covert depths of their own unrestrained passions.

This same erotic errancy is masterfully embodied in the *Furioso*'s narrative structure as a whole, which exasperates and at the same time perfects the digressionary style of narration. Instead of following a main story line, the narrative continuously disperses itself along episodic byways that intersect one another at random, without converging in a coherent, linear fashion. There is no master plot—even Orlando's pursuit of the beautiful Angelica is largely episodic—nor is there a central place that serves to localize the action (theoretically the city of Paris, under siege by the Saracens, should serve as a topographical center, but the poem only seldom takes us there). In short, Ariosto continuously veers the story off the master highways, so to speak, and diverts it into the forests. If this so-called polycentric poem has a narrative center at all, it is the eruption of Orlando's madness in cantos 23 and 24 (the *Furioso* has forty-five cantos). But Orlando's fury at the center of the poem ravages the very notion of a center, turning it instead into a vortex of self-dispossession which draws desire into an abyss of irrationality and violence. Let us turn to this "central" episode of the *Furioso* and see what is at stake there.

Orlando, the most valiant and formidable knight of Charlemagne's army, has been pursuing Angelica unsuccessfully for quite some time, but with great determination and devotion. Meanwhile she has met a frail, insignificant, and wounded Saracen warrior—his name is Medoro—and has fallen in love with him. Orlando is unaware of this, but he will discover undeniable evidence of the love affair as a result of his battle with Mandricardo, an awesome Saracen warrior. During the terrible clash between these two warriors, in which Orlando displays great prowess, Mandricardo's horse goes berserk and bolts away, carrying its Saracen rider off with it. Orlando takes off in pursuit of Mandricardo but does not succeed in finding him. Instead he wanders into a beautiful, idyllic, enchanting forest. Here he sees love lyrics carved into the barks of the trees. Composed by Medoro and Angelica, they celebrate the blissful and reciprocal love between the two. Orlando is shaken up and refuses to believe their authenticity, hoping that someone has played a malicious joke on him. Later that day, however, a shepherd who offers him lodgings for the night tells him how Angelica and Medoro enjoyed each other many a time in the very bed where Orlando was about to lay his head to rest. The shepherd unwittingly confirms the terrible truth of what the lyrics had declared, and Orlando can no longer deny it to himself. Bewildered and distraught, the paladin goes out into the moonless night and wanders forlorn through the forest, weeping like a child. All night long he weeps and wanders blindly in his grief. At daybreak, he happens to stumble into the same wood where Angelica and Medoro had signed their names to the love lyrics in the barks. The written sign of his injury drives him out of his wits, and the once courteous knight now becomes the furious Orlando.

Orlando's vengeful fury gives him a superhuman strength that he now unleashes against the forest itself. With his bare hands he uproots the trees and casts them into the river, polluting its clear waters with tree trunks and debris. His fury, like his strength, knows no bounds. Not only does he uproot huge oaks, elms, and pine trees, but with hardly an effort he also splits their trunks apart. He ravages the entire forest, which never again will afford shade for a shepherd or his flocks. For four days and nights Orlando gives vent to his suffering in this manner. On the fourth day he strips himself of all his armor and clothes and roves the countryside naked. He has become a true wild man, like Lancelot or Yvain, only wilder and more destructive.

Startled by the great din coming from the forests, shepherds gather around to see what is going on. When they spot the furious Orlando, naked and wild, they run away. But Orlando runs after them and, catching one, he snaps the head off that innocent shepherd with the ease with which one removes an apple from the branch. Then, holding it by a leg, he uses the headless body to scourge the other shepherds. Thus does the raving Orlando storm the countryside, uprooting forests, devastating farms, killing peasants, and even assaulting their livestock. For food he brings down wild boars and bears in the forests with his bare hands, feeding on their raw flesh to satisfy his bestial hunger. Thus does our Orlando go mad for love.

With Orlando diverted from the war raging around Paris, the

Christians suffer major setbacks at the hands of the Saracens. Charlemagne needs Orlando desperately, for Orlando is essentially a war machine momentarily gone berserk. His madness has disrupted the alignment of his destructive powers. Those powers are no longer aimed in the proper direction, namely toward the enemy, hence Orlando must be realigned at all costs. In other words his "sanity" must be restored. It is thanks to Astolfo that Orlando will recover his senses, for later in the poem Astolfo will journey to the moon to fetch the fragments of Orlando's alienated brain. Once restored to sanity, Orlando is able to redirect his fury against the enemy and wreck havoc with the Saracens, thus saving the day for the Christians.

The scene of Orlando's madness gives Ariosto's poem an ominous historical reference, for in the background we can see the destructive wars ravaging Italy at this time. The world of the *Furioso* is not a utopia dissociated from history; rather, it is a revelation, in the realm of literature, of the dark passions that were disrupting society and precipitating the human age into irrational wars. Politics had become an arena for absurd conflict between rivalrous desires for expansion, acquisition, and domination· the arena for an anarchic will to power. With the sort of freedom and insight that belong to literature alone, Ariosto links desire and politics together in a way that dispossesses the latter of its rhetoric of rights and reason. In the forests of the *Furioso*, the sexual impulse and the will to power are forever intersecting each other along oblique and covert paths. Desire, violence, rivalry, and warfare—Ariosto uncovers the subterranean fatality of these impulses, as well as their veiled interconnectedness. The digressionary freedom of his poem brings about unexpected intersections, not only between characters and events but also between passions. Through this digressionary style Ariosto succeeds in dispossessing the human age of its claims to self-mastery, for as he diverts the action into the forest—or into the promiscuous realm of interconnectedness—what seemed to be the case in the daylight of reality is suddenly no longer the case, and what before was a secret now becomes a scandal.

We could speak, then, of something like Ariosto's *covert realism*. This is not the disabused realism of Machiavelli, which takes its stand in the hard light of reality (the *verità effettuale delle cose,* as he called it), but rather a realism in poetic disguise which looks into the shadow of what appears in that same light. Through the comic irony of such covert realism, Ariosto preserved the seriousness of literature in an age that encouraged its irrelevance. During this period literature was in fact wholly under the sway of the rigid and artificial conventions of Petrarchism. As a literary movement Petrarchism encouraged a merely formal imitation of Petrarch's lyric commonplaces. It deliberately took flight from history and "reality" as the Petrarchists sought out the idyllic landscapes that Petrarch himself had sentimentalized with such success a century and a half earlier. Each Petrarchan poet had his Laura, with blond tresses and all; each sought to reproduce the smooth, mellifluous lyricism of "Chiare, fresche e dolci acque"; and each sought the quiet, benign forest landscape that had provided the setting for that ideal Petrarchan lyric.

This withdrawal into a purely private and merely formal lyricism represented for Ariosto the default of literature with respect to its most essential vocation. A literature that renders itself wholly irrelevant, that refuses to bring into its imaginary realm the veiled truth of the age, that flees into pastoral landscapes as into a mere utopia of lyricism—such a literature was not, for Ariosto, literature in any authentic historical sense. Ariosto's polemic against this kind of literature becomes evident precisely in the episode of Orlando's fury. Let us return to that episode.

Angelica and Medoro fall in love and are happy in one another's arms. But what does their happiness have to do with the wars raging around Paris? What does their happiness have to do with the *Furioso?* Nothing, for the two lovers effectively disappear from the poem once they find their happiness. They become in effect superfluous. They leave their lyrics behind on the tree trunks, but what of these lyrics? What of this forest that Orlando uproots in canto 23? It is the Petrarchan landscape par excellence which he devastates after his night of weeping and wandering. It is the same idyllic forest that Petrarch himself had apostrophed in "Chiare, fresche e dolci acque" and that the Petrarchists had continued to evoke in their lyrics. We alluded to this poem earlier and promised to return to it. We now return to it in the scene of Orlando's madness, for the poem that Medoro inscribed in a tree trunk leaves no doubt about the fact that he is imitating Petrarch's lyric in the Petrarchan vein. The poem begins as follows:

> Liete piante, verdi erbe, limpide acque,
> spelunca opaca e di fredde ombra grata,
> dove la bella Angelica che nacque
> di Galafron, da molti invano amata,
> spesso ne le mie braccia nuda giacque. . . .

Happy plants, green grasses, limpid waters,
sheltered cave and graced with cool shade,
where the beautiful Angelica, born
of Galafron, and loved by many in vain
lay naked in my arms, and often. . . . (Ariosto, 937–41)

This is the Petrarchism that Ariosto parodies and lays waste to in
his *Furioso,* precisely in the scene where Orlando uproots the forest
and pollutes its limpid stream with tree trunks and debris. Thanks to
Petrarch's "Chiare, fresche e dolci acque," this stream had become a
conventional metaphor for the inspired voice of lyricism, where words
flow of their own accord. Orlando uproots this lyrically animated forest and discharges its debris into the stream. As for the shepherds, or
the traditional *pastori* that had been so hospitable to Angelica and Medoro, Orlando becomes a scourge to them and to their flocks, as we
have seen. In Orlando's violence against the shepherds we get a fair
idea about Ariosto's attitude toward the pastoral nostalgias of the pre-
vailing Petrarchism. How, Ariosto is asking in these scenes, can one be
Petrarchan in times like these?

But Orlando's destructive fury contains yet another covert reference to the reality of history in his own age. It was the age that witnessed the invention of the firearm. In a famous invective of the *Furioso,* Ariosto denounces the *macchina infernale,* or infernal machine,
which makes use of gunpowder. In canto 9 Orlando kills the king of
Frisia who had invaded Holland with the firearm and throws the infernal weapon into the sea to rid humankind of its curse. It was a curse
not only because of its destructive potential but also because it deper-
sonalized warfare, going against all the chivalric codes of valor and
courage. Yet the firearm as well as heavy artillery had already given
warfare an unprecedented destructive power by the time Ariosto
wrote the *Furioso.* It is ironic that Orlando should be the one to cast
the firearm into the sea, for his indiscriminate and superhuman destruction of forests, countryside, and peasants allegorically unleashes
the power of the infernal machine. Indeed, Orlando's fury *is* the gunpowder.

The forests of the *Furioso* are literary, imaginary, extravagant, and
wondrous, but they do not provide the scene for mere diversionary
literature. They are utopic, but in another sense than Petrarch's forest
of lyricism. In the latter one enters the shadow of the modern self—its
psychological paradoxes and narcissism; in the former one enters the

shadow of the human age as a whole—the will to power that lurked beneath its geopolitics as well as its humanism. The *Furioso* has a happy ending, to be sure, but in the forests of its comic irony the modern city reveals its abandon to impulses and forces it does not control, yet which carry the comedy forward toward its conclusion.

MACBETH'S CONCLUSION

Forests recede from the civic horizon, appear through the pathos of distance, lengthen their shadows in the cultural imagination. Even John Manwood's treatise on forest laws, composed in 1592, was a work of nostalgia. The royal forests were by that time in a state of degradation, infractions all too often going unpunished. Manwood hoped that by defining its origin and purpose he could reinvigorate the old corpus of laws which had once preserved the forests' integrity, if not sanctity. In his country the problem was more severe than elsewhere. England had already been heavily deforested by the time William arrived in the eleventh century, but the clearing of woodlands (not royal forests) continued indiscriminately during Tudor and Stuart times. It was not until the seventeenth century, thanks largely to the publication of John Evelyn's *Silva* (1664), that the problem of timber shortage for Navy ships forced a new awareness on the administration about the vital economic and national importance of woodlands. Until then the English had generally congratulated themselves on their razing efforts, considering woodlands obstacles to progress or havens for thieves and other degenerates.

The changing landscape accounts at least in part for the remarkable topical inversion that we find in the work of Shakespeare: the savagery that once traditionally belonged to the forests now lurks in the hearts of men—civic men. The dangers lie within, not without. As the city becomes sinister, forests become innocent, pastoral, diversionary, *comic*. The Shakespearean comedies that take place in the forests—*A Midsummer Night's Dream* and *As You Like it*, for example—follow the comic patterns we already outlined earlier in this chapter: disguise, reversals, and a general confusion of the laws, categories, and principles of identity that govern ordinary reality. In this respect there is nothing new in Shakespeare's forests with regard to the underlying logic of comedy (which in no way means that his comedies bring nothing new to the genre). The same cannot be said, however, of his dramas about civic barbarism. Those dramas are unique for the way they bring the shadow of natural law to bear on the religious, moral, and social crises that were shaking the traditional foundations of society.

We claimed at the beginning of the chapter that the Christian era puts an end to tragedy as the highest form of wisdom, subverting its ideological basis. If we assume—and it is a questionable assumption—that tragedy, not merely as a genre but above all as an *insight*, becomes possible once again with Shakespeare, we must look in effect to the end of the Christian era for an explanation. This end is in many ways the enduring drama of Shakespeare's tragedies. Historically speaking the end of the Christian era is a prolonged and indefinite event—it represents an era in itself—and Shakespeare certainly did not see the end of it himself. What he did see, however, was the shadow of its dissolution lurking in the hearts of civic heroes.

He did not portray the dissolution so much in Christian terms as in terms of gross violations of natural law. Natural law lies at the basis of positive law; it is not the law of nature as such but rather the transcendent foundations of human social law. The depraved Shakespearean characters—Iago, Edmund, Macbeth, etc.—violate the most sacred natural bonds, and once such bonds lose their binding power Shakespeare's characters degenerate into a savagery of spirit which recalls Vico's words about those treacherous human-aged men who have been "made more inhuman by the barbarism of reflection than the first men had been made by the barbarism of sense. For the latter displayed a generous savagery, against which one could defend oneself or take flight or be on one's guard; but the former, with a base savagery, under soft words and embraces, plots against the life and fortune of friends and intimates" (*New Science,* §1106). For Vico such barbarism signaled the beginning of the end of the human age and the imminent metamorphosis of cities into forests—a return, as it were, to the lawless state of nature. In Shakespeare's work it is portrayed as an ungodly upheaval in the natural order of things, that is to say, the *lawful* order of things. It is here that the term "nature" becomes an ambiguous word. On the one hand it means the presocial or prelawful state of anarchy; on the other it means the "natural," that is, nonconventional basis of human law itself.

In a famous soliloquy of *King Lear,* the bastard Edmund declares his allegiance to nature, not to custom. He speaks of the "plague of custom" as if custom were a disease of nature; he speaks of the "curiosity of nations" as if the so-called law of nations were no more than a deviation from nature's law; and finally he speaks of "legitimacy" as if it were an artificial contrivance that has nothing to do with the "law" of his goddess. (I.ii.1–22). But we know from *King Lear* as a whole that Edmund's notion of nature as sheer will to power offends nature herself. The storm scene of act 3 appears as a cosmic response to the moral confusion that follows upon the corruptions of natural law on the part of Edmund and Lear's daughters.

Perhaps the most corrupt Shakespearean character in this sense is Lady Macbeth. Unlike Edmund, however, Lady Macbeth avows that human law has its basis in nature. Thus, in one of her speeches, she expresses her desire to be denatured, so that she might successfully, and without remorse, carry out her murderous plot against the king of Scotland:

> . . . Come, you spirits
> That tend on mortal thoughts, unsex me here,
> And fill me, from the crown to the toe, top-full
> Of direst cruelty! Make thick my blood;
> Stop up th' access and passage to remorse,
> That no *compunctious visitings of nature*
> Shake my fell purpose nor keep peace between
> Th' effect and it! Come to my woman's breast
> And take my milk for gall, you murd'ring ministers,
> Wherever in your sightless substances
> You wait on *nature's mischief!* Come, thick night,
> And pall thee in the dunnest smoke of hell,
> That my keen knife see not the wound it makes,
> Nor heaven peep through the blanket of the dark
> To cry "Hold, hold!" (I.v.41–55)

Lady Macbeth's defiance of nature has its cause in something more than a depraved will to power; it comes, in effect, from a spirit of vengeance. Nature itself has wronged her, for we know that Macbeth and his wife have no children. They are afflicted with sterility. Life is a tale full of sound and fury, signifying nothing, but this is a fact of some significance. In her speech Lady Macbeth reappropriates her own barrenness when she asks to be "unsexed." It is in this unsexed womb that she conceives all her plots and schemes. For that very reason, perhaps, they are destined to abort.

The barrenness in question has its symbolic counterpart in a natural landscape. This landscape is the heath, or waste place, where the three witches communicate their prophesies to Macbeth. This barren wasteland remains the place of origin for all the crimes that Macbeth will commit against his fellow man (crimes which, significantly enough, involve the destruction of family lineages). But the prophesies uttered there, which foreshadow Macbeth's abortive schemes and doom, ironically come to fruition. One of those prophesies has to do with a forest:

> Macbeth shall never vanquish'd be, until
> Great Birnam wood to high Dunsinane Hill
> Shall come against him. (IV.i.92–94)

It is typical that Macbeth should misunderstand the prophecy, his blindness to prophetic intent being the counterpart of his corrupted nature. There is considerable irony in his reaction to the witch's utterance:

> That will never be.
> Who can impress the forest, bid the tree
> Unfix his earth-bound root? Sweet bodements, good!
> Rebellious dead, rise never, till the Wood
> Of Birnam rise, and our high-placed Macbeth
> Shall live the lease of nature, pay his breath
> To time and moral custom. Yet my heart
> Throbs to know one thing, Tell me, if your art
> Can tell so much: shall Banquo's issue ever
> Reign in this kingdom? (IV.i.94–103)

Who can impress the forest? The word "impress" here means, among other things, to conscript—impress into military service—which is exactly what occurs when Birnam Wood moves against Macbeth. But Macbeth's question contains other connotations as well, namely, who can put his impress on the forest? Who can impose a human or political will upon the will of nature? Who can force the forest into one's service? These are questions that have been with us from the beginning of this chapter. Humankind is always "impressing" the forest in one way or another, stripping it, conquering it, cultivating it, conscripting it. Likewise the forest is always impressing those who lose their way in its labyrinth. The relation between forests and civilization during the

Christian era is largely one of impression—what we have called also the law's shadow.

The irony of this prophecy about Birnam Wood is that it refers to the visual impression of a moving forest, but Macbeth—who is impressed by visions and hallucinations throughout the play—literalizes its intent. He is the victim, in short, of his own impressions—the forest's shadow, as it were, which is peopled by the ghosts of the "rebellious dead."

In the final act of the play, as Macbeth's destiny closes in on him, the rebellious dead move against Macbeth in the impression of Birnam Wood. The soldiers of the opposing army advance toward the castle camouflaged behind boughs cut from the trees of this forest. As the forest moves against Macbeth, the play concludes in what appears to be a denouement of poetic justice. The lawlessness that Vico associated with the "nefarious forests" has here found haven in Macbeth's civic barbarism, but by the end of the play the moving forest of Birnam comes to symbolize the forces of natural law mobilizing its justice against the moral wasteland of Macbeth's nature. In this powerful image the law appears in its natural basis. As the army hides behind the boughs, they employ the same ruses of deception by which Macbeth carried out his crimes, only now the camouflage reverses the order of evil. This forest is impressed by "Banquo's issue." We see in the image of Birnam Wood the law of genealogy—the family tree, as it were—vanquishing its sterile enemy. We see the law of kinship and kingship avenging itself. We see the law of the *land* in a strangely literalistic guise.

The comic conclusion of *Macbeth* gives us a final image of the law and its own shadow—an image with which to conclude this chapter. From one point of view *Macbeth* is clearly a tragedy, but its comic, if not happy, ending recalls us to the logic we have been following all along. If *Macbeth* is tragic it is not so in the pre-Christian sense. This is not because of its comic ending. Several Greek tragedies end comically, with the triumph of justice, but justice in their case meant the reconciliation of opposing laws, each of which had their legitimate claim. When Orestes murdered his mother he was avenging his father's death, obeying the dictates of an ancient law; when the furies began to persecute him they too were avenging a law that his matricide had violated. The ending of Aeschylus's trilogy represents a triumphant reconciling of these two laws, but in *Macbeth* it is not a case of two legitimate laws striving against one another; the drama involves the law and its own corruption, the law and its own negation, the law and its own *shadow.* In this case the "walking shadow" is Macbeth himself, but as Birnam Wood moves against him, his hour on the stage is over. And we, who in this case are the spectators, move on to another epoch, another tale, and other kinds of forests altogether.

3

Michael Kenna, *Woodpile, Karlstejn, Czechoslovakia* (1989)

ENLIGHTENMENT

THE KINDS OF FORESTS DEALT WITH IN THIS CHAPTER BE-
long to several different orders. Some are as literal as the timber plan-
tations of modern forestry, others are as rarefied as Hamm's blank
dream in Samuel Beckett's *Endgame*. Some lie at the heart of darkness,
others in the light of reason. Some point forward in time, others backward. Some provoke phobias, while others inspire reveries. As we approach this sylvan diversity we must keep in mind that as surely as
things go astray in the forest so they eventually intersect again. We will
assume from the start, then, that the different kinds of forests in question will come together in one way or another to tell an overt or covert
story of the post-Christian era, into whose horizon we now pass.

The post-Christian era is broadly defined here in terms of historical detachment from the past. The first section of the chapter suggests
that the era unfolds under the Cartesian auspices of Enlightenment. If
Petrarch can be called the "father of humanism," then Descartes can be
called the father of Enlightenment. In his *Discourse on Method* Descartes compares the authority of tradition to a forest of error, beyond
which lies the promised land of reason. Once he arrives in that promised land, Descartes redefines his relation not only to tradition but also
to nature in its totality. The new Cartesian distinction between the *res
cogitans,* or thinking self, and the *res extensa,* or embodied substance,
sets up the terms for the objectivity of science and the abstraction from
historicity, location, nature, and culture.

What interests us about Descartes in this context is the fact that he
sought to empower the subject of knowledge in such a way that,
through its application of mathematical method, humanity could

achieve what he called "mastery and possession of nature." One of the ways in which this dream of mastery and possession becomes reality in the post-Christian era is through the rise of forest management during the late-eighteenth and nineteenth centuries. Forests become the object of a new science of forestry, with the State assuming the role of Descartes's thinking subject. Predictably enough, modern forestry reduces forests to their most literal or "objective" status: timber. A new "forest mathematics" goes so far as to measure them in terms of their volume of disposable wood. Method thus conspires with the laws of economy to reappropriate forests under the general concept of "utility," even in those cases where utility is conceived in aesthetic terms: forests as recreational parks, for example, or as "museums" of original nature.

Needless to say, we have by no means gotten beyond such conceptions. Enlightenment remains our dominant cultural heritage. Still today, in other words, we argue for the preservation of forests on the basis of their numerous uses and benefits. Why should we preserve the tropical rain forests? Their abundance of unique plant species, scientists argue, may one day prove useful for science and medicine. This concept of utility is more insidious and historically determined than appears at first glance, and part of the burden of the present chapter is to account for its origins.

In this sense, as well as others, the chapter goes beyond the well-known story of the subjection of nature to programmatic control and exploitation. As in the previous chapters, we will find that, here too, forests represent an opaque mirror of the civilization that exists in relation to them. In this case the various ways in which forests are conceived, represented, or symbolized will give us access to the shadow of Enlightenment ideology—its fantasies, paradoxes, anxieties, nostalgias, self-deceptions, and even its pathos. What we find in that shadow is the ghost of irony. From tragedy to comedy we now move decisively to irony as the trope which, in its several versions or declensions, holds sway over the post-Christian era as a whole. Irony is the trope of detachment. In what follows we will see in how many ways the real as well as imaginary forests of the new era reveal its darker enigmas.

THE WAYS OF METHOD

In *The Gay Science* Nietzsche recounts the parable of the madman who rushes into the marketplace at high noon with a lantern in his hand and shouts the news: "God is dead!" We have been in that marketplace before, with Zarathustra. "*We have killed him*—you and I. All of us are his murderers," declares the madman. As the people make a mockery of his pronouncement, the madman says to himself, "I have come too early . . . deeds, though done, still require time to be seen and heard. This deed is still more distant from them than the most distant stars— *and yet they have done it themselves*" (*Gay Science*, ¶125).

Suppose we stopped this madman, calmed him down, and asked him: "When and where did God die?" And suppose he were to answer: "In 1637, in part 4 of the *Discourse on Method!*" A madman, after all, can afford to be precise about such matters.

Part 4 represents a critical section of Descartes's most famous work, without doubt. It is where he reaches the conclusion: "I think, therefore I am." Before reaching it Descartes had decided to doubt the veracity of everything he ever took to be true; yet the self-evidence of this fact—"I think, I exist"—is so persuasive that it will serve as the *fundamentum inconcussum,* or unshakable foundation, for the new edifice of knowledge which Descartes wants to erect. On the basis of its certainty Descartes presumes to prove the existence of God. That is precisely where God's demise takes place, the madman might say. The certainty of the subjective existence of the *cogito* becomes the ground for the certainty of God's existence, not the other way around.

Descartes salvages a role for God in his philosophy, to be sure, since God now functions as the metaphysical guarantor of the true correspondence between my clear and distinct ideas and the external objects that those ideas represent to my mind. But such a God is no longer the Christian God of faith. He is not a God I can pray to, appeal to, kneel before, seek salvation from, or worship. Descartes's God is already cold with rigor mortis—with metaphysics. (Blaise Pascal clearly saw the demise of the Christian God in Descartes's philosophy and expressed his anguish over it throughout the *Pensées.*)

In the background of Descartes's decision to doubt the veracity of all he ever took for granted lies the Copernican revolution in astronomy, which had made a mockery of sense perception. It was a revolution in irony—irony in its most devastating version. Irony, says Vico, "is fashioned of falsehood by dint of a reflection that wears the mask of truth" (*New Science*, §408). This was the sort of ironic consciousness that became ineluctable once geocentrism was revealed as an illusion of the senses. The reliability of sense perception had of course been doubted since the very beginnings of ancient astronomy, to say nothing of Platonism, yet there was clearly something unprecedented about the Copernican revolution. All of a sudden the visible world became a deliberate delusion, a great cosmic hoax, an ironic veil of deception.

Out of such doubts, however, certainty was to emerge. In parts 2 and 3 of the *Discourse on Method,* Descartes tells the story of how he arrived at this insight. He describes the time in his life prior to his discovery of stable foundations for knowledge—the time when he was still lost in a world of unreliable opinions and beliefs, without knowing how to discriminate effectively between truth and falsehood. He had already been persuaded by the efficacy of "algebraic geometry" as a method for seeking truth, but the method still lacked a metaphysical foundation. He decided, therefore, that until such time as he found a foundation for his mathematical method he would observe a "provisional code of morals" in his practical life, remaining firm and resolute in his temporary course of action, no matter how doubtful that course may have seemed:

> In this I would imitate travelers who, finding themselves lost in a forest, ought not to wander this way and that, or, what is worse, remain in one place, but ought always walk as straight a line as they can in one direction and not change course for feeble reasons, even if at the outset it was perhaps only chance that made them choose it; for by this means, if they are not going where they wish, they will finally arrive at least somewhere where they probably will be better off than in the middle of a forest. (Descartes, 13)

Although it refers specifically to following a course of action with resolution, we could say that this analogy stands in the same relation to Cartesianism as the analogy of the cave stands in relation to Platonism. It maps out, as it were, the ways of method. Method (from the Greek *meta-odos,* or along the way) means literally the "path," hence the analogy of following a path through the forest is particularly appropriate in a treatise on method. Descartes's analogy of course brings other scenes to mind—Dante's dark forest, for example, where the "straight way" is lost and cannot be pursued. In Descartes's analogy the forest is likewise a place of error and abandon, but unlike Dante, Descartes appears confident that there is indeed a *way* to walk in a straight line through the forest.

This confidence comes from the reliability of method itself.

Dante's pilgrim depended on divine assistance to get out of the forest. It came to him in the figure of Virgil. But once it finds its foundation in the *res cogitans,* Descartes's subject of knowledge can rely strictly upon its own resources to escape the realm of randomness and error, thanks to its adherence to the linear path of mathematical analysis. Descartes's analogy of walking in a straight line through the forest is, as Michel Serres has noted, "isomorphic" with the method of algebraic geometry itself (*Le système de Leibniz,* 2:452n). Mathematical analysis follows the way of numbers and more numbers in a linear series until it reaches its final result. The triumph of method in a forest of doubt implies the ability to hold to the straight line of mathematical deduction.

But there is even more to Descartes's analogy, for the forest is a broad analogy for all that goes by the name of tradition, which for Descartes means the accumulated falsehoods, unfounded beliefs, and misguided assumptions of the past. Descartes takes his stand against tradition the moment he decides to doubt its authority and to rely upon his own personal resources in the quest for truth. This detachment from the ways of the past, and Descartes's presumption to become methodically self-reliant in matters of action and knowledge, point to the post-Christian phenomenon that goes by the name of Enlightenment. In the next section we will look at what is at stake in such detachment in more depth. Meanwhile there are good reasons to suppose that Descartes's forest refers, among other things, to tradition, or to everything that has grown up over time not by rational design but by custom. For the forest analogy in the *Discourse* distinctly recalls another analogy in the same text which compares the proper exercise of reason to the rational, geometric planning of cities. In part 1 of the *Discourse* Descartes complains that

> these ancient cities that were once merely straggling villages and have become in the course of time great cities are commonly quite poorly laid out, compared to those well-ordered towns that an engineer lays out *on a vacant plane* as it suits his fancy. And although, upon considering one by one the buildings in the former class of towns, one finds as much art or more than one finds in the buildings of the latter class of towns, still, upon seeing how the buildings are arranged—here a large one, there a small one—and how they make the streets crooked and uneven, one will say that it is *chance more*

than the will of some men using their reason that has arranged them thus. (Descartes, 6)

Just as Descartes prefers towns conceived in the mind of a single architect to those that grow up diversely over time, so too, he says, the "simple reasonings" of one individual (himself) are preferable to the knowledge one may gain from tradition and books, or the accumulated opinions of diverse people over time. These ancient cities that have grown up diversely over time, with crooked streets and uneven buildings, are the citadels of culture. For Descartes they are the results of chance, diversity, and randomness. In short, they are the forests of confusion in which Cartesian rationalism finds itself alienated, or better, "a-lineated."

If Descartes finds himself alienated in the forest—or the historically embodied world as such—it cannot surprise us that he finds himself at home in the desert. The desert in this case means the "vacant plain" of the engineer's mind, where the straight lines of geometry suffer no obstacles. It means the mind's abstraction from history—its material and cultural disembodiment. The *Discourse* in fact recounts Descartes's decision to abstract himself from his native country, to leave behind his friends and to retire in the foreign police state of Holland in order to pursue his philosophical work. Of his new abode, Descartes declares with satisfaction: "I have been able to live as solitary and retired a life as I could in the remotest deserts" (17).

Descartes composed the *Discourse on Method* (which at one point he calls a "fable") as a hagiographical tale that ends with the saint's solitary retirement into the desert. Yet an irony pervades the fable, for the straight lines of algebraic geometry, which are at home in the deserts of abstraction, finally circle back to the material world from which the Cartesian *cogito* abstracts itself. At the end of *Discourse* Descartes reveals the true ambitions of his method. Referring to certain "general notions" he had acquired from physics, he writes:

> [T]hese general notions show me that it is possible to arrive at knowledge that is very useful in life and that in place of the speculative philosophy taught in the Schools, one can find a practical one, by which, knowing the force and the actions of fire, water, air, stars, the heavens, and all the other bodies that surround us, just as we understand the various skills of our craftsmen, we could, in the same way, use these objects for

the purposes for which they are appropriate, and thus make ourselves the masters and possessors of nature. (33)

The knowledge that Cartesian rationalism seeks by way of method is not merely of the speculative sort, as in the traditional schools. It has an active and practical ambition. It is not knowledge for knowledge's sake, any more than the craftsman's technical know-how is. The ways of method promise neither salvation nor wisdom but rather *power*. They lead to the mastery and possession of nature, that is to say toward an appropriation of the power traditionally assigned to God. Reason, method, and technical craftsmanship come together at the end of the *Discourse* in a secular confession of the will to power.

The goal of mastery and possession of nature represents the highest form of practical activism. The new philosopher is more of an engineer than a saint, nor does the "vacant plane" of the engineer's fancy, where reason projects its designs, remain vacant for long, since a geometric city springs from its desert. Likewise the forests do not remain places of random confusion once mastery and possession become the agenda of the era. As we will see in the following section, when method finds a way out of the forest it returns to subject them to the rigors of method itself.

By way of conclusion we can remark that Descartes dies in 1650. In 1657 Fabio Chigi becomes Pope Alexander VII. During his eleven-year reign the pope transfigures the ancient city of Rome that had become over the course of time the sort of "straggling city" Descartes had complained about in the *Discourse on Method*. Where before there had been a labyrinth of streets, winding alleyways, historically diverse edifices, local neighborhoods, and polycentric clearings in the midst of all this, there is now the master clearing of the Piazza del Popolo with its three radically linear avenues stretching south for several miles. The master avenue in the middle, connecting the Piazza del Popolo with the equally triumphant clearing of the Piazza di Venezia, would be misnamed had it any other name than "Via del Corso." Via del Corso: the way of ways; the tautology of method; the course of the *Discourse*. How a Roman pope in the seventeenth century caught the contagion of Cartesian rationalism remains an enigma, but Richard Krautheimer's book, *Roma Alessandrina: The Remapping of Rome Under Alexander VII,* tells the full story of this urban transfiguration. Thus we return to our madman and ask him a final question: "How does one walk in a straight line through the forest?" Answer: "Methodical deforestation."

WHAT IS ENLIGHTENMENT?
A QUESTION FOR FORESTERS

In a 1784 essay entitled "An Answer to the Question: What Is Enlightenment?" Immanuel Kant gave a brief but notorious answer to the question. He defined Enlightenment as the coming of age of an age. To come of age meant, for Kant, to appeal to the law of reason as the highest legislative authority in secular affairs. But what does that imply? That Enlightenment is a historical event that at some point takes place? That it is an ideological revolution? The reform of the political constitution? All of these? Let us leave Kant's essay aside for a moment and propose our own answer to the question.

Enlightenment is a projective detachment from the past—a way of thinking which detaches the present from tradition and projects it forward into an ideal secular future ideally governed by the law of reason. The future remains Enlightenment's true heritage, while the present lags behind its republic of reason. Since the present has yet to accomplish all the social and political reforms dictated by reason, Enlightenment relates to its present age critically. Enlightenment is that which has already happened and not yet happened. It has happened to the extent that one dares to affirm the law of reason—"dare to know!" as Kant said—but it has not happened to the extent that the future must still fulfill its dictates. Enlightenment is always underway. It is an unending labor to come of age. To adopt the ambiguous metaphor used in reference to the cultural heritage of the United States—Enlightenment is the "child of Enlightenment."

The historical present of Enlightenment thus remains ambiguous. The authority of tradition continues to hold sway over the present, yet it also slowly gives way to the pressure of reason's forward march. This view of Enlightenment allows us to understand why Vico speaks of an "age of reflection" to which belongs the mode of consciousness called irony. As the trope of detachment, irony implies a critical relationship to the past. From an "enlightened" perspective, the ways of the past appear erroneous, self-deceived, and steeped in superstition. What tradition held to be true Enlightenment sees as false. (The sky was once believed to be an animate substance, but "we know better.") At the most fundamental level, then, irony demystifies the dogmas of faith and exposes their roots in falsehood. It is the trope of Enlightenment itself, which comes of age through critical reflection.

Let us turn now to our theme to see if the forests can tell the story more rigorously and concretely. Our guiding conception from the start has been that a historical age reveals something essential about its ideology, its institutions and law, or its cultural temperament, in the manifold ways in which forests are regarded in that age. Here we will focus on one of the major documents of the Age of Enlightenment, namely the French *Encyclopédie,* edited in the eighteenth century by Diderot. Under the entry for the word *forêt* in the encyclopedia, the warden of the Park of Versailles, Monsieur Le Roy, provides a typically enlightened definition of forests which we want to examine in depth here.

Le Roy opens his entry with a formal, comprehensive definition of the forest. A forest, he writes, is a wide expanse of woodlands as opposed to the smaller areas called woods (*bois*). The definition already differs significantly from Manwood's *foresta,* a juridical domain placed off-limits by royal decree and intended for the king's pleasure and recreation. For Manwood a forest consisted of four things: vert and venison, particular laws and officers. In Le Roy's definition the forest is reduced technically to "vert," the greenery. The forest is no more than a conglomerate of trees. Thus Le Roy indicates that a large forest is almost always composed of trees of all ages and species, which he enumerates as follows: *taillis,* a cluster of younger trees up to twenty-five years of age; *gaulis,* a cluster between twenty-five and fifty or sixty years; *demi-futaye,* between sixty and ninety years; and *haute-futaye,* or old-growth trees of ninety years and more.

After this formal definition of a forest, Le Roy takes a step back and sets up the terms of the approach he will pursue throughout the rest of his article. "It seems," he writes,

> that in all ages one has sensed the importance of preserving forests; they have always been regarded as the property of the state and administered in its name: Religion itself had consecrated forests, doubtlessly to protect, through veneration, that which had to be conserved for the public interest [*utilité publique*]. Our oaks no longer proffer oracles, and we no longer ask of them the sacred mistletoe; we must replace this cult by care; and whatever advantage one may previously have found in the respect that one had for forests, one can ex-

pect even more success from vigilance and economy. (Le Roy, 129)

This remarkable paragraph gives a concrete body to our abstract definition of Enlightenment as projective detachment from the past. The assertion that forests have always been viewed as the property of the state and administered in its name is a misrepresentation of historical fact, but Le Roy's error springs from an ideology that considers the state the universal, transcendent guardian of national "property." The assertion is all the more dubious in light of the author's remark that, in past ages, religion had consecrated forests so as to inspire the sort of veneration that would preserve them for the sake of the public interest. Le Roy implies here that religion functioned as a primitive agent of public administration. He demystifies its sacrality in favor of what he considers the only truly enduring sacred value, namely *l'utilité publique:* the "public interest." In this he reveals himself as a man of Enlightenment.

Le Roy's attitude toward the historical past is traversed by irony. His is irony to the second degree, for it not only sees falsehood wearing the mask of truth in the past (forests as sacred), but also the reverse. Truth, which for Le Roy means the public interest, wore the mask of falsehood in the past, hiding behind a superstitious religious sentiment of veneration. He unveils the old superstitions, but at the same time he sees some latent truth lying behind their falsehoods, namely the need for forest conservation. His irony, therefore, uncovers a deeper truth that remained concealed in the past.

The concept of coming of age assumes a new dimension here. To come of age means that truth emerges from its latency and enters the sobering light of reason. Enlightenment no longer needs the mask of false superstitions, for it can see the truth in its own proper light. Thus Le Roy comments ironically that our oaks no longer provide oracles or sacred mistletoes, and that we must replace those old (though once useful) superstitions with vigilance and economy.

Although the oak's oracle has fallen silent, its oracular function is now taken over by the enlightened encyclopedist himself, who proposes a rational agenda for the future of forest management. The agenda is articulated in the projective mode. As the rest of the entry makes clear, vigilance and economy have not yet become a reality for forest management in France. On the contrary, Le Roy indicates that present practices in France are still largely unvigilant and uneconomic when it comes to forests. By wasting the timber resource through negligence and ignorance, the present regime of forestry remains blind to the future. It does not look forward enough, failing to consult the oracle of reason which proposes long-term strategies for preserving the national timber resource well into the future.

The vital importance of forests, writes Le Roy, has been felt in all ages. This is proved by the great number of forest laws in existence. Their great number, however, only indicates their inadequacy: "Laws are by nature fixed, and the economy must continuously respond to changing circumstances," he writes. "An ordinance can only prevent crimes, abuses, depredations; it establishes penalties against bad faith, but it hardly offers instruction for ignorance" (129). Laws in themselves cannot do the work of vigilance and economy, for they do not see clearly into the future. Proof of this can be found in the widespread degradation of the French forests, the high price of fuelwood, and the extreme scarcity of wood for construction and manufacture. (In effect, while the price of commodities fluctuated greatly during the eighteenth century in France, the price of timber skyrocketed steadily throughout the century, a clear indication of the dwindling supply of wood for all purposes [Corvol, 50].)

The issue, then, has to do with the correction of ignorance in matters of forestry. The restoration of forests is a long-term project that demands the most rigorous empirical knowledge. Forest management calls not merely for preventive laws but above all for expertise, well-informed judgment, and long-term perspectives that can see beyond the horizon of a single generation. Le Roy:

> While woods must be regarded as the property of the state [le bien de l'etat], due to their general utility, a forest is often nothing other than a cluster of woods belonging to many different particular owners. From these two points of view come different interests, which good administration must reconcile. The state needs wood of all sorts and for all time; it must above all carefully cultivate large trees. If one exploits woods for present needs, one must also conserve them and plan in advance for future generations. On the other hand, the particular owners are anxious to profit from their woods, and at times their eagerness is justified. . . . It is therefore necessary that those who are charged with overseeing the maintenance of forests by the state be very experienced, have

seen and observed much, and know enough not to outrage
the owners; furthermore they must know the workings of
nature, so that they may fulfill the spirit of the law and not
only its letter. (Le Roy, 129)

The interest of the owners is oriented toward immediate exploitation.
The state has its own interest in exploitation as well, yet it must also
guard the public interest in general, and for all time. Le Roy believes
that the interests of all parties involved, as well as the public interest of
future generations, cannot only be reconciled but also enhanced by
competent forest management. Everything depends upon the forester's enlightenment, his overcoming of that "ignorance" which Le Roy
associated with forest laws of the past.

Now the forester attains his expertise through direct experience
and observation of many woods and terrains ("One cannot learn except by closely following traditional experiences . . . and by observing
many different woods and terrains" [129–30]). Our encyclopedist here
reveals his allegiance to the dominant philosophical spirit of the *Encyclopédie,* which upholds the primacy of *expérience* in matters of knowledge. The *Encyclopédie* as a whole is a grand apology for sensism, empiricism, and a proto positivism of sorts. In this sense it seems directly
opposed to Descartes's mathematical deductionism and suspicion of
sense data; but in truth it merely dispenses with Descartes's metaphysics while remaining within the sphere of the Cartesian distinction between the subject of knowledge and its objects of analysis. However
one comes to know the object—through empirical observation or logical deduction—the subject retains its subjectivity as the organizing
principle of knowledge. An identical "humanism" underlies both
Cartesian rationalism and the encyclopedia's empiricism, a humanism
that finds fulfillment in what Descartes called the mastery and possession of nature.

Le Roy, then, characterizes the enlightened forester as someone
who derives his knowledge from observation and experience, basing
his judgments not on speculative principles but rather on the empirical
nature of varying local conditions. As he declares in his criticism of the
inflexible forest laws of the past, "economy must continuously respond to changing circumstances." The forester is a man of economy
par excellence. His knowledge of different terrains, the growth characteristics of various species, climatic conditions, etc., serves to refine
his judgment with regard to his single most important task, namely

the prescription of the right *time frames* for the cutting of trees. In questions of forestry, all is in the timing.

Le Roy elaborates what is at stake in firsthand knowledge of the growth rates of trees. We know, he says, that the cutting of woods rejuvenates their growth, and that, once cut, they will continue to grow annually up until a certain point. To maximize the benefit to be gained from a particular wood one must know exactly the cycle of its growth and the point at which it ceases to grow at the optimum rate. One must leave the wood standing until such time as it reaches that point. On the other hand, the benefit to be gained is even more considerable (*l'avantage devient plus considerable*) if one cares foremost for the *preservation of the soil* in which the trees have their roots. Excessive rejuvenation alters growth and exhausts the earth. Since every terrain has a certain depth, beyond which the roots cannot reach, excessive cutting will only hasten the moment when trees begin to decay. The forester must command such knowledge in all its empirical detail if he is to prescribe the timing of the cut. He must decide to leave some woods untouched for several generations, so that large-growth trees can flourish and be exploited for their appropriate purposes in the future; he must know which terrains are best suited for which species of trees, and he must know the optimum variety or quantity of species for a given area. This knowledge leads to an enlightened public administration of woodlands:

> Public vigilance is thus obliged to oppose the misconceived avidity of particular owners who would want to sacrifice the duration of their woods to the profit of the moment; it is the guardian of the rights of posterity; it must concern itself with its interest and manage from afar those interests: but it would be dangerous to exaggerate this principle, and one must distinguish here between the use of *taillis* and the reserve of *futaies*. The *taillis* being an object of revenue, one must not delay their cutting beyond the well-established annual progression of which we spoke: in that way one renders equanimously what is due to the present generation as well as to the generation that follows. The owner is recompensed for the waiting imposed on him, and the soil of the woods is conserved as much as possible. (130)

A rational approach to forest management, grounded in empirical knowledge of the matter, will reconcile the varying interests by managing the public interest in general. The public interest is not intrinsically opposed to the private interest of the owners; it represents and even subsumes the long-term interests of all. It is *universal*. It transcends, yet includes, the immediate and particular interests within society as a whole. Because of its universality, it guards the rights of posterity (by "rights" Le Roy means essentially *interest*). The rights of posterity are not opposed to the rights of the present generation; on the contrary, rights by nature safeguard the rights of all. The rights of posterity serve, therefore, as a regulatory principle of enlightened forest management, which, given the slow transgenerational growth of forests, must project its designs far into the future.

At this point we can no longer postpone the critical question: What does Le Roy mean by the "public interest"? Of what is the forester a guardian? The answer is not far off; it lies in the recurring concept of usefulness, or *l'utilité publique*. Forests are useful for many human purposes: heating, energy, manufacture, shipbuilding, revenue, and even more intangible things such as aesthetic pleasure, landscape, parks, and so forth. In the Age of Enlightenment the forest is subsumed altogether under this concept of usefulness. Given that Enlightenment is so much a part of our cultural heritage, we fail at first glance to grasp the revolutionary aspect of this new, all-embracing concept of usefulness. Lurking in the concept of course is the idea of profit—forests as a source of revenue and taxation—and we know that considerations of profit would soon come to dominate the entire European enterprise of forest management by the state as well as by the particular forest owners. Enlightenment presides over the reduction of forests to the status of a material resource in need of strict management. This view of the forest as mere material resource is so prevalent in our encyclopedist that he projects it back into the past, inviting us to believe that religion once conspired to consecrate forests so as to preserve so precious a commodity.

In order to gauge the novelty of the concept of the forest's usefulness, we have only to compare it to Manwood's concept in his treatise on the Forest Law. For Manwood a forest was essentially an asylum from the human world, a natural sanctuary where wildlife could dwell securely in the king's protection. It had nothing to do with the public interest, nothing to do with usefulness. On the contrary, forests marked the limits of human exploitation of the wilderness. The royal ban on forests protected them for the sake of their wildlife, which in turn was related to the king's "delight and recreation." We must understand Manwood's word "recreation" in the radical sense. In the royal sanctuaries the king engaged in a ritual chase that symbolically *re-created* his role as conqueror and subjugator of the wilderness.

In Le Roy's article forests are stripped of the symbolic density they may once have possessed. They are reduced to the most literal of determinations, namely "a great expanse of woodlands . . . composed of trees of all sorts." Le Roy never once mentions the issue of wildlife. *The forest as habitat has disappeared.* If habitat is not an issue for Le Roy it is because the forest has already been conceived of in terms of timber. This timber, in turn, has been conceived of in terms of its use-value. Use-value, in turn, has been linked to the concept of "rights"— the rights of the state, the rights of the private owners, and the rights of posterity. Nowhere is there any mention of the rights of the forest's wildlife. By contrast, Manwood's definition of the forest is dominated precisely by what he considers the natural rights of the beasts of pleasure, guaranteed by and inseparable from the divine right of sovereignty itself.

At first glance it seems strange that Le Roy, a game warden, would maintain such a conspicuous silence about the forest as a natural habitat, defining it as merely a sum total of trees. Upon reflection, however, it seems less strange, for Le Roy's article merely instantiates the hyperhumanism of the French *Encyclopédie* as a whole. This is the same humanism that announced itself at the beginning of the human age and that prepared the way for Descartes's enterprise. In his entry for the word *Encyclopédie,* Diderot took the occasion to reflect upon and clarify the philosophy of the *Encyclopédie.* His article affirms the old humanistic faith in terms that are by now familiar to us: "Man," he writes, "is the sole and only limit whence one must start and back to whom everything must return." For this sort of enlightened humanism, shared by Le Roy, there can be no question of the forest as a consecrated place of oracular disclosures; as a place of strange or monstrous or enchanting epiphanies; as the imaginary site of lyric nostalgias and erotic errancy; as a natural sanctuary where wild animals may dwell in security far from the havoc of humanity going about the business of looking after its "interests." There can be only the claims of human mastery and possession of nature—the reduction of forests to utility.

Le Roy's article manifests the mentality that comes to dominate the future of forest management in Europe and the United States. In this sense Le Roy indeed functions as the new forest oracle. Soon after

Le Roy wrote his article for the *Encyclopédie,* the definition of a forest as a wide expanse of woodlands composed of trees would give way to an even more reified concept: the forest as a quantifiable volume of usable (or taxable) wood. The usefulness of the forest becomes measured in terms of a quantifiable mass. Its enduring maximum availability, and its continuous renewal, become the predominate concerns of a new *science* of forestry.

The science was born in Germany in the latter half of the eighteenth century. New methods of forest management, based on mass or volume of wood, replaced the old area-based forestry. These methods were made possible by the founding of "forest mathematics," a technical science by which foresters could calculate the volume of wood in a given topography, project the growth rates of forests far into the future, and prescribe time frames for the felling of trees according to precise mathematical charts. Algebra, geometry, stereometry, and xylometry came together to form the *Forstwissenschaft* (forest science) of sustained-yield forestry. Foresters became state scientists, and a new category of professional came into being: the *Forstgeometer,* or forest geometer, who measured the borders of forests, drew up maps, and calculated the essential data. The founding heroes of the new forest mathematics—names like Hartig, Cotta, Beckmann, and others—turned German forestry into a truly rigorous science of measurement and quantification. The subjection of forests to mathematical analysis was a triumph for German forestry and kept it far in advance of any other nation's into our own century. As late as 1938 Franz Heske, addressing himself to American foresters, could affirm: "For all time, this century [nineteenth] of systematic forest management in Germany, during which the depleted, abused woods were transformed into well-managed forests with steadily increasing yields, will be a shining example for forestry in all the world" (Lowood, 342).

It is not our intention here to review the technical history of modern forest management. We must nevertheless remark that the reduction of forests to quantifiable volumes of wood brought about the transfiguration of forests themselves. Natural forests, with their diverse species and ages of trees, were gradually replaced by forests of uniform types, with prescribed planting times. The new monocultural forests were established according to the abstract concept of the "normal" forest: an ideal forest whose random and natural variables were reduced to a minimum. Henry Lowood, in his seminal work on the birth of German forest mathematics, describes the results as follows:

The German forest became an archetype for imposing on disorderly nature the neatly arranged constructs of science. Witness the forest Cotta chose as an example of his new science: over the decades, his plan transformed a ragged patchwork into a neat chessboard. Practical goals had encouraged mathematical utilitarianism, which seemed, in turn, to promote geometric perfection as the outward sign of the well-managed forest; in turn, the rationally ordered arrangement of trees offered new possibilities for controlling nature. (341)

We have followed many circuitous paths since the beginning of this study; along this one we arrive back at Descartes, who presumed to find his way out of a forest of randomness and confusion by following the straight line of method. In his *Discourse on Method* Descartes employed a mere analogy, but we are now in the position to see to what extent the analogy takes on a literal dimension of its own. Algebra and geometry, which served as the basis of Descartes's method for pursuing indubitable truth, become the basis of the new science of forestry. Thanks to such method the forest ceases to be the place of random errancy and becomes an orderly chessboard. As it becomes a calculable quantity, it also becomes geometric. How do you walk in a straight line through the forest? To begin with you plant your trees in rectilinear rows, as German foresters did. Algebraic geometry suffers no obstacles. The straight lines of geometry come to the forests of Enlightenment, and the ways of method prevail.

We may remark, finally, that the legacy of such enlightened attitudes toward forests still dominates governmental policies today. The United States in particular is the "child of Enlightenment" in this respect. Its approach to forestry is based largely on the French and German models. But then again, the United States is the child of more than one parent. It has Puritanism, Enlightenment, Romanticism, and more as part of its heritage. We could say that a war is being waged today in the United States between Monsieur Le Roy and John Manwood. The war is between two fundamentally opposed concepts of the forest. One is the concept of the forest as resource; the other of the forest as sanctuary.

These opposing concepts are presently confronting one another over the issue of the spotted owl in the old-growth forests of the Pacific Northwest. In the United States we do not have laws that protect habitats, yet since passage of the Endangered Species Act, we now have laws that protect endangered animal species. Those who appeal to the Endangered Species Act in their fight to protect the habitat of the spotted owl are the Manwoodians, so to speak, who envision the forest as a sanctuary for wildlife, or an asylum from the pitiless logic of economy which governs the institutions of enlightened society. In this sense the spotted owl has become a symbol of the forest's ghostly and posthumous existence in an age of the forest's twilight. Like Hegel's owl of philosophy, it appears at the end—but at the end of what? The end of the remnants of old-growth forests? The end of poetry? The end of the history of the imagination's relation to the domain that has so often provided asylum from the light of reality? What is it that this owl symbolizes? In David Lynch's television series, "Twin Peaks," set in the vicinity of the old-growth forests of the Pacific Northwest, Special Agent Dale Cooper is told by the oracle of supernatural forces that "the owls are not what they seem." Perhaps this owl is the spirit of evil that still lurks in the woods, but one way or another it needs an asylum, and those who are fighting to turn the forests into natural sanctuaries for the owl—whatever the owl is, whatever it seems or does not seem to be, whatever it announces the end of—these Manwoodians of today are among those whom Nietzsche had in mind when he spoke of the overman as "the meaning of the earth."

Those who oppose the Manwoodians are, in a word, nihilists. They are of course not nearly as enlightened as our encyclopedist Le Roy, since logging practices in America are for the most part neither vigilant nor economic over the long term, yet for them, as for Le Roy, the forest as habitat has disappeared altogether. The forest as habitat has become irrelevant, in essence, "useless."

The Manwoodians of today are forced, however, to speak the language of those whom they oppose. This is precisely the language of usefulness. In their efforts to preserve the forest sanctuaries, they must remind science as well as governments that one day the abundant diversity of plant species that exist nowhere else but in the forests will prove useful and beneficial for such things as treating cancer or other diseases. They must contrive a thousand convincing or unconvincing arguments in favor of the utility of forest conservation. For the moment this is the only language that has a right to speak, for it speaks of the "rights," that is to say economic interests, of humanity. It remains to be seen whether one day a less compromised, less ironic language will become possible—a language of other rights and other interests, a language, in short, of other worlds.

We have already remarked that forests appear in manifold and at times even antithetical ways during the Age of Enlightenment, which may raise some doubts about the identity of the phenomenon in question. Similar doubts may also arise with regard to the identity of a particular individual, who at one time speaks as a man of Enlightenment and at another as a rebel in revolt against the presumptions and mendacity of his age. Jean-Jacques Rousseau is such an individual (better perhaps, a "dividual"). He is fraught with contradictions not only for those who reckon with the coherence of his doctrines, but above all within himself, especially when it comes to his discourse about forests.

Is it really the narcissistic dreamer, the apologist for natural innocence, the critic of institutional society, who authored the *Projet de constitution pour la Corse* (Project for the Constitution of Corsica)? In this treatise of 1765 Rousseau speaks like a true votary of the *Encyclopédie,* championing the rule of reason, advocating *prévoyance,* or foresight, and calling for empirical exactitude in the management of Corsica's political and economic future. The first word of the treatise's title—*Projet*—already points to the spirit of enlightened projection which informs the document. Projection into the future was not Rousseau's dominant passion; rather the reverse. We know him as one who mystified human origins and denounced progress as a corruption. But its spirit of optimistic projection is not the only anomalous aspect of Rousseau's treatise. The author's reduction of nature to its status of usefulness—its potential exploitation for social and political purposes—is even more striking in the case of one who otherwise believed himself the favorite child of a generous, but much-abused, Mother Nature. In the *Projet de constitution pour la Corse,* Corsica's natural geography is apprehended primarily in economic terms. Referring to the island's capacity for almost total economic self-sufficiency, Rousseau emphasizes the importance of an enlightened and programmatic management of its various resources, above all its abundant forests. In this last regard he sounds much like our encyclopedist Le Roy. Addressing himself to the Corsicans, he writes:

> One will begin by assuring oneself of the most necessary raw
> materials, namely wood, iron, wool, leather, hemp, and flax.
> The island abounds in wood for construction as well as heat-
> ing, but one must not trust in this abundance and abandon
> the cutting of forests to the sole discretion of the owners. As

the island's population grows and the fellings increase, there will come a rapid degradation of woodlands, which can be repaired only very slowly. On this score one can learn the lesson of foresight from the country in which I live. Switzerland was once covered with woodlands so abundant that it was almost smothered. But because of the expansion of pasturelands and the establishment of industry, they were cut down with neither measure nor rule [*sans mesure et sans règle*]; now those immense forests reveal only denuded rocks. Fortunately, alerted by the example of France, the Swiss saw the danger and ordered their activities as much as they could. It remains to be seen whether their precautions are not already too late; for if, despite their precautions, their forests diminish daily, it is clear that they must ultimately perish.

By planning well into the future Corsica will not have to face the same danger. It is necessary to establish early on an exact policemanship of the forests and to regulate cutting in such a way that reforestation equals consumption. One must not follow the example of France, where the owners of waters and forests (who have the right to fell at will) have an interest in destroying the forests. . . . One must foresee the future from afar: though it is not now the time to establish a navy, the time will come when it will be necessary to do so, and at that moment one will realize the advantage of not having given up to foreign navies the beautiful forests that lie near the sea. One must exploit or sell the old forests which no longer profit, but one must leave standing all those that are still thriving; in their own time they will have their use [*ils auront dans leur temps leur emploi*]. (*Projet*, 926–27; my translation)

Here too, as in Le Roy's entry in the *Encyclopédie,* the forest appears solely as a potential resource of exploitation. Even the *belles forêts* of the Corsican coast are viewed with an eye to their eventual use in the construction of a national fleet. Is this, then, really Rousseau—the denouncer of *homo faber,* of human self-determination, of the great "city of man" as it was imagined in its ideal future by Enlightened humanism—is this really the Romantic rebel speaking?

The contradictory elements in Rousseau's work as a whole derive from his resolve to be a critic of the age of critique. This resolve places him squarely within the crisis of irony. We spoke of Enlightenment as a critical relation to the historical present by virtue of a detachment from the past which is projected into the future. Rousseau shares the anxiety of his age—namely, projective detachment—but he generally tends to reverse the positive and negative terms of the historical trajectory. In the primordial past, claims Rousseau, lies the lost natural innocence of man (its image serving as the measure of critique for the present). The future, in contrast, merely precipitates history into the nihilistic abyss of human "progress," or alienation from the original state of human happiness. One could say that in Rousseau one finds a *dédoublement,* or redoubling, of Enlightenment irony as he sets out to unmask the ideals of Enlightenment and to vindicate the more authentic truth of the state of nature, which the age of reason covers over and falsifies.

This leads us to two remarks. First, Rousseau's reduction of nature to mere resource for enlightened exploitation in his *Projet de constitution pour la Corse* cannot be the only or even the main way in which nature reveals itself to this poet of nostalgia. On the contrary, nature as utilizable raw material for the human project remains distinctly opposed to Rousseau's doctrine of nature as the benevolent origin and guardian of the human soul in its natural authenticity. The second remark is more like a question that pervades Rousseau's speculations about origins. If these origins have long been lost, falsified, covered over by human artifice and social contracts, how does Rousseau presume to recover them? Everywhere one looks the original state of nature has been erased, both inwardly and outwardly, by history. In his *Discourse on the Origin and Basis of Inequality Among Men* (1755) Rousseau claims that it is impossible to determine empirically what the state of nature was all about, or even to conjecture scientifically about man in his primordial state. All such attempts to approach the matter externally are doomed to futility. In the preface to that work he writes:

> What is still more grievous is that, since all the progress of the human race continues to move it farther away from its original state, the more new knowledge we amass, the more we deprive ourselves of the means of acquiring the most important knowledge of all, and in a sense, it is by studying man that we have made ourselves unable to know him.

In the same preface Rousseau suggests that the only way to come to know "natural man" is to delve reflectively into one's own inner self and to discover there, through natural intuition, the traces of that original human nature so disfigured and corrupted over time, and yet so imperishable in its truth. This truth lies well beneath the alienated surface of history and social evolution, well beneath the manners, conventions, ideas, and prejudices of the age, yet it somehow remains accessible to the soul's natural sensibility. If human nature cannot be empirically demonstrated, it may nevertheless be truthfully intuited.

By activating the resources of such intuition in the *Discourse on the Origin of Inequality,* Rousseau presumes to discover within himself an image, or scene, or sentiment of nature truer than that which science could ever achieve. Intuition enables him to imagine "natural man" wandering solitary through the great primeval forests of the earth, living a simple, innocent, and, most importantly, *happy* life. These forests sustained his human needs and assured him of his natural joy in being alive. Rousseau's intuition, or reflective introspection, also enables him to discover in human nature two primordial "principles": the first, he writes, "makes us ardently interested in our own well-being and self-preservation, while the other gives us a natural repugnance to seeing any sentient creature, especially our fellow man, perish or suffer" (140). These insights represent the foundation for Rousseau's idea of prelapsarian human nature, when human beings roamed the primeval forests carefree and happy.

We are more concerned here with the basis of Rousseau's intuition than his speculations about "natural man" wandering the forests as a happy savage. What is the basis of such intuition and how does it function? What is it that provokes its revelations? How does Rousseau liberate the resources of an intuition that has the power not only to overcome the disfigurements of time and history but also to discover the two primordial principles of human nature? For answers to these question we can turn to a passage from Rousseau's *Confessions* which describes the circumstances surrounding the composition of his *Discourse on the Origin of Inequality.* It is in the latter work that the forest appears as the imaginary scene of origins. It is in the *Confessions,* however, that we may begin to understand how the forest becomes for Rousseau the indispensable correlate of his intuitions. The relevant passage occurs in book 8:

> [I]t was in that year, I think, of 1753, that the Dijon Academy proposed "The Inequality of Mankind" as a subject for discussion. I was struck by this great question and surprised at

the Academy's daring to propose it. But since they had the courage, I thought that I might be bold enough to discuss it, and set about the task.

In order to think this great matter out at my leisure, I went to Saint-Germain for some seven or eight days with Thérèse, and our landlady, a decent woman, and another woman friend of hers. I think of this trip as one of the most pleasant in my life. The weather was very fine; those good women undertook all the trouble and expense; Thérèse amused herself in their company, and I, without a care in the world, came in at meal times and was unrestrainedly gay over table. For all the rest of the day, wandering deep into the forest, I sought and I found the vision of those primitive times, the history of which I proudly traced. I demolished the petty lies of mankind; I dared to strip man's nature naked, to follow the progress of time, and trace the things which have distorted it; and by comparing man as he has made himself with man as he is by nature I showed him in his pretended perfection the source of his true misery. Exalted by these sublime meditations, my soul soared toward the Divinity; and from that height I looked down on my fellow men pursuing the blind path of their prejudices, of their errors, of their misfortunes and their crimes. Then I cried to them in a feeble voice which they could not hear, "Madmen who ceaselessly complain of Nature, learn that all your misfortunes arise from yourselves!"

Rousseau goes on to recount how, upon his return to Paris, he becomes disgusted with the vain presumptions of human society and how, in order to get relief from his oppressions and to continue to ponder the truth of nature, he would wander for hours in the Bois de Boulogne, a wooded park on the margins of the city:

I found so little gentleness, open-heartedness, or sincerity even in the company of my friends, that in my disgust for that turbulent life I began to long ardently to live in the country and, seeing that my profession did not allow me to settle there, I hastened to spend the few hours that I had free away from the town. For some months, immediately after my dinner, I would go and walk alone in the Bois de Boulogne,

thinking over the subjects for works to be written and not returning till night. (*Confessions*, 362–63)

Let us return now to the original scene of intuition. The forest of
Saint-Germain is no longer the primeval forest of ancient times, yet
the *natural affinity* between this groomed forest and its remote prototype allows for Rousseau's vision of the state of nature. Here under the
lofty trees, in the dimness of the light of reason, intuition conspires
with the forest's suggestive environment to reach beyond time, beyond history and its institutions, to the truth of "natural man" in his
intimate connection to the source of his nature. The origin wells up in
Rousseau's imagination as the forest of Saint-Germain closes in around
the reflective self, yielding to intuition direct access to the recesses of
time. The forest of Saint-Germain could be called the preserve of
imagination's storehouse of images of remote antiquity. Intuition conspires with the forest's presence to produce in the mind an image of
origins. Or better, in the forest's recesses the solitary wanderer wanders through the recesses of time itself. The forest of Saint-Germain
becomes, quite literally, the *phenomenon* of origins.

The least we can remark is that this forest has for Rousseau a
wholly different aspect than the forests of Corsica, for which he prescribes an enlightened policy of vigilance and economy. The forest of
Saint-Germain reveals itself not in usefulness but in its communion
with the self's intuitive recollection of a prelapsarian human nature.
The difference between these two modes of apprehension comes from
the difference between finding oneself inside or outside of the forest.
In the former case, when Rousseau is enclosed by its towering mysteries, the forest becomes the scene of insight, or the place where the
glimpse of truth takes place. In the latter case the genetic secrets fold
up and disappear behind the forest's forbidding exterior, which confronts the outsider in its brute aspect of mere raw material.

We can also remark that Rousseau's rebellious social discourse has
an essential need to generate itself on the margins of the city, from
within the forest's enclosure. This need has as much to do with the
forest's suggestive environment as it does with the forest's topical marginality with respect to the city, for Rousseau needs to situate himself
in an eccentric space. When he returns to the city of Enlightenment
after his week in Saint-Germain he feels spiritually detached from the
vain and pretentious society of Paris, and he hastens to spend several
hours a day walking in the Bois de Boulogne, "thinking over subjects

for works to be written." Continuing to search out the proper context for his meditations, Rousseau finds it in the forests of a municipal park. These daily walks on the margins of the city offer us a spatial image of Rousseau's detachment from his age. It is an ambiguous measure, to be sure, for he remains at once inside and outside of the city during his forays into the parks. Furthermore, his "detachment" signals at the same time his subjection to the age, since Enlightenment, as we have suggested in so many versions, is essentially a mode of detachment.

This ambiguity—of Rousseau's position within Enlightenment—not only underlies the apparent incongruity between the enlightened author of the *Projet de constitution pour la Corse* and the denouncer of human progress; it also makes of Rousseau's sentimental forest the scene of irony in the historical sense we discussed earlier. We remarked that Vico's characterization of irony as being "fashioned of falsehood by dint of a reflection that wears the mask of truth" is not as obvious or straightforward as it seems. As the trope that governs reflective consciousness in general, irony refers to the capacity to perceive the beliefs of earlier epochs as falsehoods wearing the mask of truth. We saw an example of such historical irony at work in Le Roy's article in the *Encyclopédie,* where the author declared that in earlier times religion would consecrate forests so that veneration might preserve a vital material resource for posterity. Le Roy went on to declare that in our enlightened age we must replace those ancient cults with "vigilance and economy," implying that with our historical emergence from ignorance we no longer need to rely on falsehoods to get on with the business of managing our affairs.

In Rousseau's case this sort of historical irony turns upon itself in an act of reflection. During his meditations in the forest of Saint-Germain he *inverts* the ideals of Enlightenment: "I demolished the petty lies of mankind; I dared to strip man's nature naked, to follow the progress of time, and trace the things which have distorted it; and by comparing man as he has made himself with man as he is by nature I showed him in his pretended perfection the source of his true misery." It is precisely in this *comparison* that the trope of irony turns upon history as a whole and strips human progress, invention, science, and civility of their masks, exposing the "petty lies" of the age. Such irony reaches deep into the heart of the matter—into the heart of the forest, as it were—for by unmasking the petty lies of science, progress, civilization, knowledge, reason, and so forth, Rousseau asserts that all the efforts of humankind to take responsibility for itself and to forge for itself a social world are masks of falsity which disguise their own inauthenticity and alienate the intrinsic truth of man's nature. From this perspective history as a whole appears condemned to a fatal irony.

The question that remains to be asked is why such irony raised to the second degree finds itself at home in the forests—not in the wild forests but rather in municipal forests? The answer lies in Rousseau's will to criticize, which motivates his thinking far more than any will to truth. The ancient state of nature which he envisions through introspective intuition need not be real or demonstrable. Indeed, Rousseau can even affirm that perhaps the state of nature as he imagines it never truly existed. Yet Rousseau needs the idea or image of that state to denounce his fellow men and their progressive ambitions. Rousseau's dominant passion is that of denunciation. Expressed otherwise, he is more intent on the act of stripping men of their pretensions than of discovering their naked nature. The idea of a naked human nature serves merely as an imaginary term of comparison within the broader logic of Rousseau's critique of human society in its institutional forms. The process of unstripping compares man as he had made himself with man as he is "by nature." This constant and merciless comparison figures as the work of historical reflection: the work, essentially, of irony.

To the extent that he strips away all the guises in which man has masked his "true nature" throughout his social evolution, and to the extent that this stripping away engages in analysis, critique, detachment, indeed, in the prose of reason itself, Rousseau fully belongs to the ironic age he presumes to denounce. His various attempts to ironize his age, or to unmask its claims to progress and denounce its historical triumphalism, merely aggravate the disease for which he seeks a cure.

This sort of ironic irony finds the scene of its reflection in municipal forests. Whether at Saint-Germain or the Bois de Boulogne, the scene lies on the parameters of Enlightenment, where the light of history is refracted and diffused by the fringe of forest that defines the boundaries of its clearing. Rousseau moves back and forth from the light to its shadows, from the city to its wooded parks, from the society of men and women to their negative reflections in the soul of the "solitary wanderer," from reason to passion back to reason again. The movement is one of reflective consciousness, and its chiaroscuro is historically circumscribed, so circumscribed, in fact, that the dreamer who laments the constructs of human progress and envisions the innocence of origins in the forest of Saint-Germain is the same author of the treatise that puts the *belles forêts* of the Corsican coast on standing reserve for their eventual transformation into a national fleet. Affirmation in Rousseau's case has its ground in negation; the dialectic it entails comprehends the relation between nature and history, truth and falsity, innocence and corruption, forests and cities. In Rousseau's doctrine the latter terms appear as negative. But a more decisive analysis of these apparent oppositions reveals that they belong to one another as surely as the Bois de Boulogne belongs to Paris.

CONRAD'S BROODING GLOOM

In many ways the nineteenth century remains the most modern century to date: a century of nostalgia, to be sure, but also of visions of future alternatives which history for some reason never fulfilled. It dreamed of a truly radical and redeemed modernity, but one which failed to materialize, or which failed to consolidate its spiritual gains. History made—is making—a mockery of our presumption to become truly modern. As the millennia comes to a close, the nineteenth century appears to us (at least to some of us) like brooding storm clouds drifting over a drought-stricken land without discharging their moisture. It was a century that came and went like a cluster of illusions.

The following two chapters of this study deal with the nineteenth century from multiple perspectives, but at this juncture in our analysis we will move directly to the threshold of the twentieth, staying with our theme of irony, Enlightenment, and historical detachment from the past. At this threshold we confront a question that has been with us from the outset of this chapter, namely: What does the wilderness have to do with the Western metropolis? More concretely, where are the ancient, virgin forests in relation to London, for example?

" 'And this also,' said Marlow suddenly, 'has been one of the dark places of the earth.' " Marlow, the narrator of Conrad's *Heart of Darkness,* speaks from the deck of a boat anchored in the Thames river in the last year of the nineteenth century. He is thinking of the time when the Romans arrived on the banks of the Thames and confronted an abominable wilderness of savagery, disease, and death. Now it is the British and their European kinsmen who carry the torch of empire "to the uttermost ends of the earth" (*Heart of Darkness,* 27–29).

No one could imagine more vividly than Joseph Conrad the wilderness of the West in prehistoric times. During his long seafaring career he had seen the remote frontiers of forested worlds in their savage state; he had also seen how those same worlds became European colonies; and he had firsthand experience of the Western "conquest of the earth," as he called it. Hence Conrad exercises a special authority when he declares that the Western races—as if under the impulse of a moral imperative—knew how to overcome the sylvan wilderness; how to rise above its gloom; how to seek the open radiance of a luminous ideal. Worshippers of the light, believers in ideas, lovers of the open horizon—these strong and indomitable Western races subdued the forests long ago. Now Western Enlightenment spreads abroad, bringing its light to places that have yet to conquer the darkness. The light of that torch is fueled by morality—the European virtues of faith, heroism, and self-sacrifice.

In *Lord Jim,* a book published in the first year of the new century, Marlow offers a striking symbol of the moral idealism by which the Western races have overcome the gloom. This symbol is Jim, a young romantic who has made himself the "lord" of the native forest people of Patusan in a remote region of the Eastern Pacific. In Patusan Jim has gained for himself a new life in the sunlight. Prior to his going there he had been cast into the depths of darkness and disgrace by an ignominious act of cowardice. As chief mate of the *Patna* he, along with the rest of the crew, had jumped from the ship when it seemed that it was about to sink in the dead of night, abandoning its unsuspecting Asian passengers. The *Patna* remained afloat, however, and when it was rescued by another vessel the incident became common knowledge among the seafaring community. Thereafter Jim found himself desperately looking for a second chance to prove to himself that he was indeed a hero, or that it was not his true self that had jumped from the ship in that moment of distraction. Jim got that second chance in Patusan, a place far from the white man's world and memory. Nor did he fail to exploit it. He confronted extravagant dangers with legendary courage; he defeated in battle the oppressors of the Patusan people; and he becomes the benevolent, enlightened lord of Patusan. When Marlow goes to visit him in his remote haven, he perceives in Jim something symbolic of his race as a whole:

> He stood erect, the smouldering brier-wood in his clutch,
> with a smile on his lips and a sparkle in his boyish eyes. I sat
> on the stump of a tree at his feet, and below us stretched the

land, the great expanse of the forests, sombre under the sunshine, rolling like a sea, with glints of winding rivers, the
grey spots of villages, and here and there a clearing, like an
islet of light amongst the dark waves of continuous tree-tops.
A brooding gloom lay over this vast and monotonous landscape; the light fell on it as if into an abyss. The land devoured the sunshine; only far off, along the coast, the empty
ocean, smooth and polished within the faint haze, seemed to
rise up to the sky in a wall of steel.

And there I was with him, high in the sunshine on the
top of that historic hill of his. He dominated the forest, the
secular gloom, the old mankind. He was like a figure set up
on a pedestal, to represent in his persistent youth the power,
and perhaps the virtues, of races that never grow old, that
have emerged from the gloom. I don't know why he should
always have appeared to me symbolic. Perhaps this is the real
cause of my interest in his fate. I don't know whether it was
exactly fair to him to remember the incident which had given
a new direction to his life, but at that very moment I remembered very distinctly. It was like a shadow in the light.

(*Lord Jim*, 161–62)

Dressed in white, Jim appears here in the guise of a marble statue
symbolizing moral rectitude—the spiritual power of his race to overcome the abyss of the forest's darkness. Yet the symbolism is troubled.
It belongs to the dream world in which Jim now levitates without having come any closer to self-knowledge with regard to the abyss within
himself. Marlow cannot help remembering the "incident" that
brought Jim to Patusan in the first place—his precipitous jump from
the *Patna*. "It was like a shadow in the light." Even here in the radiance
of his historic hill (where he won a major battle against his enemies),
Jim is still in the "everlasting deep hole" that he jumped into a few
years earlier. He now believes that he has climbed out of
that hole once and for all, but we know from the outcome of the novel
that the hole will in fact swallow him up again with the first fluttering
of the veils of illusions which Patusan has momentarily wrapped
around him.

Just as Jim's moral transcendence precipitates into the shadow of
the past which lurks in the present light, so too his symbolic stature
becomes shrouded in irony. The figure on the pedestal is nothing more

than a beautiful illusion, a deception. The elevated symbol cancels its own symbolism in the shadow it casts. In that shadow, a truth lies concealed: that Jim's race does grow old, that it does not always emerge from the gloom, that it has an incorrigible habit of daydreaming. That this race, in short, knows how to deceive itself on a pedestal.

Let us read that sentence again: "A brooding gloom lay over this vast and monotonous landscape; the light fell on it as if into an abyss." In *Lord Jim* the "brooding gloom" hangs over the forests of Patusan; but no one who has read *Heart of Darkness* can fail to recall its opening pages in Conrad's choice of words here. In *Heart of Darkness,* written a year earlier, the same phrase recurs in three variations, referring not to the gloom from which Jim's race has "emerged" but rather to the gloom that now hangs over the city of London: "Only the gloom to west, brooding over the upper reaches, became more sober every minute, as if angered by the approach of the sun." This gloom broods over the modern metropolis in the "dawning" twentieth century of the Western world: "The sun sank low . . . stricken to death by the touch of that gloom brooding over a crowd of men." Again: "And farther west on the upper reaches the place of the monstrous town was still marked ominously on the sky, a brooding gloom in sunshine, a lurid glare under the stars" (*Heart of Darkness,* 27–29). What do forests have to do with London? With the West? With the twentieth century? The West was once dark, then it saw the glory of Enlightenment. Now it declines, it sinks back into the shadows from which it arose. What is the nature of this decline? Why, in other words, does Conrad envelop "the biggest, and the greatest, town on earth" in a gloom that evokes the forest landscape?

The symbolism of *Heart of Darkness* may hold some clues. To begin with, its story recalls Vico's theory of the decline of civic society into what he called the "barbarism of reflection." Vico's theory held that in the later stages of cultural evolution, when irony begins to corrode the moral foundation of institutions and when no ethical imperative can effectively restrain the "bestial" inclination of human beings, enlightened men begin to "turn their cities into forests and the forests into dens and lairs of men." Such oversocialized men, we recall, are "made more inhuman by the barbarism of reflection than the first men had been made by the barbarism of sense. For the latter displayed a generous savagery, against which one could defend oneself or take flight or be on one's guard; but the former, with a base savagery, under soft words and embraces, plots against the life and fortunes of friends and intimates."

The barbarism of reflection entails deceit, the "soft words" of irony. Veils of benevolent rhetoric conceal treacherous intentions. A shadow lurks at the heart of Enlightenment. *Heart of Darkness* unveils this shadow, this deceitful rhetoric; but in this case the rhetoric is that of humanitarian idealism, which European societies promoted as moral justification for the Western conquest in Africa.

The novel's juxtaposition of civilized Europe with the wild forests of Africa suggests that barbarism lurks not so much in the African natives as in the hearts of the Europeans, who conceal a savagery of greed and violence beneath the public colonial rhetoric about "saving the savages from their benighted ways." As it moves deeper and deeper into the interior of the African forests—the wilderness that the West had long ago turned into the centers of modern Enlightenment—Marlow's narrative suggests that the African "savages" are intrinsically more "civilized" than their self-appointed saviors, who presume to bring their efficient methods of administration to the dark continent. The only positive heroes in this sombre story are the cannibals on board Marlow's steamboat. Along with the natives enthralled to Kurtz, they are the only ones who possess what Vico as well as Conrad considered the primordial moral virtue: *restraint.* Decadence begins with the loss of restraint.

But the loss of restraint results from an even more grave and serious loss, namely the loss of faith. In several moments of the narrative Marlow insists that only on the basis of an unshakable faith can a modern European withstand the abomination of the wilderness and exercise restraint under conditions of extremity. "Principles won't do," he declares, "Acquisitions, clothes, pretty rags—rags that would fly off at the first good shake. No; you want a deliberate belief" (p. 69). Instead of such a deliberate belief, Marlow discovers among the African colonists its conspicuous absence. He discovers a spiritual vacuity, an "everlasting deep hole" of nihilism. Marlow is deliberately vague about the nature of the redemptive faith to which he appeals. It does not seem to be religious per se. The following passage, addressed not only to his fictive audience on board the boat, but also to the cosmopolitan reader of *Heart of Darkness,* is a masterful exercise of vague allusion:

> You can't understand. How could you?—with solid pavement under your feet, surrounded by kind neighbors ready to

cheer you or to fall on you, stepping delicately between the
butcher and the policeman, in the holy terror of scandal and
gallows and lunatic asylums—how can you imagine what
particular region of the first ages a man's untrammelled feet
may take him by the way of solitude—utter solitude without
a policeman—by the way of silence—utter silence, where no
warning voice of a kind neighbour can be heard whispering
public opinion? These little things make all the difference.
When they are gone you must fall back upon your own innate strength, upon your own capacity for faithfulness. Of
course you may be too much a fool to go wrong. . . . Or you
may be such a thunderingly exalted creature as to be altogether deaf and blind to anything but heavenly sights and
sounds. Then the earth for you is only a standing place—and
whether to be like this is your loss or your gain I won't pre-
tend to say. But most of us are neither one nor the other. The
earth for us is a place to live in, where we must put up with
sights, with sounds, with smells, too, by Jove!—breathe
dead hippo, so to speak, and not be contaminated. And
there, don't you see? your strength comes in . . . your power
of devotion, not to yourself, but to an obscure back-breaking
business. (85–86)

This sermon from *Heart of Darkness* is, among other things, a decisive commentary on the character of Jim in the later novel. Jim is one
of those "thunderingly exalted creatures" for whom the earth is too
unclean a place. He is a Romantic, a hero of the ideal, a "butterfly";
but he is defenceless against the earthliness of the earth. He too, in his
own way, lacks restraint in the moment of crisis, precisely because he
lacks the "faith" or "innate strength" that would allow him to withstand corruption. At bottom Jim never actually climbed out of the
"everlasting deep hole" of his self-deception. He merely covered it up,
or veiled its abyss, with an irony that would ultimately make his second fall inevitable. Thus the forest he overlooks on the top of his hill
"symbolizes"—if we may use such a word in the present context—the
dark "hole" concealed at the core of Jim's nature.

Heart of Darkness delves more frankly into the historical dimensions of this hole, yet it does so through a similar forest symbolism. In
the forests of Africa the hole in question comes to represent something
like Western nihilism at the dawn of the new century. Of one of the

agents at the Central Station, Marlow says: "I let him run on, this papier-mâché Mephistopheles, and it seemed to me that if I tried I could poke my forefinger through him, and would find nothing inside but a little loose dirt, maybe" (56). There is more to the remark than an image of moral bankruptcy. The loose dirt indicates that this soul is not only vacuous but that it has been unearthed. This papier-mâché individual belongs among the emissaries of the enlightened West who have come literally to unearth the African continent.

The unearthed hole or cavity, like a festering wound in the depths of the forest, symbolizes the colonial enterprise. Marlow is exposed to this literal hollowness the moment he steps foot on the continent: "I avoided a vast artificial hole somebody had been digging on the slope," he says, "the purpose of which I found impossible to divine" (44). Through the symbolic gateway of this cavity, dug up senselessly by the colonists, he will descend deeper and deeper into the heart of darkness. At the bottom of the cavity—the Inner Station of the Trading Company—Marlow will meet Mr. Kurtz, the "remarkable man" whose voice our narrator has been so anxious to hear, hoping for a redemptive idea within the folds of Kurtz's eloquence. This darling of Europe and the Trading Company ("All Europe had contributed to the making of Kurtz" [86]) is a true genius. He came to Africa with progressive ideas, a moral mission, and an exalted rhetoric about enlightened administration. But in the African interior Kurtz discovers that his true genius lies neither with his ideas nor with his eloquence. It lies rather in the extraordinary efficiency of his "unsound methods," which give up the pretensions of Western administrative practices and follow, as Marlow puts it, "no method at all." In other words Kurtz's genius lies in his ability to dig up the earth in search of ivory. In Kurtz, Marlow meets the most unearthly of colonial unearthers:

> Ivory? I should think so. Heaps of it, stacks of it. The old mud shanty was bursting with it. You would think there was not a single tusk left either above or below the ground in the whole country. "Mostly fossil," the manager had remarked, disparagingly. It was no more fossil than I am; but they call it fossil when it is dug up. It appears these niggers do bury the tusks sometimes—but evidently they couldn't bury this parcel deep enough to save the gifted Mr. Kurtz from his fate. (84–85).

If Marlow could not understand the purpose of that vast artificial hole he almost fell into on his arrival, it was because he had still not discovered the purpose of the European presence in Africa. At the heart of darkness the hole reveals its purpose. The unearthing of the earth yields resources, in this case ivory. But by virtue of a perverse symbolism, Kurtz, as he digs up the earth for ivory, delves into the moral cavity of his administrative genius and uncovers its skeletal nihilism. By the time Marlow sets eyes on him, this "gifted man" looks strangely like the bone of disinterred ivory himself: "It was as though an animated image of death carved out of old ivory had been shaking its hand with menaces at a motionless crowd of men made of dark and glittering bronze" (99).

At the end of his journey—his "nightmare," as he calls it—Marlow will go and visit Kurtz's Intended, or fiancée, who lives in Brussels. Like London, Brussels is a European metropolis juxtaposed to the forests in *Heart of Darkness*. In this case the juxtaposition is symbolized by the ironic relation between Kurtz and his Intended. Kurtz has been dead a year when Marlow goes to visit the mournful Intended, but his memory lives on both in her and in Marlow. Since Marlow assumed responsibility for Kurtz's "burial" in the spiritual sense (the body itself was buried in some "muddy hole" along the banks of the Congo river), he must visit the Intended in order to consign once and for all the still disinterred memory of Kurtz in the majestic tomb of this woman's devotion to him.

The last ritual in Marlow's task as caretaker leads him to a "high and ponderous door, between the tall houses of a street as still and decorous as a well-kept alley in a cemetery." The setting is appropriately described. Not only does it evoke a neatness and efficiency of management in stark contrast with the inefficient administration that reigns in Africa, but Marlow has referred to Brussels throughout his narrative as the "sepulchral city." He could just as easily have spoken of a sepulchral Europe. If the forests of Africa are the place of naked unearthing, of disinterment, of the disclosure of an abyss at the heart of the savior civilization, the European city is the place where the abyss is obscured, or buried. Only at the end of the novel, then, do we fully understand why London, at the beginning, was enveloped in a "brooding gloom" that evoked a forest landscape. The gloom is funereal, sepulchral, mournful.

If Kurtz knew how to unearth the African continent and delve into the cavity of his own nihilism, his Intended knows how to bury what has been left exposed. Kurtz and the Intended belong most intimately to one another, like the duplicity of irony itself. She embraces Kurtz's rhetoric of greatness, genius, and sacrifice, but with the special privilege of being spared the trial that would put its eloquence to the test. She is an idealist, but like Kurtz and Jim, and like the world and epoch to which she belongs, she cannot bear very much reality. Face to face with this creature of earnest illusion, Marlow himself cannot bear to witness the collapse of yet another ideal, the extinguishing of yet another light (the light which, in the dusk, has gathered around her white forehead). When she asks him about Kurtz's last words, he lies to her. This deliberate lie—that Kurtz's last word was her name and not that infernal whisper, "The horror!"—consummates a nightmare. Marlow conspires with the Intended's self-deception. Only by virtue of the lie's power to conceal, to cover over, to *bury the truth,* can the fragile fabric of a self-deceived civilization hold together.

Marlow's lie conspires with the irony of the sepulchral city. For Marlow to have spoken the truth would have amounted to a dangerous lack of irony—dangerous because, in the final analysis, irony is what safeguards the more complex, paradoxical truth of the age. But this lie is the most disturbing of conclusions to such an epic, if only because nothing is more disgusting to Marlow than a lie:

> You know I hate, detest, and can't bear a lie, not because I am straighter than the rest of us, but simply because it appals me. There is a taint of death, a flavour of mortality in lies— which is exactly what I hate and detest in the world—what I want to forget. It makes me miserable and sick, like biting something rotten would do. (57)

Marlow is a man for whom irony is a rotten fruit that he is forced to bite into, for there is nothing else to feed on at this extremity of knowledge. Irony is the innermost truth of a civilization that knows how to lie to itself about itself, or how to bury under deceptive veils a truth that would otherwise destroy it. Marlow succumbs before a fatality—the decaying nature of the civilization that enlisted Kurtz in its mission of conquest. His lie is at once a renunciation as well as an impotent act of protest. It bites into the rotten fruit, conspiring with the principle of decadence; yet it also revolts against mendacity and exposes it, within the economy of the narrative, as the ongoing strategy by which the West lives with itself.

The juxtaposed relation between the primitive forests and civilized Europe, then, is at once analogical and topographical. The African jungles are literally remote from Europe, yet their wilderness provokes the most intimate cultural confession—a failure in the power of devotion, a failure of the idea, a failure, in essence, of European morality. In *Heart of Darkness* forests appear as the locus of this revelation. What the forests' darkness reveals is precisely what remains concealed under the gloom that broods over the metropolitan crowd of men, namely Western nihilism at the turn of the twentieth century. Conrad's heart of darkness—the heart of the forests within and without—exposes nihilism not so much as the savagery and greed that lie beneath the humane postures of colonialism, but as the absence of a redemptive idea in the West's conquest of the earth.

"The conquest of the earth," says Marlow, "which mostly means the taking it away from those who have a different complexion or slightly flatter noses than ourselves, is not a pretty thing when you look into it too much. What redeems it is the idea only. An idea at the back of it; not a sentimental pretence but an idea; and an unselfish belief in the idea—something you can set up, and bow down before, and offer a sacrifice to . . ." (31–32). Instead of such an idea, Marlow discovers in the African jungles that Europe's conquest of the world amounts to a simple unearthing of the earth, an unrestrained global assault on nature and native cultures.

During his career as a seaman Conrad witnessed the brutal scene of assault the world over. He wrote works like *Heart of Darkness* and *Lord Jim* at the threshold not only of a new century but also of a new epoch of planetary conquest, which had amassed unprecedented means for a totalized dominion over the earth. Conrad was at a loss before the global magnitude of the phenomenon; he was unable to conceive of "an idea at the back of it." Such an idea, whether moral or spiritual, is not forthcoming in his work. Its absence is conspicuous, above all in a story like *Heart of Darkness.* We must conclude, therefore, that Conrad remained not only a pessimist but also a nihilist with regard to the global future that was taking shape at that moment of history. He knew that the older ideas and faiths were inadequate, superfluous, superannuated. *Lord Jim* in particular testifies to the ultimate irrelevance of the moral codes of the past (Brierly's suicide is eloquent on this score), for there was something unprecedented about the modern conquest, so unprecedented that it rendered any analogy between the ancient Romans and the modern European colonists dubious.

This analogy in fact breaks down before certain irreducible historical differences between the Roman conquerors and the European colonists. It breaks down precisely where Marlow alludes to the need for a redemptive idea in the conquest of the earth. About the Romans Marlow remarks: "They were no colonists; their administration was merely a squeeze, and nothing more I suspect. They were conquerors, and for that you want only brute force. . . ." (31). But we modern Europeans, he suggests, are not like the Romans in this respect. We do not have the serenity of mere conquerors, for the history of Europe since Roman antiquity has been predicated on faith in redemption, a devotion to the idea, a drive toward idealism, a morality of sacrifice. We are not Romans because we have been Christianized, spiritualized, internalized. The Romans had no need to believe, only to triumph. We on the other hand are subject to a historical imperative that demands belief, even if it is no longer Christian belief. One way or another we must believe, even if it means to make believe. Hence a failure of faith in our case can only take the form of a corrosive irony.

This sort of corrosive irony was profoundly offensive to Conrad, yet he had no choice but to embrace it, for he was not in a position, historically speaking, to imagine an ethic or a faith adequate to the enormity of global conquest. In the final analysis Marlow remains a bewildered moralist who belongs to the century that is setting with the sun that goes down over London in the opening pages of *Heart of Darkness*. The unearthing of the earth on a planetary scale—the global assault on the frontiers of nature and non-Western cultures—gives a hollow resonance to all prior rhetoric of the cross, all traditional codes of morality, and all private conceptions about the good and honorable. The nihilism of a work like *Heart of Darkness* lies in the failure of Marlow's private code of morals to achieve a credible reference to the global future of the new century.

At the end of his journey Marlow finds himself in a hopeless position precisely because he cannot see clearly through the dark with the lens of his own moral wisdom. His ultimate gesture—lying to Kurtz's Intended—can only ironize the irony that veils the truth about his civilization. His ability finally to ironize his age and its presumptions perhaps indicates a higher wisdom than he possessed before the journey into Africa, but even this higher wisdom cannot overcome the irony that revolts it. By ironizing the irony that holds sway over the age Conrad succeeds in dramatizing its historical inevitability, hence he reveals in the realm of literature something like a "truth." But such truth is neither positive nor redemptive; it is the same truth that insinuates a shadow into the light of Jim's transcendence on top of the hill overlooking the forests of Patusan.

ROQUENTIN'S NIGHTMARE

Earlier in this chapter we found intimations of global conquest in Descartes's reference to the "mastery and possession of nature" through scientific method. We discussed the so-called death of God and saw how Descartes proposed the *res cogitans* as the new foundation for knowledge. Having briefly characterized the method by which Cartesian rationalism presumes to arrive at indubitable truth in the sciences, we went on to analyze the analogy in the *Discourse on Method* which compares resolute action to walking in a straight line through the forest, suggesting that the analogy contains a broad reference to Cartesian method in general. In our discussion of the rise of forest management during the eighteenth and nineteenth centuries we found that Descartes's analogy takes on a strangely literal significance once forests are apprehended in terms of wood volume and subjected to rigorous mathematical calculation. The discussion of Conrad and the colonial conquest of Africa, in turn, gave us a glimpse into the underside of the Western ethic of method, resource management, and efficient administration. We now turn to a twentieth-century doctrine that in many ways embodies the afterlife of Cartesianism in the post-Christian era, namely Jean-Paul Sartre's existentialism.

In a brief essay of 1946 ("L'Existentialism est un humanism") Sartre states that existentialism is a humanism. By humanism he means, at bottom, a form of Cartesianism. The undeniable certainty of the fact "I think, I exist" is the basis of existentialism, he writes. But whereas Descartes had tried to deduce the existence of God from this "indubitable" truth, existentialism, according to Sartre, confronts bleakly and without compromise the unjustifiability of human existence—its abandon in a world devoid of God or any higher court of appeal than itself. Even reason loses its legislative authority for existentialism, since the latter realizes that there is no sufficient reason for things to be rather than not to be. In Sartre's version of existentialism human beings are condemned to a stark freedom—the freedom to make what they will of their own individual existence. The doctrine, therefore, conceives of itself as a call to human beings to "come of age"—to free themselves from the tutelage of false authorities and live up to the fact that each one of us is handed over to himself or herself without appeal to any transcendent ground. The subtle complexities of Kant's idea of Enlightenment give way, in Sartre, to a clear and distinct doctrine of self-consignment and responsibility.

In fairness to Sartre we must keep in mind that his statement of 1946 was a simplification of the philosophical basis of existentialism. It is to his credit that he had the courage to reduce his ontology to a manifesto in order to boldly articulate its moral and social consequences. The manifesto, however, left Sartre open to several attacks and he later repudiated its validity. These considerations do not change the fact that existentialism is a humanism, nor that it has its roots in Cartesianism, nor that Sartre was essentially a disillusioned rationalist who discovered that the assumptions of rationalism were ultimately ungrounded. Nor, finally, does it change the fact that, as a humanist, Sartre suffered from the same sort of forest phobia whose traces we detected in Descartes's *Discourse on Method*. One way or another humanism abhors the forest, especially when it is an exasperated humanism like Sartre's. On this score there is more to be learned from Sartre's novel *Nausea* (1938) than from his formal statements in the essay of 1946, or from the ontology of *Being and Nothingness* (1943). It is to that early novel that we now turn as we continue to probe the issue of forests, Enlightenment, and nihilism.

Roquentin, the lonely existentialist hero of Sartre's *Nausea,* is someone who no longer shares the naive optimism of Cartesianism yet who remains nevertheless a Cartesian. He is a rationalist in revolt. He revolts against the fact that words, grammar, concepts, definitions, equations, in short, the entire bureaucracy of human knowledge, cannot account for the *existence* of concrete things. Every individual thing, insofar as it exists, stands outside the cloister of human consciousness and confounds the latter with the enigma of its being-there. A stone that Roquentin holds in his hand as he walks along the seashore is enough to induce in him a state of nausea, which means at bottom intellectual bewilderment. However thoroughly one might define the stone's properties—its color, weight, shape, and other such abstractions—its *existence* remains wholly inexplicable and impenetrable by the mind. Existence transcends conceptualization. It is absurd, contingent, without foundation or reason, and ultimately unjustified. In Sartre's novel, nausea is the symptom of the mind's acknowledgement of its inability to construe, in good faith and without self-deception, any human meaning out of existence. Nausea is the gloom of humanism, which in its more positive moods affirms that the human constructs that give meaning to the world correspond in some essential way to the existence of phenomena.

A stone, however, is finally less offensive to an exasperated humanist like Roquentin than a tree. The climactic crisis of nausea in Sartre's novel comes about when Roquentin wanders into a park and finds himself in the presence of a chestnut tree, whose sheer existence is more irrefutable and more absurd than anything else he has encountered so far in the novel. The tree's muteness, its immovable posture, its downward-reaching roots and rising branches, its refusal to refine the materiality of its existence into a transparent concept—all this humbles and offends Roquentin, filling him with disgust. This single tree, with its knarled roots and chaotic network of branches, figures as a synecdoche for the forest itself. And nothing, as we have already suggested, disquiets a rationalist more than a forest.

What color is the root of the tree? It seems to be black, yet Roquentin knows that black is a relative concept that belongs to the apparatus of subjectivity, not to the thing itself. "Black? I felt the word deflating, emptied of meaning with extraordinary rapidity. Black? The root was not black . . . black, like the circle, did not exist" (*Nausea*, 130). What *does* exist is the root of the tree. Distressed by this observation, Roquentin kicks the root but cannot split off the bark. The grotesque thingness of the thing continues to confront him with the absurdity of its being-there until Roquentin, vanquished by his own frustrations, concludes that everything that exists—including human beings—exists *de trop*, in excess. In excess, that is, of consciousness.

Here, then, is a rarefied version of forest phobia. Opacity and rootedness—these are the qualities of the tree that induce the nausea in Roquentin. A stone is opaque, but a tree is more so. Rootedness, or better yet, begottenness, aggravates the opacity of existence. It is not by chance, therefore, that it is the *root* of the tree that inspires in Roquentin the following anguished reflections, which summarize the philosophical premises of existentialism:

> This root—there was nothing in relation to which it was absurd. Oh how can I put it in words? Absurd: in relation to the stones, the tufts of yellow grass, the dry mud, the tree, the sky, the green benches. Absurd, irreducible; nothing—not even a profound, secret upheaval of nature—could explain it. Evidently I did not know everything, I had not seen the seeds sprout, or the tree grow. But faced with this great wrinkled

paw, neither ignorance nor knowledge was important: the
world of explanations and reasons is not the world of existence. A circle is not absurd, it is clearly explained by the ro-
tation of a straight segment around one of its extremities.
But neither does a circle exist. This root, on the other hand,
existed in such a way that I could not explain it. . . . This
root, with its colour, shape, its congealed movement, was
. . . below explanation. (129)

What lurks in this confession is the humanist's terror of a world that
transcends human grounding. Here is a tree whose existence cannot
be accounted for either by the *res cogitans* or by the latter's efforts to
reduce the world to intelligibility through mathematics or history. Roquentin inhabits the cloister of human consciousness, but beyond it the
world of nature exists independently, autonomously, indifferently.

Where do such realizations lead our protagonist? They lead him,
predictably enough, ever deeper into the subterfuges of the humanly
constructed world. Any other sort of world—the world of nature, for
example—terrifies him. Roquentin is thus condemned to the city, for
the city remains the ultimate fortress of any humanism whatsoever. In
the city one has cleared the forests, cast them to the margins, buried
them under the pavement. For Roquentin the city is a refuge or asylum
from nature, yet even this humanized environment fails to put him
completely at his ease. In another dramatic passage of *Nausea* Roquentin declares:

The houses, I walk between the houses, I am between the
houses, on the pavement; the pavement under my feet exists,
the houses close around me. . . . I am. I am, I exist, I think,
therefore I am; I am because I think, why do I think? I don't
want to think anymore, I am because I think that I don't want
to be, I think that I . . . because . . . ugh! I flee. (100)

But Roquentin has nowhere to flee. The pavement under his feet
exists. This *fundamentum inconcussum* is the paved road of the modern
city, yet even here Roquentin is trapped; the houses close around him;
he wants to leave, but he has nowhere to go, for outside the city lies
the vegetation, the forest, the horrendously irreducible fact of the nonhuman world, as absurd and impenetrable as the gnarled root of the
chestnut tree. The cities are under siege, they are giving way to the
forests, and Roquentin must inhabit them while they last. Toward

the end of *Nausea* the existential confessions of Roquentin come to a
conclusion with the following admission:

> I am afraid of cities. But you mustn't leave them. If you go
> too far you come up against the vegetation belt. Vegetation
> has crawled for miles toward the cities. It is waiting. Once
> the city is dead, the vegetation will cover it, will climb over
> the stones, grip them, search them, make them burst with its
> long black pincers; it will blind the holes and let its green
> paws hang over everything. You must stay in the cities as
> long as they are alive, you must never penetrate alone this
> great mass of hair waiting at the gates; you must let it undu-
> late and crack all by itself. In the cities, if you know how to
> take care of yourself, and choose the times when all the beasts
> are sleeping in the holes and digesting, behind the heaps of
> organic debris, you rarely come across anything more than
> minerals, the least frightening of all existants. (156)

These are Roquentin's thoughts at the moment he decides to end his
self-imposed exile in the provincial town of Bouville and return to the
metropolis of Paris. The confessions of a humanist, a Cartesian, a cosmopolitan. Rarely has a long tradition of thought—the forest phobia
of rationalism—been given such a telescopic formulation. The end of
Vico's order of institutions, when forests begin to overrun the cities, is
in sight. Nausea amounts to a vision of vegetation, a nightmare of
nature. It is the dread of a civic hero who, like Gilgamesh, looks beyond the walls of the city to the green paws of existence.

WASTELANDS

Sooner or later we will have to come up with a less ironic name than
"greenhouse effect" for the choking of the atmosphere with carbon
dioxide. Green is the wrong color. The color is ashen. One-tenth of
the carbon dioxide emitted into the atmosphere comes from the fires
of deforestation in Brazil alone. That is a lot of green rising in smoke.
The earth is on fire; it has a fever. Perhaps we should call it the "fever
effect" rather than greenhouse effect. But beyond its name, this "effect" is part of a worldwide phenomenon that will mark the ecological
legacy of the twentieth century: desertification. Roquentin's nightmare—his vision of vegetation crawling toward the cities waiting to
place its "green paws" over everything—is strangely out of touch with

the times, for it is the desert that is extending its domain over the realm of vegetation.

"The wasteland grows," wrote Nietzsche over a century ago, "Woe to him who harbors wastelands within." But as we remarked earlier in another context, such things are as mirrors: if a monkey looks in no apostle will look out. If desertification occurs within, the forests cannot survive without. Soul and habitat—we are finally in a position to know this—are correlates of one another. It is not by accident, then, that the "wasteland" figures as one of the dominant emblems, or landscapes, of modernist literature, from Eliot's poem by that same name to Dino Buzzatti's *Deserto dei Tartari*. T. S. Eliot's poem "Gerontion," originally part of *The Wasteland* and separated out in later revision, ends with the verse: "Thoughts of a dry brain in a dry season." The season in question is the epoch under critique in *The Waste Land*, which opens with the famous verses:

> April is the cruelest month, breeding
> lilacs out of the dead land, mixing
> memory and desire, stirring
> dull roots with spring rain.

We have been taught, among others by Eliot himself, to read *The Waste Land* as a testimony of despair over a civilization in spiritual decay. But that is only one aspect of the testimony. Poetry does not only monitor spiritual states of being, or what one used to call the "spirit" of an age; it also registers the spiritual effects of a changing climate and habitat. As the external environment undergoes transformations, poets often announce them in advance with the clairvoyance of seers, for poets have an altogether sixth sense that enables them to forecast trends in the weather, so to speak. Like oracles, they may couch their message in the language of enigma. And like oracles, the meaning of their message becomes fully manifest only after the events it foretells have unfolded. Modern poetry at its best is a kind of spiritual ecology. The wasteland grows within and without and with no essential distinction between them, so much so that we might now say that a poem like Eliot's *The Waste Land* is in some ways a harbinger of the greenhouse effect. Or better, we can say that the greenhouse effect, or desertification of habitat in general, is the true "objective correlative" of the poem.

But poets are not always reliable in this regard. In retrospect it seems clear that a modernist writer like James Joyce, whose literature exploited the almost limitless resources of the sayable, never really heeded the "nature" of the times. His luxuriant forest of prose does not grow in the desiccated ground of the modern habitat but rather in some garden of nostalgia. His work thrives on the illusion of plenitude—the plenitude of nature, of the vigorous body, of meaningfulness in every dimension of being. On the other hand the bleak essentialist literature of a writer like Samuel Beckett seems truly to reflect, or preannounce, the changing climate of the times. In his case the ecology of the sayable is reduced to an authentic poverty. The failure of his word to flourish in any grand sense reveals, in its minimal flower, the depleted resources of the ground that lies outside the writer's window.

This window of the soul, so to speak, appears in one of Beckett's plays as one of the bleakest mirrors in modernist literature. In *Endgame,* Hamm periodically asks Clov to go look out of the window of their room, and each time he does so Clov reports that nothing has changed: the habitat lies wasted, devoid of trees or signs of life. At one point during the play Hamm falls asleep and his mind drifts back in thought to some mysterious recollection or fantasy. When he wakes up he mutters to himself: "Those forests!" These two words, left uncommented, refer to some impossible space beyond the world, beyond the wasteland that exists both inside and outside of the room. Hamm's cryptic utterance as he awakens from the dream of some other world barely intrudes into the action of play, yet it may well hold the secret of the drama as a whole: "Those forests!" Which forests? The forests of Vico's giants? The forests of pre-Cartesian "prejudices"? Or the forests that are disappearing as this sentence is being read?

As for Ezra Pound, since we are speaking of modernist writers, it would seem at times that he tried to defy the growing wasteland in a mad attempt at cultural and historical reforestation. In his *Cantos* he created a true wilderness of beauty, but one that dried up and exhausted its sources almost as quickly as it flourished. Pound struggled to the death against the inhospitable climate of the times, and those same times reduced his efforts to ashes. In the fragments that end the *Cantos* he offers his most intimate confession of all:

> M'amour, m'amour
> what do I love and
> where are you?
> That I lost my center
> fighting the world.

> The dreams clash
> and are shattered—-
> and that I tried to make a paradiso
> terrestre. (Pound, 802)

Like "those forests" in Hamm's dream, the green dream of an earthly paradise pertains to other times and climates than those which suffer from greenhouse effects. Meanwhile Pound lost his center fighting the world—the desiccated land outside Hamm's window—attesting in his failures that green is not the color of the age.

Like many of Beckett's works, *Endgame* dramatizes an end that cannot come to an end: an end endlessly prolonged. Whatever the nature of the end in Beckett's vision, it drags on indefinitely. This failure of the Christian era to achieve the end of that which is already over—the faith in redemption, in humanism, in history, in progress, in "man"—is one more dimension of nihilism. The word *nihil* in Latin means "nothing." It is that which is left over after the story is over yet continues to drag on. In Beckett's work the *nihil* refers, among other things, to the absence of a grammatical tense to describe this strange state of affairs. In part 1 of *Molloy* the narrator, who is agelessly old and whose decrepit life cannot come to an end, says: "My life, my life, now I speak of it as something over, now as of a joke which still goes on, and it is neither, for at the same time it is over and it goes on, and is there any tense for that?" (*Molloy,* 47).

Molloy hopes that by returning home to his mother in his great old age—by returning to his origins—he may close the circle of his life. The "last leg" of Molloy's odyssey takes him through a dark and "towering" forest in his native province. Up until this point Molloy had only one good leg, relying on crutches and a bicycle for his mobility, but in the forest he loses the use of even that leg and takes to groveling through the woods in an absurdly determined way: "Flat on my belly, using my crutches like grapnels, I plunged them ahead of me into the undergrowth, and when I felt they had a hold, I pulled myself forward, with an effort of the wrists" (121). Does Molloy make any forward progress through the forest in this manner? It is not clear. All Molloy knows is that he must be wary of Descartes's advice about walking in a straight line:

> And having heard, or more probably read somewhere, in the
> days when I thought I would be well advised to educate my-

self, or amuse myself, or stupefy myself, or kill time, that
when a man in a forest thinks he is going forward in a
straight line, in reality he is going in a circle. I did my best to
go in a circle, hoping in this way to go in a straight line. . . .
And if I did not go in a rigorously straight line, with my system of going in a circle, at least I did not go in a circle, and
that was something. (115)

By going in a circle he hopes to go in a straight line and reach the
end of the road, but his movement is neither linear nor circular. His
movement is like the grammatical tense that does not exist to describe
a life that is over but that nevertheless drags on. The forest in *Molloy* is
an allegory for this impossible paradox, or paralysis of life. But is it
really a forest that Molloy grovels through in his last desperate attempt
to make an end of it all? In part 2 of the novel we learn from Moran—
the agent who has been commissioned to seek out Molloy—that Molloy could hardly have been lost in a forest. At most it was simply a
meager clump of trees, for the native region of Molloy's wanderings is
in essence a wasteland. Moran informs us: "The land did not lend itself
to cultivation. . . . The pastures, in spite of the torrential rains, were
exceedingly meagre and strewn with boulders. Here only quitchweed
grew in abundance, and a curious bitter blue grass fatal to cows and
horses" (184). This is the true landscape of Molloy's forest. Part 2 of
Molloy demystifies the landscape of part 1, just as its narrator, Moran,
demystifies the fiction of his own report: "It is midnight. The rain is
beating on the windows. It was not midnight. It was not raining"
(241). In short, desertification.

At the end of his narrative Molloy indicates that the forest ends in
a ditch—a sign of human cultivation? Of a grave? It is in any case a
boundary, and in this ditch Molloy's journey comes to a provisional
end. What sort of end we do not know. In the distance Molloy sees the
steeples and towers of a town, but he makes no effort to get out of the
ditch. "Molloy could stay," he says, "where he happened to be" (124).
Help is apparently on the way, but history meanwhile will stay where
it is—in a ditch at the edge of the forest.

4

Caspar David Friedrich, *Winter Landscape with Church* (1811)

FORESTS ᴏꜰ NOSTALGIA

IF IT IS TRUE THAT THE POST-CHRISTIAN ERA DETACHES IT-
self from the past, frees itself to some extent from the inertia of tradition, "comes of age" under the auspices of reason, it is also true that it
experiences its freedom as a deprivation as well as a gain. Early in the
last chapter we saw how freedom from the past implied freedom for
an enlightened future. The countercurrent of Enlightenment's drive to
inherit the future is nostalgia. As the ancestors fall silent in their
graves; as the age-old traditions and landscapes of the past recede into
vanishing horizons; and as the sense of historical detachment begins to
doubt its original optimism—nostalgia becomes an irrevocable emotion of the post-Christian era.

From this nostalgia perspective, which laments the condition of
loss, however imaginary or impossible its object of longing, human
mortality and history appear as the unfolding of nihilism, or as our
steady alienation from the spontaneity, joy, and authenticity of origins.
In the nostalgic look back toward a remote and originary past, forests
loom large indeed in the post-Christian imagination. In Rousseau's
case we saw how the poet's nostalgia gave rise to a general theory of
humanity's fall into the corruption and deprivations of social history,
and how Rousseau envisioned his garden of prelapsarian origins as a
primeval forest. In the present chapter we will explore variations of
this sort of nostalgia that conceives of forests in terms of some originary plenitude—of presence, innocence, community, or even perception.

More specifically, we will approach the nostalgic imagination
with reference to romanticism, symbolism, and the Brothers Grimm's

recovery of folklore tradition. In general we will find that forests have the psychological effect of evoking memories of the past; indeed, that they become figures for memory itself. They are enveloped, as it were, in the aura of lost origins. This is by no means a phenomenon peculiar to modernity (we have seen versions of it in antiquity). Nevertheless there is something new in the nostalgic countercurrent of the post-Christian era. We will find here that forests and origins "correspond" with one another through the medium of recollection, and that the former provide a sort of correlate, or primal scene, for poetic memory itself.

As we focus on the relation between forests and memory in this context, we will also find that the nostalgic attitude is merely a declension of the irony that holds sway over the post-Christian era as a whole. In the nostalgic eye forests are ringed with a halo of loss (they still are, today more than ever), yet the pathos of loss is permeated with a reflective irony that belongs to the ambiguous shadows of Enlightenment. Our discussion of Rousseau made it clear that however much Rousseau presumed to repudiate the presumptions of Enlightenment, he too belonged to its historical detachment from the past. Nostalgia, in other words, is an ambivalent stance: it cannot but evoke the condition it laments, and by the same token it cannot but present its lost paradise (or forests) as anything but imaginary, inaccessible, or unreal.

This is not to doubt the authenticity of nostalgia, nor to condemn its pathos to superfluity, nor even to deny that its objects of loss once existed. On the contrary, by the end of this chapter it should become clear that nostalgia keeps open the vision of historical alternatives; that it keeps alive the expectation of grace; or that it perpetuates the quest for a poetry which has as its vocation the redemption of the vulgar and deadly prose of modern realism. Only in the last and concluding chapter of this study, however, will we be in a position to fully determine what it means, in our own age, to keep the eye of poetic vision open.

FORESTS AND WORLD IN WORDSWORTH'S POEM

If John Manwood's name somehow inspired him to author a treatise on the Forest Law, and if there is any reason to believe that a name can sometimes inspire a vocation, then perhaps it is worth pondering the name of William Wordsworth in this context. Wordsworth learned the lesson of Rousseau's doctrine of natural innocence and translated it into a poetic idiom whose goal was to vindicate the worth of the simple word. He spoke of the "naked dignity of man" as well as of the "naked and simple" language that corresponds to it. Just as Rousseau had presumed to strip away the artificial social constructs that corrupt the original innocence of the human soul, so too Wordsworth strove to dismantle the artifice of poetic neoclassicism, with its attendant dogma about poetic diction, decorum, the hierarchy of genres, and the formal rules of composition. Through this effort he aimed at leading poetry back to the immediacy of everyday language and the natural spontaneity of speech. For Wordsworth the simple word had the power to draw nearer to the inner life of nature—to the creative source of life itself, which links human nature to nature as a whole.

For Wordsworth the intrinsic power of the poetic word to renaturalize human sentiment, or to run as the great countercurrent of history back toward the sources of simplicity and happiness, promised to overcome the brutal dispersion of an urban age through recollection and to rediscover the dignity of the creature who had made a mess of its attempts to create a world of its own making. As with Rousseau, forests play an important role in the poet's rhetoric of renaturalization. The poem "Lines Written in Early Spring," composed in 1798, evokes a simple forest scene:

> I heard a thousand blended notes,
> While in a grove I sate reclined,
> In that sweet mood when pleasant thoughts
> Bring sad thoughts to the mind.
>
> To her fair works did Nature link
> The human soul that through me ran;
> And much it grieved my heart to think
> What man has made of man.
>
> Through primrose tufts, in that green bower,
> The periwinkle trailed its wreaths;
> And 'tis my faith that every flower
> Enjoys the air it breathes.
>
> The birds around me hopped and played,
> Their thoughts I cannot measure—
> But the least motion which they made,
> It seemed a thrill of pleasure.

The budding twigs spread out their fan,
To catch the breezy air;
And I must think, do all I can,
That there was pleasure there.

If this belief from heaven be sent,
If such be Nature's holy plan,
Have I not reason to lament
What man has made of man? (Wordsworth, 80–81)

The speaker in the poem finds himself in privileged proximity to what is authentic and enduring in nature, enveloped by its tangible presence and exuberant vitality as he sits in the grove. The thousand blended notes are the sounds of the forest, which not only harbors a diversity of living things but also blends them into a unity that sounds like the harmony of music. Here the pleasant thoughts that nature inspires bring sad thoughts to the mind as well. These sad thoughts have to do with what "man has made of man," as opposed to what nature made when she first created him. It is clear from the rest of the poem that the pleasant and sad thoughts do not blend together like the thousand notes of the grove but coexist in the poet's mind in a sort of discord.

Nature claims as her own creation the "human soul that within me ran." To say that nature "linked" this soul to her "fair works" is a way of saying that the human soul has its being in this link to the source of its genesis. Such linkage between nature and her creatures manifests itself in the "blending" of the sounds of the forest. Much like Rousseau in his moment of introspective intuition in the forests of Saint-Germain, the poet here rediscovers his soul by virtue of the countercurrent that flows against the temporal or historical fall into alienation. This countercurrent is often figured in Wordsworth's poetry as the movement of recollection, although this poem does not explicitly allude to recollection as such. Perhaps this is because the poet finds himself in a place that has already gathered within its enclosure that which recollection otherwise re-collects.

But it is precisely at the moment the poet rediscovers "the human soul that within me ran" that thoughts of the man-made world began to grieve him. They grieve him because the man-made world has severed the link, strayed from the source, detached itself from what otherwise assures man's harmony in the order of nature. They grieve him for another reason as well. The poet knows that he too is a man and that, however persuasive his feeling of appurtenance to nature, he is condemned to the legacy of what man has made of man. The one who grieves is already conditioned in advance by the man-made world. If nature originally created man, man in turn takes over the creative process and makes of himself something unearthly. The poet, then, speaks here both as a child of nature as well as a citizen of the city. His alienation is none other than his historicity, haunting his mood as the measure of his remoteness—a remoteness at the heart of his sensation of intimacy.

The coexistence of these sentiments of appurtenance and alienation insinuates itself repeatedly throughout the three stanzas that follow. Wordsworth invokes his famous pleasure principle—the idea that a spontaneous joy of being pervades the vitality of all living things, indeed, that their vitality *is* their joy, in such assertions as: "every flower / Enjoys the air it breathes"; "the least motion which they made, / It seemed a thrill of pleasure"; "there was pleasure there." In each case, however, he must qualify his declaration: "'tis *my faith* that every flower . . ."; "Their thoughts *I cannot measure* . . ."; "And *I must think,* do all I can. . . ." The qualifications dramatize both the proximity and the distance that define the poet's link to nature at this moment. They amount to a confession that he cannot really know nature from within, but only from without. Appearances *seem* to corroborate his impressions, but the poet will never ultimately know whether the appearances correspond to the inner truth of nature's being, for he has access only to his own inner being. Yet when he turns within himself he finds that pleasant thoughts and sad thoughts, joy and grief, celebration and lament, are commingled. This troubled interiority, then, would not seem to correspond to the exuberant nature around him.

The discordance arises out of the necessary historicity of human life, or the poet's awareness of transience, aging, and ultimately death in those things that most concern him, including himself. Nature passes away and returns, erodes and rebuilds itself without concern for what it leaves in its wake. But a human being is pervaded by care, which in turn is grounded in temporality. The difference between human care and nature's indifference establishes the measure of human alienation.

One of Wordsworth's most acclaimed sonnets, "The World Is Too Much with Us," addresses this alien historicity directly. What is remarkable about the poem, among other things, is its historical perspective, or better, its suggestion that as consciousness evolves through history human beings become more and more excessive of the world.

> The world is too much with us; late and soon,
> Getting and spending, we lay waste our powers;
> Little we see in Nature that is ours;
> We have given our hearts away, a sordid boon!
> This Sea that bares her bosom to the moon,
> The winds that will be howling at all hours,
> And are up-gathered now like sleeping flowers,
> For this, for everything we are out of tune;
> It moves us not.—Great God! I'd rather be
> A Pagan suckled in a creed outworn;
> So might I, standing on this pleasant lea,
> Have glimpses that would make me less forlorn;
> Have sight of Proteus rising from the sea;
> Or hear old Triton blow his wreathéd horn. (Wordsworth,
> 270).

To declare that the world is "too much" with us is both paradoxical and enigmatic, for it implies an excessive fullness in the world by virtue of our presence within it. But the "too much" of human presence does not refer to plenitude, rather to emptiness. We have emptied out our nature, given our hearts away, spent what we have received. Far from adding itself to the plenitude of nature, human existence exceeds it and thus becomes a sort of nullity at the edge of things.

The condition of excess appears as a historical one. Wordsworth's sonnet suggests that only now, in the age of irony, have human beings evacuated and thus exceeded the world. In previous ages, when consciousness embraced a more innocent "creed," nature did not appear so forbidding and alien, or so reduced to its mere objective status. In those "pagan" times the sea revealed itself anthropomorphically, in the form of Proteus rising from its depths, or Triton blowing his horn. Nature then was more humanized because humanity itself was more naturalized. The capacity for anthropomorphism was a gift from nature, a "getting" that we since have spent.

What is left, after the spending, is irony's detachment. As it reflects upon itself, human consciousness discovers its exclusion from the world, its inability to rehumanize or reanimate it anthropomorphically. The Sea now "bares her bosom to the moon." It reveals itself in its bare objecthood as a mere body of water. Having stripped away the veils of anthropomorphism, irony reduces the world to its reified state, while the subject—in this case the poet—finds himself suspended in the empty space of his own exteriority with respect to the world.

Much of Wordsworth's poetry deals with the remorseless passage of both personal and historical time, the former serving as an analogy for the latter, and vice versa. In either case the past appears as the age of natural spontaneity. Time flows out and away from the source, while poetic recollection becomes, in Kierkegaard's words, "the countercurrent of eternity flowing backward into the present." As Kierkegaard's remark about poetic recollection suggests, this countercurrent does not flow back so much into the chronological present but rather into presence as such. Presence means more than the mere objective presence of the sea, the sky, the moon. It means above all the presence of the origin, the fullness of time itself, which is what Rousseau presumed to intuit in his moments of sentimental introspection. Wordsworth's poetry correlates this presence with recollection of the past, suggesting thereby that the origin lies deep in the reaches of the has-been and that its presence is repeatable, or recuperable, only through poetic memory.

In our discussion of Rousseau we were led to ask about the landscape of intuition; here we may ask about Wordsworth's landscape of "the source," or the presence of the origin. We may do so by comparing the two poems we have already cited and discussed. To begin with their similarities, we find that they both allude to human historicity as the measure of exclusion from nature. By turning into the self the poet discovers the soul's link to nature but also his condemnation to the man-made world. This man-made world is not comprised merely of "Steamboats, Viaducts, and Railways"—technological inventions which mar the beauty of natural landscapes but which Wordsworth can nevertheless praise in a sonnet that goes by that title—nor does it encompass merely the world of human laws and institutions. The man-made world means first and foremost the historical modes of consciousness which determine our relation to nature and which lead, in the long run, to irony. In both of these poems, therefore, and throughout Wordsworth's corpus as a whole, the poet's meditations revolve around the historical fatedness of his personal as well as historical lack of spontaneity.

The difference between the two poems, on the other hand, lies in a difference of landscapes and magnitudes. In "The World Is Too Much with Us," we have the open sea, the vast night sky, the moon, the dormant but violent winds: a landscape, in short, of the sublime. Here the exclusion of the spectator from the spectacle of nature is absolute. The earlier poem, "Lines Written in Early Spring," portrays a much different landscape: that of a natural enclosure, a grove, a bower, in short, a forest. Here the presence of nature has none of its alienating grandeur. We are privy to a scene of intimacy rather than intimidation, and as the poet draws near, absolutely near, to the inner life of things—as near as is humanly possible without the leap into mysticism—he almost seems to close the gap that separates the human soul from the inner being of nature, but not quite. A haven from the sublime, the grove's enclosure offers the closest possible proximity to the presence of the source.

It would seem, then, that we have answered our question about the landscape of the source. That landscape is the forest. It would be excessive to argue that the forest is the privileged locus of Wordsworth's recollective poetry as a whole, but there is no doubt that, in Wordsworth's poetry, forest imagery evokes the deepest "feeling" of proximity to nature. In "Tintern Abbey," for example, the poet describes a moment of recollection which is actually the recollection of a recollection. He states that when he had been far away from the place where he now finds himself again—that is to say, when he had been in the city—he would often recall its "beauteous forms" and would sometimes fall into those special moods of recollection, in which, "with an eye made quiet by the power / Of harmony, and the deep power of joy, / We see into the life of things." This recollective vision, which looks into the life of things, recalls the experience in the grove described by "Lines Written in Early Spring." Yet conscious of the irony of his position, the poet cannot confirm his feelings of communion without a note of doubt. This same doubt appears in "Tintern Abbey," marked by the qualifying "if," immediately after the verses just cited about looking "into the life of things":

> If this
> Be but a vain belief, yet, oh! how oft—
> In darkness and amid the many shapes
> Of joyless daylight; when the fretful stir
> Unprofitable, and the fever of the world,
> Have hung upon the beatings of my hears—
> How oft, in spirit, have I turned to thee,

> O sylvan Wye! thou wanderer through the woods,
> How often has my spirit turned to thee! (Wordsworth, 133)

Perhaps this belief that he saw into the life of things is a vain one. But vain or not, the poet lives by this creed. In the man-made world the poet would often "turn" in recollection to the Wye river. This "turn" is in every sense a re-turn, not only in memory to a familiar scene from the personal past but also in "spirit." In those moments of recollection the soul spiritually returns against the currents of time and history back toward the source of its nature. The source is ultimately invisible, and yet it offers an image of itself in the "sylvan" river. The Wye river flows from the heart of the forest, down through Wales into Southwest England into the Severn estuary, and from there into the open sea of the Bristol channel. It is against the current of this river that the soul returns, from the alienating openness of the sublime (the open sea of "The World is Too Much with Us") to the intimate enclosure of origins in the forest. This "sylvan" river winding through the woods is the ultimate correlate of poetic recollection. The forest is its imaginary source—the source of time itself.

Yet all this is taking Wordsworth at his word. Whatever his word is worth, it involves a special form of irony. Recollection does not merely recall the presence of the origin, it in fact engenders it through its ironic mediations. It is in the city that Wordsworth recollects the scene of nature, and it is only by recollecting his recollection that he relates to the presence of nature in "Tintern Abbey." Likewise in "Lines Written in Early Spring," it is by virtue of his historical remoteness from nature that he has an experience of nature's proximity in the forest. The consciousness of "what man has made of man" divorces the poet from nature but at the same time lies at the source of his nostalgia for origins. The nostalgia, in turn, is what draws nature into its presence, allowing its "thousand blended notes" to sound their harmony. In other words, nature derives its mode of presence from the man-made world, in this case the city. Nature has no being apart from its modes of revelation, which are given by historicity.

Wordsworth avows as much in "The World is Too Much with Us" when he states that he would rather be "a Pagan suckled in a creed outworn" so that nature might appear to him in its spontaneous aspects. The modes of nature's presence derive from modes of human consciousness, and these latter are historically determined. In other words, Wordsworth's romantic "creed" is not a creed at all—it is a consciousness conscious of the loss of creed. However much it may want to retrieve spontaneity or the presence of the origin through poetic recollection, it remains a testimony of civic irony. The forests of its nostalgia come to presence in images and words that speak less about nature and more about what man has made of man.

THE BROTHERS GRIMM

In discussing the Brothers Grimm we will try to avoid rehearsing clichés about the Germanic tendency to mystify forests as sanctuaries of origins, race, community, and so on. This will not be easy, however, for the careers of Jacob and Wilhelm Grimm conjure up Tacitus's remark in the *Germania* about the ancient German Suebi: "The grove is the center of their whole religion. It is regarded as the cradle of the race and the dwelling-place of the supreme god to whom all things are subject and obedient" (Tacitus, 134). The Grimms shared this atavistic sentiment. Their consuming interest in old German literature and folklore led to what one might call a philological mystification of German forests, if only because forests loom so large in the songs, legends, and tales they collected and transcribed during their career as scholars.

Many of the fairy tales in their *Children's and Household Tales*—after the Bible, the highest selling book in the West since its publication in the nineteenth century—contain themes and narrative patterns we have encountered already, whether it be in hagiography, chivalric romance, or medieval outlaw legends. Here too it is not our intention merely to rehearse them. What we must bear in mind above all is the larger context. To distinguish the Grimms' fairy tales from the various traditions that often inform them, we must pay special attention to the historical circumstances of the brothers' enterprise of collecting the tales. As for distinguishing the brothers' attitude toward forests from that of their German ancestors, we must keep in mind that the Grimms were not Suebian barbarians carrying on in the forests but philologists of the post-Christian era, broadly defined.

Within this broader historical context, the Grimm brothers belong to a more circumscribed one—that of Romantic historiography. The latter represents an attempt to liberate the past from the grand narrative schemes of classical historiography and to resurrect the inner *life* of the past, in all its concrete fullness. As opposed to merely reviewing historical events and the deeds of dynastic individuals, Romantic historiography sought to recover what one might call the "life-worlds" of cultural tradition. It emphasized the importance of historical documents dealing with laws, customs, and economy, for example; and it looked to poetry and folklore as vital reserves of cultural memory. One of the assumptions of this new historiography was that the "spirit" of the past lay with the people, not their rulers; with ways of life, not wars and conquest; with values and beliefs, not aristocratic fashions; with national character, not international characters. For the Romantic historian the past was more an affair of the land than of courts.

This shift of emphasis gave forests a new sort of importance or, better, mystique, in the Romantic imagination. Thanks to their imposing presence in folklore and legends, forests came to be viewed as having genetic as well as symbolic connections to memory, custom, national character, and ageless forms of popular wisdom. Their topical marginality with respect to the grand narrative of courtly history lent forests a strange kind of "documentary" authority. Thus Jules Michelet, one of the most sublime of Romantic historians, was fascinated by forests. Among his many books there is one entitled *La sorcière,* dealing with the figure of the witch in both pagan and Christian religion. Focusing on the witch's ambiguous status, Michelet sought to come to terms with her alternative and outcast wisdom, which belonged to the profane, eccentric space of the forests.

In this context we must return again to Giambattista Vico, who traverses this study in so many ways. Michelet was "seized by a frenzy," as he put it, when he read Vico's *New Science,* discovering in the work the "great truth" that individuals and historical events are largely irrelevant to understanding the past when compared to the anonymous forces of social evolution. We may also mention in this regard Fustel de Coulanges, author of the French masterpiece *The Ancient City* (1861), which tells the story of those "silent revolutions" of antiquity which had changed the laws and institutions of ancient society. Such notions of an anonymous history were Viconian through and through, for Vico had argued that history is determined by gradual mutations in the customs, laws, institutions, beliefs, languages, and modes of thought of peoples as a whole. Vico spoke of an "ideal eternal history traversed in time by the histories of all nations" (*New Science,* §393). His theory of "Poetic Wisdom" held that the modes of thought of ancient peoples were essentially poetic, not prosaic. This notion of Poetic Wisdom became especially critical for a historian like

Michelet, concerned as he was with questions of national character and popular wisdom. Michelet spoke of Vico as the "golden bough" allowing him to descend into the realm of "infernal shades" and resurrect the spirit of the past. And sure enough, the way back into the realm of the past led to the forests of remote antiquity—the forests where Vico searched for the origins of Poetic Wisdom.

We bring up Vico in this context because he also lies in the background of the Grimm brothers' careers as philologists. The connection with Vico is perhaps only indirect, but substantial nevertheless, for the singlemost important influence on Jacob and Wilhelm Grimm during their formative years as scholars came from their law professor at the University of Marburg, Friedrich Karl von Savigny. The brothers went to study law in Marburg in 1802 and 1803, respectively, and Savigny, founder of the so-called historical school of law, became their master and mentor. Savigny was, among other things, one of Vico's early enthusiasts. He considered Vico his predecessor in the historical approach to jurisprudence. Savigny believed that a nation's laws are rooted in the ancient customs and language of its people and that only by understanding the history of those customs and language could one truly understand the spirit of law. He encouraged the Grimms, therefore, to research the popular origins of German culture. Like Vico, Savigny placed a heavy emphasis on philology in the study of law. The idea that law has its basis in customs and language was one of the major contentions of the *New Science*. In the following axioms from book 1, for example, Vico boldly articulates the philologico-historical approach to law:

XVI

149 Vulgar traditions must have had public grounds of truth, by virtue of which they came into being and were preserved by entire peoples over long periods of time.

150 It will be another great labor of this Science to recover these grounds of truth—truth which, with the passage of years and the *changes in languages and customs,* has come down to us enveloped in falsehood.

XVII

151 The *vulgar tongues* should be the most weighty witnesses concerning those ancient customs of the peoples that were in use at the time the languages were formed.

XVIII

152 A language of an ancient nation, which has maintained itself as the dominant tongue until it was fully developed, should be a great witness to the customs of the early days of the world.

153 This axiom assures us that the weightiest philological proofs of the natural law of the gentes . . . can be drawn from Latin speech. For the same reason *scholars of the German language can do the like,* since it retains this same property possessed by the ancient Roman language.

Passages such as these make it easy to understand why Savigny would have considered Vico a misunderstood predecessor of his historical school of law. They also enable us to understand the crucial emphasis Savigny placed on the role of customs and language. According to Vico the study of language yields knowledge of ancient customs, and the latter, in turn, yields knowledge of the basis of a nation's laws. Relying on Tacitus's claims in the *Germania,* Vico argued that German, like Latin, is a privileged language to the extent that it evolved autonomously, without contamination from foreign languages. Such "native" languages were, for Vico, a "storehouse of etymologies" which allowed the philologist to recover not only the *roots* of words but also the origins of the customs and natural law of antiquity.

Savigny shared this assumption, believing that national culture was a holistic phenomenon that came into being through the *Volk* and that law was the original and enduring bond that united the people as a whole. The influence of Savigny on the Grimm brothers was decisive, for he encouraged their already intense philological interest in ancient German literature and folklore—an interest that was further inspired by German romantics like Ludwig Tieck and Clemens Brentano, who in turn were inspired by Herder's cultural historicism. The brothers were to place greater emphasis on language than on law as the unifying bond of national culture, yet Savigny's mentorship at Marburg University put them on the track that would lead to their project of collecting popular tales and legends of folklore. In his book *The Brothers Grimm: From Enchanted Forests to the Modern World,* Jack Zipes summarizes the Grimm brothers' philological vocation:

> What fascinated or compelled the Grimms to concentrate on old German literature was a belief that the most natural and

pure forms of culture—those which held the community together—were linguistic and were to be located in the past.
Moreover, modern literature, even though it might be re-
markably rich, was artificial and thus could not express the
genuine essence of *Volk* culture that emanated naturally from
the people's experience and bound the people together. . . .
[T]hey began to formulate similar views about the origins of
literature based on tales and legends or what was once oral
literature. The purpose of their collecting folk songs, tales,
proverbs, legends, and documents was to write a history of
old German *Poesie* and to demonstrate how *Kunstpoesie* (re-
fined literature) evolved out of traditional folk material and
how *Kunstpoesie* had gradually forced *Naturpoesie* (natural literature such as tales, legends, etc.) to recede during the Renaissance and take refuge among the folk in an oral tradition.
According to the Grimms, there was a danger in this development that the natural forms would be forgotten and ne-
glected. Thus, the Brothers saw their task as literary historians to preserve the *pure* sources of modern German literature
and to reveal the debt or connection of literate culture to the
oral tradition. (Zipes, 32–33)

Zipes argues persuasively that the brothers' nostalgia for origins
and "fatherland" was psychologically linked to the early death of their
father. What interests us here about their nostalgia is its association of
Germanic culture with the forests. The Grimms conceived of forests
as symbolic preserves of the popular and oral traditions they set out to
recover through their sustained philological work. In 1813 the brothers even published a journal entitled *Altdeutsche Wälder,* or *Old German
Forests,* which explicitly linked German forests to the genesis and continuity of authentic German culture. We may cite Zipes again on the
nature of this association:

It was as though in "old German forests" the essential truths
about German customs, laws, and culture could be found—
truths which might engender a deeper understanding of
present-day Germany and might foster unity among German
people at a time when the German principalities were divided
and occupied by the French during the Napoleonic Wars. The
Volk, the people, bound by a common language but dis-
united, needed to enter old German forests, so the Grimms

thought, to gain a sense of their heritage and to strengthen the ties among themselves. (45)

All of the foregoing considerations allow us to approach the forests of the Grimms' fairy tales from the broader perspective of our study as a whole. It is precisely the forests' association with a lost unity which we want to focus on here. We have seen the same association at work in antiquity, and we will see it at work again in nineteenth-century doctrines of symbolism (discussed in the next section). The case of the Brothers Grimm is somewhat special, however, insofar as the lost unity in question is specifically cultural, social, and national. It is of course literary as well, for the German forests are genetically related to so-called *Naturpoesie*. But *Naturpoesie* as the Grimms understood it was not a separate "discipline" of the arts; it was the natural and popular spirit of unity itself. Let us turn to some of the fairy tales to get a better idea of what this lost unity is all about.

Anyone familiar with the Grimms' fairy tales knows how prominently forests figure in the collection as a whole. These forests typically lie beyond the bounds of the familiar world. They are the places where protagonists get lost, meet unusual creatures, undergo spells and transformations, and confront their destinies. Children typically "grow up" during their ventures in the forests. The forests are sometimes places of the illicit—Little Red Riding Hood learns her lesson in the forest, telling herself at the end of the tale: "Never again will you stray from the path by yourself and go into the forest when your mother has forbidden it" (Grimm, 104)—yet more often than not they are places of weird enchantment. But in what way do the tales associate forests with the phenomenon of unity?

A man whose wife has died marries a widow. His daughter is pretty, hers is ugly. The malicious stepmother, intent on bringing about the death of the former, makes her a thin paper dress and sends her out into the forest in the dead of winter to collect strawberries, giving her only a piece of bread to eat. Strawberries do not grow in winter, but the girl, being obedient, sets out through the snow into the forest. She comes across a cottage and knocks at the door. Three little gnomes who live there invite her in and ask her to share her bread with them, putting her generosity to the test. She does so gladly, and they reward her by granting her three wishes that will come true: She will grow more beautiful each day; every time she speaks gold coins will fall out of her mouth; and a king will take her for wife. The jealous stepsister also sets out into the forest (but dressed in fur with bread and butter and cake to eat), and she too comes to the cottage of the gnomes. She, however, refuses to share her meal. She will become uglier; toads will fall from her mouth; and she will die a miserable death ("The Three Little Gnomes in the Forest").

The tale is simple enough. The forest gnomes, who hold the power of destiny in their hands, reward generosity and punish selfishness. In other words, they reward the girl who upholds the bonds of community, founded on sharing. As in most of the tales, reward and punishment are modes of reciprocity. Reward goes to the girl who shares the spirit of reciprocity by which the human community is held together, while punishment is the appropriate response to the self-interest of the stepsister. In another tale—"A House in the Forest"— the three daughters of a poor woodcutter get lost on separate occasions when they are sent into the forest to bring their father his noontime meal (the birds eat the trail of seeds, lentils, and peas which the father leaves for them to follow). Lost in the forest at nightfall, the oldest daughter sees a light and approaches the house. Inside is an old man with a long white beard and three animals: a chicken, a rooster, and a spotted cow. The old man has plenty of provisions and tells the girl to prepare a meal. She does so but neglects to feed the animals. That night, when she goes to sleep, she falls through a trapdoor into the cellar. The next day the same scene repeats itself with the second daughter. The day after that, however, the third daughter refuses to sit down to eat her dinner before she has taken care to feed the animals. She then says her prayers and goes to sleep. When she awakes she finds herself in a royal palace and discovers that the old man is actually a prince over whom a wicked witch has cast a spell. His animals were once his servants. Only a maiden who showed kindness to humans as well as animals could have broken the spell. The girl, of course, marries the prince. This tale adds another dimension to the theme of community, for it invokes not only social bonds between people but also natural bonds between humans and animals. Animals are typically what animate the enchanted forests of the Grimms' fairy tales, bringing them alive with a strange but usually friendly presence. The forests in this sense represent the ancient unity of nature—the unity and kinship of the species. Protagonists who show consideration for the sylvan creatures are typically recompensated for their kindness by being helped or saved by those same creatures.

Let us focus on one more tale that brings these motifs together in a remarkable way, "The Two Brothers." The title already indicates that it is not an indifferent tale by any means, for this story about twin brothers conjures up the strong fraternal bond between the Brothers Grimm themselves. It is also the longest tale of the collection. We will abbreviate it considerably, but if the following summary remains quite long nonetheless, it is because several of the tale's details are crucial to its coherence as well as to the deeper significance we will attempt to extract from it.

There were once two brothers, one rich and evil-hearted and the other poor and kind-hearted. The latter brother had two twin boys. When the twins inadvertently eat the magic heart and liver of a golden bird, whose miraculous powers their uncle had hoped to appropriate, the uncle tells his brother that his sons are in league with the devil. With reluctance the father takes the young twins deep into the forest and abandons them there, for he is afraid of the devil. A huntsman, who has no children of his own, comes across them in the forest and says, "I shall be your father and bring you up." Once the boys have grown up under the guardianship of their foster father, the latter decides to put their huntsmanship to the test, to see if they are ready for independence. Passing the test the boys ask him permission to leave home and travel the world.

They take off together and come to a huge forest. As they wander through it they exhaust their provisions and begin to search for animals to hunt. One of them spots a hare, but when he raises his gun to shoot the hare declares: "Dear huntsman, if you let me live, / two of my young to you I'll give." The hare runs off into a bush and delivers two of her young to the brothers. The young hares are so endearing that the brothers do not have the heart to kill them. The same scene repeats itself with a fox, a wolf, a bear, and a lion. This coterie of paired young animals uses its various resources to procure food for the brothers and remains by their side. When the brothers eventually decide to separate from each other in order to seek employment, they divide the animals so that each has a hare, fox, wolf, bear, and lion. The older brother goes east, the younger west. Before parting, however, they stick into a tree a knife given to them by their foster father. The opposed sides of the blade, one facing east and the other west, would indicate in the future whether the brothers were alive or dead, depending on whether their side of the blade is bright or rusted.

The younger brother arrives with his animals at a city and discovers that the king's daughter is about to be handed over to an evil dragon that demands a virgin every year, threatening to lay waste to the entire country if the demand is not met. The king has promised to give his daughter's hand in marriage to the one who slays the dragon, but many valiant knights had already lost their lives attempting it, and the king's daughter is the only maiden left in the land. When she is led to the dragon's mountain and left there, the brother appears to take up the challenge. A furious combat with the dragon ensues in which the brother, with the help of his animals, cuts off the dragon's seven heads and tail. Having rescued the princess (and winning her affection in the process), he severs the dragon's tongues and wraps them in her handkerchief. At this point they, and all the animals, fall asleep from fatigue on the mountain. The king's marshal, who had been watching from a distance, climbs the mountain and finds that the dragon has been slain. He promptly cuts off the brother's head and then threatens the princess with death if she dares tell the truth about what has happened. Claiming to be the dragon slayer, the marshal is engaged to the princess and is scheduled to marry her one year and one day from that date.

Meanwhile the animals are in despair over their master's death. But the hare knows of a place where a root grows that cures all sorts of wounds. The brother's head is placed back on his body, and, with the aid of the magic root, he is brought to life again. The brother and his animals take up their travels again, and a year later they find themselves back in the same city. The brother learns from an innkeeper that the princess is to be wed to the dragon slayer the next day. He makes a huge wager with the innkeeper that he will be the one to marry the princess, a wager that he goes on to win by presenting himself at the wedding ceremony with the dragon's seven tongues. The truth comes out; the brother marries the princess; and the marshal is sentenced to be torn apart by four oxen. When the brother sends for the innkeeper, he not only allows him to keep the house and property the latter had lost in the wager but returns to him the thousand gold pieces the innkeeper had lost in a prior wager.

The story continues, for the happily married brother goes hunting one day and follows a beautiful white doe deep into an enchanted forest, where he gets lost and meets up with a witch who transforms him and his animals into stones. Meanwhile the other brother has decided to see what has become of his younger twin and returns to the crossroad where they had planted the knife into a tree. Finding that the side of the blade facing west is half-rusted and half-bright, the older brother goes off in search of his twin. Arriving in the kingdom he is mistaken for his missing brother, learns of the latter's excursion to the enchanted forest, and decides to keep silent about his true identity. He even spends the night in his brother's bed, but he places a double-edged sword between him and the princess. The next day he goes into the enchanted forest, meets the witch and constrains her to restore his brother and all the other stones in her pit to life. The brother, his animals, and several other merchants, artisans, and shepherds are brought back to life.

The brothers and their animals are reunited again, but on the way back to the palace, as the older brother recounts how he kept silent about his identity and even spent the night in the other's bed, the younger brother is seized by a fit of jealousy and cuts off his brother's head with his sword. He is promptly overcome by remorse, for his brother had after all saved his life. The hare dashes off to fetch the magic root, and the dead brother is brought back to life. They return to the palace and enjoy a great feast. That night, when the younger brother goes to bed, his wife asks him why he had placed a sword between them the night before. He realizes then how faithful his brother had been to him, and the tale comes to an end.

So much for the abbreviated summary of the longest tale in the Grimms' collection. We will not approach it here as one tale among others but rather as an allegory for the Grimm brothers' philological endeavor to recover the *Naturpoesie* of German traditions. We have seen how the Grimms believed that popular culture lies at the root of "high culture," and that as the former began to disappear during the Renaissance it took refuge in the oral tradition. In the preface to their *Children's and Household Tales,* the Grimms employ the analogy of a great storm that lays waste to a wide cultivated field, leaving only a small patch of it intact. This small patch is the remnant of the once vast tradition of folk wisdom. The storm is modernity itself, which has almost completely effaced that tradition, destroying its vitality and thereby ravaging the basis of the authentic unity of German culture. The Grimms conceived of their philological enterprise as an effort to restore that lost unity by recovering whatever remained of the original tradition. Hence it is not only the theme of fraternal bonding that invites us to approach "The Two Brothers" as an allegory for the Grimms' enterprise; it is above all the theme of *restoration.*

This theme has two main articulations in the tale: restoration of life on the one hand and unity on the other. To begin with unity, it is obvious that the tale relies upon the dialectic of separation and reunification. Two brothers are divided at the outset of the tale: one is rich and evil-hearted, the other poor and kind-hearted. The twin sons are abandoned by the latter in the forest. Later, when they set off together to seek their fortunes, the twins relive the scene of their own abandonment in the forest: "Dear huntsman, if you let me live, / two of my young to you I'll give." The animals they intend to shoot abandon their young twins just as the brothers' father had, but like the brothers who found a foster father in the forest, these young animals will find foster parents in the two brothers. Nevertheless this reunification gives way to division again, for when the brothers decide to go their separate ways, they divide the animals between themselves and plunge a knife into a tree at the crossroads.

The knife cuts through this tale with a powerful symbolism. The two sides of its single blade represent the unity of the fraternal bond, without doubt, and its symbolism recurs in another context when the older twin places "a double-edged sword" between himself and his brother's wife, thereby reaffirming the bond. The kinfe's symbolism has an ambiguous edge, however, for its blade also indicates the brothers' separation—their departure in opposite directions. Likewise the double-edged sword can sever, divide, and kill. The younger brother will draw his sword and cut off the older's head in a fit of jealousy. Furthermore it is with the same sword that the younger brother previously cuts off the seven heads of the dragon and severs its tongues, thus liberating the land from the dragon's malice.

Severance is followed by restoration. The brothers' severed heads are in both cases restored to their bodies; peace is restored to a kingdom after the slaying of the dragon; a princess is restored to her father; and finally, the brothers and their animals are reunited after a period of separation. We cannot fail to notice, however, that division is the means by which disruptive evil is dealt with, or overcome. The dragon is horribly dismembered, first by the brother and later by his animals, "who tore the dragon to pieces" (Grimm, 236). The marshal who killed the sleeping brother is executed by being torn apart by four oxen. These acts of disunification are dialectically related to reunification, which in most cases entails the restoration of life. The brothers are brought back to life by the magic root. The witch who turns living creatures into inanimate stones with a switch is forced by the older brother to reanimate them with the same switch (the switch is in this sense like the sword, which kills and also preserves). The final episode of one brother's decapitation of his twin seems at first glance gratui-

tous or jarring, yet it is essential to the theme of the tale, for it recapitulates the pattern whereby division is followed by a restoration of the
bonds of unity.

If "The Two Brothers" can be approached as an allegory for the
Grimm brothers' philological enterprise, it is because it so overtly
dramatizes the theme of loss and recovery. The Grimm brothers saw
as their task the restoration of the lost unity of German culture and the
reanimation of the folk tradition from which it originated. We mentioned that they associated cultural origins with the German forests,
believing that the customs, beliefs, language, law—the entire ancient
basis of German community—were intimately related to the forests.
Thus they believed that the reanimation of German culture could
come about by returning in spirit to the forests that gave life to the
popular traditions. In the minds of the Grimm brothers modernity had
ravaged, divided, or taken that life away, but just as "The Two Brothers" thrives on the motif of restoration and reanimation, so too the
Grimms thrived on their faith in a miraculous healing process by
which the original unity of German culture could be restored to integrity.

It is in their nostalgia that the Grimms belong to the ironic modernity of German history. It is not an exaggeration to say that the myth
of a lost unity holds sway over modern German history as a whole,
from the Germans' first attempts to create a unified nation to its most
recent efforts at reunification, with National Socialism in between.
German history during this period could be characterized as a prolonged attempt at cultural, national, social, spiritual, or racial reunification. But like the dialectical patterns dramatized by "The Two
Brothers," Germany's nostalgia is pervaded by the trauma of division,
or severance. Where does this trauma come from? To what extent is it
a self-fulfilling prophecy? Is the very concept of "reunification" not
profoundly ironic? The prefix *re*-places it squarely in the horizon of
irony, for the lost unity that Germans have typically yearned for is a
fairy tale of modernity. It has always already been lost—it exists only
in this loss. It is *engendered* by an enduring sense of loss, which, as we
know, has ways of reinventing the past. What is striking in the case of
the Brothers Grimm is the persistent dream of recovery. This dream is
distinctly modern in nature. It has done more to devastate Germany
and divide it against itself than all the so-called ravages of modernity.
Indeed, the dream of recovery is Germany's nightmare, brought on by
a failure to acknowledge the irony lurking in the forests of its fairy tale

of origins. Irony that does not deem itself ironic is the most dangerous irony of all.

To this day forests continue to symbolize Germany's heritage—the stronghold of its cultural origins, of its ancient bonds of community, and of its collective national possession. In 1852 a contemporary of the Brothers Grimm, the folklorist Wilhelm H. Riehl, wrote:

> In the opinion of the German people the forest is the only *great possession* that has yet to be completely given away. In contrast to the field, the meadow, and the garden, every person has a certain right to the forest, even if it only consists in being able to walk around in it when the person so desires. In the right or privilege to collect wood and foliage, to shelter animals and in the distribution of the so-called *Losholz* from communal forests and the like, there is a type of communist heritage that is rooted in history. Where is there anything else that has been preserved like this other than with the forest? This is the root of genuine German social conditions. (Cited by Zipes, 60)

Even as he wrote those words, the "great possession" of the German people was already being given away. Private ownership was already beginning to assert its exclusive rights and to defend the forests against trespassers. Moreover, the Germans were on the verge of developing the new science of forestry, with its "forest mathematics" that would maximize the timber yield of German forests. The "communist" possession of the German people was becoming an affair of economic profit for the state as well as for the private forest owners. Already in 1842 Karl Marx, as editor of the *Rheinische Zeitung,* had written a long article—"Proceedings of the Sixth Rhine Province Assembly. Third Article: Debates on the Law of the Thefts of Wood"—in which, for the first time in his career, he addressed the question of the material interest of the masses, precisely with regard to the question of the endangered "customary rights" of the poor to collect wood from the forests. The Sixth Rhine Province Assembly had just voted in favor of laws that would protect the interests of the forest owners and make the gathering of dead wood in the forests a crime. In this extraordinary article, which would cost him his job as editor of the newspaper, Marx went so far as to compare the forest owner's possession of his forest to the tree's possession of its branches, arguing that the customary rights of the poor to collect fallen wood has its basis in the analogical relation of the poor to dead wood:

> Fallen wood provides an example of this. Such wood has as little organic connection with the growing tree as the cast-off skin has with the snake. Nature itself presents as it were a model of the antithesis between poverty and wealth in the shape of the dry, snapped twigs and branches separated from organic life in contrast to the trees and stems which are firmly rooted and full of sap, organically assimilating air, light, water and soil to develop their own proper form and individual life. It is a physical representation of poverty and wealth. *Human poverty senses this kinship and deduces its right to property from this feeling of kinship.* (Marx, 234)

Marx appealed to the mythic authority of past customs, but his plea in favor of the poor's customary rights to gather dead wood in the forests of nascent capitalism did nothing to hinder the new laws designed to protect the private interests of the owners. Since then things have changed even more dramatically for the "old German forests." At the present moment the great German "possession" is literally dying. Those wealthy "trees and stems which are firmly rooted and full of sap, organically assimilating air, light, water and soil to develop their own proper form and individual life" are turning into the "dry, snapped twigs" of poverty in a protracted process of biological degradation. Despite all the efforts of the German Green Party to remystify the German forests as the heritage of the fatherland and the keeper of its spirit, there is not much Germany can do about what they call *Waldsterben,* or the dying forest, for the death of the trees is caused by acid rain. Acid rain knows nothing about national boundaries, cultural unity, or the communal possessions of fatherlands.

Meanwhile the German nation is being put back together again like the brothers whose severed heads are reattached to their bodies. Whether political reunification will reanimate the old German forests is doubtful, for in this case it would seem that reanimation depends on more than a magic root, or the switch of a witch.

FORESTS OF SYMBOLS

Already by Tacitus's time the German barbarians were looking back to the forests as the "cradle of their race," much the way the myth of

Arcadia in Virgil's *Aeneid* looks back to an antecedent epoch when men were born of oaks. Tacitus reminds us that certain groves were "the dwelling-place of the supreme god to whom all things are subject and obedient" (Tacitus, 134). These groves, he informs us, were also the sites of theophanies. A veiled goddess would appear to her devotees in a clearing, for example, riding in her chariot.

The sacred groves of Europe's barbarian prehistory give a new meaning to the phrase "cathedral forest," which has become something of a commonplace these days. The Gothic cathedral visibly reproduces the ancient scenes of worship in its lofty interior, which rises vertically toward the sky and then curves into a vault from all sides, like so many tree crowns converging into a canopy overhead. Like breaks in the foliage, windows let in light from beyond the enclosure. In other words, the phrase "cathedral forest" entails more than just a casual analogy; or better, the analogy has its basis in an ancient correspondence between forests and the dwelling place of a god.

It was not only in the Germanic north that forests once housed a god. Even in historic times most sanctuaries in Greece possessed their adjacent grove. Sometimes the grove itself was the sanctuary. From the iconography we gather that a single tree, or group of trees, would sometimes be enclosed by a wall marking off the space of the temple. Votives would arrive in procession to these sanctuaries and invite their goddess to appear by dancing ecstatically around her sacred tree. At the height of their ecstasy the goddess would reveal her presence. Rituals such as these point to the phenomenon of tree worship, so prevalent among various pagan religions. Thanks to the documentary work of Sir Arthur Evans we know that on Crete, for example, both wooden and stone pillars were used to harbor the souls of sacred trees. In his report "Mycenaean Tree and Pillar Cult," Evans reconstructs the rituals by which the soul of a tree was transferred to, or made to inhabit, a column.

The correspondence between columns and trees leads one to suspect that the archaic Greek temple is not unlike the Gothic cathedral in its religious symbolism. Why, after all, is the Greek temple dense with columns? What purpose do the columns serve beyond their architectural function? If a single column once symbolized a sacred tree, a cluster of columns may well have symbolized a sacred grove. What we know for sure is that the temple's network of columns enclosed a holy shrine where the god's presence was preserved in his image. A temple was the dwelling place of the deity. If we stand back and look at it from this symbolic perspective, something fugitive begins to stir in the shadows of the Greek temple . . . something like the prehistoric groves of theophany.

What are these correspondences all about? Why does the symbol—be it the cathedral, the column, or the temple—traverse their distance? How is it that forests can become dense with symbolism, understood as the reunification of that which ordinary perception obscures or differentiates? These are questions that could lead us in many directions. In the present context, however, they lead us to the poetic doctrine of correspondence, which belongs to nineteenth-century French symbolism. The doctrine is typically associated with a famous poem by Charles Baudelaire in *Les fleurs du mal*:

CORRESPONDENCES

Nature is a temple where living pillars
Sometimes let out confused words.
Man passes there through forests of symbols
Which observe him with a familiar gaze.

Like long echoes confounded from a distance
In an obscure and deep unity,
Vast as the night or as clarity itself,
Scents, colors, and sounds respond to one another.

There are perfumes fresh as the flesh of children,
Sweet like oboes, green as prairies,
—And others corrupt, rich, and triumphant,

Having the expansion of infinite things,
Like amber, musk, bergamot, and incense,
Which sing the transport of the mind and the senses.

The first words already announce the symbolist doctrine of the poem as a whole. Nature *is* a temple, not like a temple. If the utterance relies on an analogy, the analogy in turn relies upon the natural affinity of its terms of comparison. Nature is a temple because it preserves within its forestial enclosure the original familiarity that makes analogies between different things possible. When two or more things correspond with one another through symbolic analogy, they are already prerelated by kinship. In Baudelaire's forests of symbols, the "living pillars" observe the observer with a "familiar" gaze, for these symbolic forests, whatever they may be, are the guardians of primordial relations, however remote or forgotten.

When Baudelaire declares that nature is a temple, therefore, he is not looking at nature with the eyes of a poet who simply forges comparisons. He is looking at nature with imaginary eyes that see familiar eyes gazing back at him from a strange, indeterminate distance. Whatever the nature of the distance that "confounds echoes" in an "obscure and deep unity," Baudelaire was devoted to it. His nostalgia for childhood, for the beyond, for the remote frontiers of other worlds and imaginary shores, in short, his nostalgia for *elsewhereness,* combined with an acute modern sensibility, gives Baudelaire's poetry and prose their unmistakable blend of reverence and sarcasm. Baudelaire in effect abhorred literal objects when they were reduced to mere objecthood. Too near at hand and too deprived of the "familiarity" of distance, the literal object was deathly. The utterance "Nature is a temple" takes us beyond the realm of literal objects and into the forests of symbols, where ordinary sense perception undergoes a metamorphosis and becomes suffused with memory, analogy, and association.

Within this temple of nature objects look back at you, lose their mere objectivity, and enter the "expansion of infinite things." They assume what Walter Benjamin called an "aura" that contains vague reminders of a lost kinship between subject and object. The deadly Cartesian separation between the *res cogitans* and *res extensa* gives way, in the forests of symbols, to an ecstatic psychological state—a "transport of the mind and senses"—which recovers the realm of correspondences in their predifferentiated unity.

Thus in the forests of symbols a "confusion" of the senses comes about. Scents, colors, and sounds "respond" to each other. Symbols are the guardians of these ancient correspondences. For Baudelaire it is a question of correspondence between perceptions more than between things, but the two ultimately coincide. For a symbol is not a thing but rather a conspiracy between things, reunifying what habitual modes of perception differentiate—the five senses, for instance, or body and mind. Baudelaire's forests of symbols represent the mutual implication of all perceptions, indeed the mutual implication of all living species, which underlies the phenomenon of correspondence. We must assume, therefore, that the forest of symbols is not one symbol among others but rather the symbol of symbolism itself.

(Symbolism could be seen, in short, as a flight from the sublime, which represents a landscape of unconditional oppositions: finite and infinite, earth and sky, male and female, animate and inanimate, subject and object. In the horizon of the sublime the subject of experience confronts its own exclusion from the immensity of the elements. The forest of symbols, on the other hand, is the realm of inclusion, of the intimate appurtenance of all things within a greater network of kinship. Precisely for this reason, however, we cannot speak of an "opposition" between the forests of symbols and the landscape of the sublime, since oppositions of this sort belong to the realm of the latter.)

When nature ceased to be a temple of correspondences it became for Baudelaire an abomination. That is why, in the essay entitled "In Praise of Cosmetics," Baudelaire can speak of nature in wholly negative terms. "Nature can counsel nothing but crime," he writes. "It is this infallible Mother Nature who has created parricide and cannibalism, and a thousand other abominations that shame and modesty prevent us from naming" (*The Painter of Modern Life,* 32). Nature in the literal sense appears only as the ground of the flowers of evil: "Crime, of which the human animal has learned the taste in his mother's womb, is natural by origin. Virtue, on the other hand, is artificial, supernatural . . ." (ibid.). In such statements Baudelaire seems to uphold the traditional connection between beauty and moral virtue. He declares that the lover of beauty loves not what is natural but, in essence, what is supernatural. Beauty belongs not to the literal body-object but rather to the veils of analogy that transfigure the body-object's natural state and associate it with some other order of being.

This is why Baudelaire saw in the art of costume and cosmetics an agent of exalted mysticism. The painted face of a woman is wondrous, he argues, not because makeup enhances her natural beauty but because it symbolizes the body-object, transforming it into a dream image. What we love in a woman's beauty, claimed Baudelaire, is the disclosure of distance, or beauty's disclosure of distant worlds. Through cosmetics, distance comes to presence in a woman's face. The more contrived and artificial the made-up face appears, the better, for an excessive artificiality distinguishes her face from nature in the literal sense and evokes, as if by magic or incantation, the supernatural realm.

The supernatural realm that we supposedly love over against nature is nothing other than nature resymbolized. When it ceases to be a temple, nature has merely lost its natural symbolism. To restore to nature its natural symbolism was, in Baudelaire's view, the mystical function of cosmetics. A woman who applies rouge to her cheek engages in a natural sacrament. Her colored cheek now corresponds to the sunset, to fire, to fruit, to the red clay of the earth. Her accentuated lips are the curvature of a horizon. The black mascara around the eye and on the eyelashes forms an image full of depth and wonder. "Its black frame," Baudelaire writes, "gives the eye a more decisive appearance of a window open onto the infinite" (*Painter,* 34).

This window open onto the infinite is not the same window that Baudelaire speaks of when he criticizes naturalist painters who reproduce a landscape as it appears objectively to the eye that looks out the window of a country house. Nor is it a window that one simply looks through into some receding utopia. This cosmic window is an eye whose depth and distance look back at you with a familiar gaze. The woman's darkened eye is a clearing in the forests of symbols—a cosmetic *lucus.* Gazing back at you in the midst of that surrounding darkness, it assumes the symbolic gaze of those "living pillars" of nature's temple. The mysticism of cosmetics, then, restores to nature its aspect of the temple, bringing the forests of symbols to a woman's face.

The art of cosmetics which Baudelaire so admired is linked to the most natural or primitive forms of animism. The supernaturalism of cosmetics and costume is associated by Baudelaire with the wisdom of the so-called savage cultures of the forest. His essay in praise of cosmetics in fact serves as an occasion for him to attack his contemporaries for their presumed superiority over cultures that have not yet lost the natural symbolism of nature:

> Those races which our confused and perverted civilization is pleased to treat as savage, with an altogether ludicrous pride and complacency, understand, just as the child understands, the lofty spiritual significance of the toilet. In their naif adoration of what is brilliant—many-colored feathers, iridescent fabrics, the incomparable majesty of artificial forms—the baby and the savage bear witness to their disgust of the real, and thus give proof, without knowing it, of the immateriality of their soul. Woe to him who, like Louis XV (the product not of a true civilization but of a recrudescence of barbarism), carries his degeneracy to the point of no longer having a taste for anything but nature unadorned. (32)

The child, who is not yet denatured, and the "savage" of the forests, both of whom know the ways of nature's magic, stand over against the barbarism of a civilization that has declined into the most unnatural forms of naturalism, or what is worse, materialism. In other words, Baudelaire's loathing was directed not so much against nature as against the vulgar and deadly literalization of nature by his contemporaries, who cultivated such naturalism in the domains of fashion and aesthetics. With their emphasis on the literal and observable, they lost touch with the more distant reaches of sense perception, or so Baudelaire believed. By habit they reduced the indefinite to the definite, the symbolic to the objective, the poetic to the prosaic, the distant to the adjacent. Baudelaire did not share their sentimental nostalgia for "nature unadorned" but looked back to a far more ancient temple of nature, which the age had reduced to a litter of ruins.

But why should forests haunt the mind like some mystical dream or nightmare that every now and then spreads its long, prehistorical shadows over the ordinary clarity of things modern? On the basis of what "data of prehistory," to borrow a phrase from Walter Benjamin, does the forest become dense with associations and monstrous fears? The forest is at once a temple of living pillars and a scene of horror, an enchanted wood and a wood of abandon. In one of Mallarmé's reflections on symbolist literature, the forest comes forth once again as the symbol of symbolism, yet this time in another version:

> [We symbolist writers have] abolished the pretension, aesthetically a mistake, even though it dominates the masterpieces, to include on the page of the subtle volume anything other than the horror of the forest, for example, or the thunder muted amid the foliage; not the intrinsic and dense wood of trees. (*Crise de vers*, 355–66)

Mallarmé presumed to convey in his poetic word only the horror and terror of Vico's giants under a thundering sky, leaving to other writers the naturalistic representation of the forests, where the awakening takes place. Yet this horror is not different from the emotion of reverence in Baudelaire's "Correspondences." Horror and reverence are declensions of the same bewilderment—the bewilderment of being fully *alive*. When one is fully alive, the entire world is alive. The observed observes. The forest becomes a congeries of eyes.

The second verse of Baudelaire's poem speaks of "confused words" emitted by the living pillars of nature's temple. What sort of language do they speak? This is the enigma pondered by Törless, the adolescent protagonist of Robert Musil's novel *Young Törless* (1906).

The same enigma will intrigue Törless even in his adulthood, when he grows up to become the protagonist of Musil's later novel *The Man Without Qualities*. The following passage occurs in *Young Törless*:

> Törless was still gazing out into the garden. He thought he could hear the rustling of the withered leaves being blown into drifts by the wind. Then came that moment of utter stillness which always occurs a little while before the descent of complete darkness. The shapes of things, which had been sinking ever more deeply into the dusk, and the blurring, dissolving colours of things—for an instant it all seemed to pause, to hover, as it were with a holding of the breath. . . .
>
> "You know, Beineberg," Törless said, without turning around, "when it's getting dark there always seems to be a few moments that are sort of different. Every time I watch it happening I remember the same thing: once when I was quite small I was playing in the woods at this time of evening. My nursemaid had wandered off somewhere. I didn't know she had, and so I still felt as if she were nearby. Suddenly something made me look up. I could feel I was alone. It was suddenly all so quiet. And when I looked around it was as though the trees were standing in a circle round me, all silent, and looking at me. I began to cry. I felt the grownups had deserted me and abandoned me to inanimate beings. . . . What is it? I still often get it. What's this sudden silence that's like a language we can't hear?"
>
> "I don't know the thing you mean. But why shouldn't things have a language of their own? After all, there are no definite grounds for asserting that they haven't a soul!"
>
> Törless did not answer. He did not care for Beineberg's speculative view of the matter.
>
> But after a while Beineberg went on: "Why do you keep on staring out of the window? What is there to be seen?"
>
> "I'm still wondering what it can be." But actually he had gone on to thinking about something else, which he did not want to speak of. That high tension, that harkening as if some solemn mystery might become audible, and the burden of gazing right into the midst of the still undefined relationships of things—all this was something he had been able to endure only for a moment." (*Young Törless*, 25–26)

Törless's vulnerability to such twilight moods "was the first hint of a psychological development that was later to manifest itself as a strong sense of wonder" (28). The wonder awoke for the first time in his childhood, when he saw the trees staring at him with the "familiar gazes" of Baudelaire's forests of symbols. Törless's sense of an animate presence in the forest figures as the prelude to his subsequent bewilderment about the arbitrary, unstable definitions of reality:

> The fact was that later he was to have—and indeed to be dominated by—a peculiar ability: he could not help frequently experiencing events, peoples, things, and even himself, in such a way as to feel that in it all there was at once some insoluble enigma and some inexplicable kinship for which he could never quite produce any evidence. (ibid.)

In *Young Törless,* the forest symbolizes this indeterminacy. The novel has other symbols running through its narrative—the window, for example, or the worm—yet the forest is not just one symbol among others. It is, once again, the symbol of symbolism.

This is borne out just after the twilight scene. When Törless and Beineberg leave the cake shop from whose window they have watched twilight descend on the garden, they do not return to their military boarding school but follow a path along a river: "Beineberg stopped. The farther bank was thickly wooded . . . the trees had the menacing look of a black, impenetrable wall. Only if one looked carefully did one discover a narrow hidden path leading straight on and into it" (31). On this path the boys penetrate deeper into the woods, deeper into the "symbolic" darkness of the human psyche, until they reach a clearing. There, in a dimly lit house, is the prostitute. She is like a forest witch out of the Grimms' fairy tales. She embodies all that is suppressed or unconfessed in the bourgeois world to which boys belong and which the rigors of military school are preparing them to take charge of. The young whore haunts, fascinates, disgusts, attracts. She is an anti-mother figure, but she is also confused in Törless's mind with his mother. She awakens primal passions pent up under the surface of the public world. She arouses lust as well as hatred. She belongs to the forest. From this point on, Törless's adolescence will become deeply perturbed by the subterranean world of depravity, guilt, and malice which lurks just under the surface of institutional society.

T. E. Lawrence once said of the desert that it is a place without nuance, only of light and dark in their opposing contrast. We might remark that the forest, on the other hand, is all nuance. It blurs distinctions, evoking the lost kinship between animate and inanimate, darkness and light, finite and infinite, body and soul, sight and sound. Törless's "peculiar ability" to experience indeterminate correspondences between things developed during his adolescence, but its origins reach back to a scene in his early childhood, when the forest came alive and rendered the familiar world uncanny. An alienated dimension of experience suddenly opened up as memory's other worlds gathered round and stared at him. From that moment forward Törless would grow up to experience in events, things, and people "some insoluble enigma and some inexplicable kinship for which he could never quite produce any evidence." In other words he would continue to wander through the temple of nature listening to the echoes—those "long echoes confounded from a distance / in an obscure and deep unity"— which sound nostalgically in Baudelaire's poem. This unity is "vast as the night or as clarity itself." It is beyond the mere contrast of light and dark. It is where the differentiated senses recover their original oneness, where "scents, colors, and sounds respond to one another," and where body and mind liquidate their boundaries. Törless senses that this kinship exists, yet he cannot quite produce any evidence for it. This is not surprising, for the forest does not offer evidence. At most it lets out "confused words" to which only the symbol can respond.

WAITING FOR DIONYSOS

A shaft of light falls from the canopy into chasms of the forest, gathering the darkness around it. Like a lucent tree trunk it reaches into depths of oblivion. Ancestral ghosts—their former worlds—hover in the penumbra of the haze, looking back into the eyes of recollection. The scene suggests that memory belongs to the world of its analogues, in this case the forest. Memory inhabits external things as much as the internal regions of the human psyche. For Marcel Proust the taste of a madelaine brought to life a lost era of his childhood; in one of Baudelaire's "spleen" poems, the spring loses the "adorable scent" that once animated the reveries of recollection; for the English poet John Clare the felling of a familiar elm tree amounted to a devastation of the memory that inhabited the place where the tree had stood for generations. When the analogues of memory disappear from the world, sense perception can no longer conspire with recollection to recall forgotten antiquities.

We have explored scenes of recollection and nostalgia in Rousseau, Wordsworth, the Brothers Grimm, and to some extent in Baudelaire; and we have seen how in each case they were related to forests. In Baudelaire's "Correspondences," the forest figures symbolically as the potential depth of sense perception. The word "spleen" in his work refers to the deprivation of the depth of experience. In this sense it figures as the loss of the forests of symbols. Spleen is the ever-present menace of "modernity," a term that Baudelaire in fact coined.

In what follows we will continue to ponder the enigmas of these various correspondences: recollection and sense perception; past and presence; memory and forests; spleen and modernity. The Italian poet Giacomo Leopardi (1798–1837) offers us a way into their obscurity. Not only is memory the dominant theme of his lyrics but in his life-long notebooks, the *Zibaldone di pensieri,* he speculated about the psychology of recollection in ways that cannot fail to interest us at this point in the discussion.

Both his poems and his notebooks reveal that Leopardi had an intense abhorrence for the present. When stripped of its connections with the past, the present represented for him a form of spiritual death, or what Baudelaire would call later spleen. In part this revulsion was rooted in Leopardi's personal temperament and metaphysical outlook; but it also had connections to his attitude toward the Italy of his time, which had long ago ruptured the bonds with its Roman past and, in its failure to become a unified nation, had moved to the margins of the cultural life of Europe. Leopardi lamented this historical severance from the past and conceived of national unity as a cultural reunification that would revitalize the correspondences between modern Italy and its bygone imperial history.

The same logic of correspondence holds true for experience at the most ordinary, personal level. Like Baudelaire, Leopardi abhorred objects perceived in their naked or literal actuality, devoid of the imaginative associations that would create a penumbra of depth about them. Only when memory pervaded the ordinary perception of objects could Leopardi feel liberated from the otherwise deathly quality of mere chronological time. In one of his notes from 1828 he writes:

> To the sensitive and imaginative man, who lives, as I have
> lived for a long time, feeling and imagining continuously, the
> world and its objects are in a certain sense double. He will see
> with his eyes a tower, a countryside; he will hear with his ears

the sound of a bell; and at the same time with his imagination he will see another tower, another countryside, he will hear another sound. In this second sort of objects lies all the beauty and pleasure of things. Sad is the life (and yet such is life for the most part) that sees, hears, senses only simple objects, [namely] those of which eyes, ears, and the other senses receive a mere sensation. (30 Novembre, 1 Domenica dell' Avento). (*Zibaldone,* 1162)

The "second sort of objects" which accompanies the perception of simple objects belongs to the reservoir of personal memory. The sight of a simple tower evokes in the mind an image of some other tower, either seen or imagined before. As the two images fuse together through psychological association, the horizon of perception takes on another dimension. Perceived stereoscopically, the tower evokes another place and another context; perhaps it even evokes the same place and the same context, but at a different moment in time. It is enough to recall an earlier perception of the same tower to experience the effect of doubleness that Leopardi describes here. This sort of "poetic experience" of the world and its objects belongs not only to poets but to the deepest core of human experience in general. Leopardi believed that poets merely reconfigure in a verbal medium the potential sensory depths of ordinary human experience.

But how do poets go about conveying in their poems the sensory depths of experience which, after all, reside in one's personal memory? If memory is personal, how can readers share in the poet's associations? For his answer Leopardi turned to the shared heritage of the Italian people—their language. Like the Brothers Grimm he believed that language was the most essential cultural bond of a nation. In composing his poem, therefore, Leopardi knew that the poet must rely above all on *words* to re-create the phenomenon of depth. Words belong to the collective heritage of a people. Language is the property not of any individual, but of a race, community, or nation; it is thus a reserve of collective memory.

Leopardi strove to imbue his lyrics with the collective memory embedded in language itself. He chose words he believed would produce in the reader that resonant sense one has when bare reality is supplemented by memory, that poetic feeling of doubleness, depth, and vagueness. In his reflections on poetic composition Leopardi distinguished between what he called *termini* and *parole,* "terms" and

"words." *Termini,* he says, "merely offer a single idea of the object signified." *Parole,* on the other hand, are words that signify the idea of an
object but offer "certain accessory images as well." Such *parole* are
words with metaphorical origins that reach back into the ancient history of the Italian language and hence into the depths of racial memory
("race" understood in a cultural, not a biological sense). They are
words dense with overtones, latent meanings, etymological suggestion, and multiple connotations. Such *parole,* claimed Leopardi, are
generic to the highest degree. Their lack of specificity allows for a
maximum freedom of association in the mind of the reader. *Lontano,
antico, notturno* (distant, ancient, nocturnal)—these are the sort of generic words that Leopardi considered deeply poetic, because full of
resonant vagueness. They achieve their poetic effect by bridging the
gulf of time that separates the present from a lost "national" past.

Leopardi summarizes the experience of memory after which he
aspired in the concept of *il vago,* or the indefinite. "The words *notte,
notturno* [night, nocturnal]," he writes, "are extremely poetic, because
objects at nighttime are blurred and the mind perceives only a vague,
indistinct, and incomplete image of both the night and of what it contains." Leopardi here describes *il vago*—the blurring of objects or the
horizon that contains them—in terms of a "night effect" (ibid., 1180).
In an extended entry in his notebooks, Leopardi cites numerous examples of indirect or obstructed light, the perception of which he links
to the experience of *il vago:*

> From that part of my theory of pleasure which states that ob-
> jects seen only halfway, or with certain obstructions, etc.,
> awaken in us *indefinite* ideas is explained why I like the light
> of the sun or the moon seen in a place from which they can-
> not be seen, or one cannot discern the source of the light; a
> place only partially illuminated by such light; the reflection of
> such light, and the various material effects that derive from it;
> the penetration of such light in places where it becomes un-
> certain and impeded, and is not easily distinguished, as
> through a canebrake, in a forest, through closed shutters,
> etc., etc.; such light seen in a place, object, etc., where it does
> not enter and strike directly, but is refracted and diffused by
> some other place or object, etc., where it does strike; in a
> hallway seen from inside or outside, or in a loggia, etc., those
> places where the light is mingled etc., etc., with shadows, as

under a portico, in a lofty and overhanging loggia, among cliffs and gullies, in a valley, on hills seen from the shady side, on such a way that their tops are golden. . . . (20 Settembre 1821). (ibid., 633)

Although the forest is mentioned in only one clause of the passage, one could say that it remains the "primal scene" of this entire phenomenology of light effects. It is not just one place among others where "one cannot discern the source of the light" but the most ancient scene in cultural memory of diffused illumination. All the other examples of obstructed or broken light "correspond" to the forest scene, as it were. If Leopardi mentions the forest with extreme discretion in his catalog it is because discretion is the essence of *il vago*.

Such discretion is also the essence of Leopardi's poetics of the *parola,* or evocative word. Let us look at an example. In an early poem, "To the Moon" (1819), Leopardi describes his return to the same spot where, one year earlier, he had come to weep and lament the sorrows that afflicted his youth. From a hillside he addresses the moon, which spreads its illumination over a valley forest, just as it had done on that night a year ago:

> O gracious moon, I remember how,
> A year ago today, I came to this hill
> Full of sorrow to gaze at you:
> And you hung then over that forest
> Just as you do now, illuminating it all.
> But your face appeared nebulous and tremulous
> To my eyes because of the tears
> That soaked my brow; for my life
> Was full of travail then, nor does it change,
> O my delightful moon. And yet I rejoice
> At the recollection, and at the renewal
> Of my sorrow. O how pleasing it is
> In youth, when hope still has a long,
> And memory a short, course,
> To remember things past,
> Though they be sad and the grief still last. (*Canti,* 96)

To translate a poem from one language to another of course always involves difficulties. But Leopardi relies so deliberately on the historical, psychological, and etymological associations of his words within the mind of the native speaker that his poems in any other language than Italian are like corpses deprived of their source of animation. Lost in this poem's translation, among many other things, are the linguistic and sonorous correspondences between the "turning" of the year (*volge l'anno*) and the face of the moon (*volto*); between *rammentare* (literally, to re-mind) and *rimirare* (literally, to gaze again); and even between *ricordanza*, "recollection," and *corso,* "the course." Thematically, however, the poem is simple enough: although the sorrows of the past year have not ceased to trouble the poet's life, the mere recollection of that night a year ago, and its continuity with the present night, fills him with happiness. This happiness in sorrow is paradoxical. It comes from the "double tower" effect. One night recalls another night of the past. The correspondence between the two nights opens the depths of time, liberating the present from its imprisonment in the mere chronological instant. Animated by this correspondence with the past, memory casts a veil of vagueness over the present moment. The reference to the poet's tears, which causes the moon to appear "nebulously" to his eyes, links this vagueness to the very medium of visual perception.

But in order to convey the experience of memory *in the poem* and to create the corresponding associative horizon for the reader—who after all does not share the poet's personal associations—Leopardi must rely upon the psychological effect of words as well as images. In the most generic words possible he describes the scene: a hill, the moon, a valley, a forest. This landscape is not indifferent. It embodies the recollective experience conveyed in the poem. The disclosed depths of memory, which grace the moment on the hill, are gathered visually before our eyes in the depths of the valley, where the forest lies illuminated by the gleaming moon. The word *selva* (forest), with all its "indefinite" evocations in the mind of the Italian reader, is the indispensable *parola* of the poem. It is the *parola* that evokes the horizon of memory and draws the poem as a whole into the rich vagueness of its associations. If you take the word away, the poem loses the ever-so-elusive suggestion of those depths of remote origins, which precede the linear dispersion of personal or historical time. Time's cyclical repetition, embodied by the moon, shines upon the woods in a chiaroscuro image pervaded by indefinite associations.

In the same year that he wrote "To the Moon," Leopardi also wrote one of the most extraordinary lyrics of modern poetry: "The Infinite." In this poem the correspondences we have been discussing come together to dissolve the chronological moment in a sea of temporal and spatial totality. The poem describes this process of dissolution:

THE INFINITE

Always dear to me was this lonely hill,
And this hedgerow, which from many sides
Bars the gaze from the utmost horizon.
But sitting and looking out, endless
Spaces beyond that hedge, and superhuman
Silences, and profoundest quietude,
I in my mind forge for myself: where the heart
Is all but terrified. And as I hear
the wind rustle between these plants,
That infinite silence to this voice I go on
To compare: and I recall the eternal,
And the dead seasons, and the present, living one,
And the sound of her. So in this
Immensity my thought drowns:
And shipwreck is sweet to me in this sea. (*Canti*, 93)

The experience of the infinite described in the poem arises from the *comparison,* or correspondence, between the sound of the wind and the "infinite silence" imagined in the poet's mind. The intersection between the dimension of the here and now and the dimension it evokes in the poet's imagination is expressed grammatically in the play of demonstrative pronouns. "This hedgerow" becomes "that hedgerow" by the fifth verse. "This" wind corresponds to "that" infinite silence. By the end of the poem, the totality of time and space has dissolved into "this immensity"—an immensity that is no longer localizable as here or there. The immensity is the collapse of the distinction between the two.

The last verse of the poem alludes to a shipwreck. This is the "sweet" shipwreck of finite, linear time. By virtue of the fact that it comes as the *fifteenth* verse of the poem, the last verse also alludes to the shipwreck of the sonnet form. Its excess dissolves the formal boundaries of the sonnet and liberates prosody for the experience of the infinite, which the poem produces from out of its own immanent transcendence of formal time. It was not for nothing that Leopardi was the first European poet to write free verse. In this case free verse "corresponds" to a different experience of time: not time's linear formality but its indeterminate totality.

The maritime image that ends "The Infinite" is remarkable for other reasons as well, for it turns a land poem into a sea poem by dissolving the formal opposition between the elements. When Leopardi speaks of "this sea," he is referring to the ecstatic dissolution of form, boundary, identity, restraint, and differentiation. This ecstatic dissolution goes by the name of Dionysos, the mystery god of excess, orgiastic rapture, and visionary delirium—the god of the forests, as we have seen. The most Dionysian poet of the nineteenth century was no doubt Arthur Rimbaud, who sought poetic vision in a "systematic derangement of the senses." In his poetic pursuits, Rimbaud attempted to make artistically productive the loss of his bourgeois provincial identity—a loss experienced in running away to Paris shortly before the revolutionary upheavals of the Commune and his tempestuous relationship with Paul Verlaine.

Reversing Leopardi half a century, Rimbaud will turn sea into land in what became the first free-verse poem in French literature:

MARINE

The chariots of silver and copper—
The prows of steel and silver—
Beat the foam,—
Uprooting the stumps of the brambles.
The currents of the moor,
And the vast ruts of the backward surge,
Run in circles toward the east,
Toward the pillars of the forest,
Toward the boles of the jetty,
Whose corner is battered by whirlwinds of light. (196)

The poem reveals through its symbols the originary kinship between the elements by which they correspond to one another. In this visionary delirium of perception they appear in their predifferentiated unity, which in its own way corresponds to Leopardi's infinite sea of dissolution. Both Rimbaud and Leopardi are in this sense Dionysian. Rimbaud's poem speaks from within the sphere of that disordering of the senses which dissolves identities, formal boundaries, or the principle of individuation. The ecstatic perception of the poem presumes to see the primordial implication and promiscuity of all things—their involvement in some universal orgy that points in the direction of the forest. Rimbaud's "currents of the moor" run eastward toward the "pillars of the forest." They run, in effect, toward Baudelaire's forests of symbols, with their "living pillars" that look back at you. These forests of symbols belong to Dionysos.

The nostalgia for Dionysian rapture—its promise of rebirth in the intimate implication and correspondences of all living things—also finds expression in one of the most canonical lyrics of English literature: Shelley's "Ode to the West Wind." Shelley's poem associates the elements in such a way as to establish their irrevocable inclusion in one another. According to Shelley's note, this poem was "conceived and chiefly written in a wood that skirts the Arno, near Florence." As with both Leopardi and Rimbaud, it is crucially linked to a political dissatisfaction with the present and the given order of things. Yet it is also a remarkable forest poem. It evokes a great cosmic forest that embraces land, sky, and even the subsurface life of the sea. The wind disperses the dead leaves of the autumnal wood and ferries seeds to their "dark wintry beds," where life will be reborn in spring. Clouds in the sky are compared to leaves shaken loose from "the tangled boughs of Heaven and Ocean." The poet even speaks of forests at the bottom of the Atlantic: "The sea-blooms and the oozy woods which wear / the sapless foliage of the ocean." These aquatic forests "sympathize" with the forests of the land, hence they too "tremble and despoil themselves" in the autumnal season.

But the evocation of this forest of cosmic correspondences leads, predictably enough, to the poet's lament about his own exclusion from the universal cycle of death and rebirth. His consciousness of linear mortality precludes his participation in the primordial correspondence. Therefore he pleads to the wind for liberation from human time: "Oh! lift me as a wave, a leaf, a cloud. . . . Make me thy lyre, even as the forest is." It is a prayer, in effect, to the same wind that Leopardi heard rustling through the plants on his lonely hill, or to the wind that becomes a whirlpool of light in Rimbaud's "Marine." Better yet, it is a prayer to Dionysos, the god of vegetation, dispersion, and cyclical rebirth. In the second stanza of the poem Shelley in fact compares the clouds of an approaching storm to the hair "of some fierce Maenad," or frenzied votary of Dionysos. He then goes on to offer *himself* to Dionysos, that his scattered words might carry (like embers) light and life across the winter night.

T. S. Eliot once remarked that humankind cannot bear very much "reality." If reality means the literal and objective presence of things, we have something to learn about its unbearability from the poets who sought asylum in the forests of symbols. Wordsworth sensed in the forests the presence of the origin, which the cities cast into oblivion. For Baudelaire the temple of nature saves us from the denatured naturalism of the age—its loss of the depths of experience. Leopardi's work as a whole suggests that we have memory so as not to perish of contemporaneity. For the young Rimbaud "reality" amounts to nothing more than the bankruptcy of poetic vision. In his "Ode to the West Wind," Shelley longs for liberation from the conditions of isolated subjectivity and for reinclusion in the cosmic forest of creation. But we cannot forget that, even in his grove, Wordsworth's mood was troubled by the thought of "what man has made of man"; that Baudelaire was also the poet of spleen; that Leopardi ended his life as the most radical pessimist of the nineteenth century, defeated and embittered by the nihilism of linear time; that Rimbaud soon gave up poetry altogether and even repudiated its visionary ecstasies; and that Shelley's nostalgias for cosmic inclusion led to laments about his impoverished times.

One way or another the poets of nostalgia all testify to the unbearable yet ineluctable detachment of the age—its loss of the forests of symbols. How, then, does one bear the unbearable? In this case, by reminding oneself that it is unendurable, that is to say abnormal and unlikely. In the short run the poet has little choice but to hold vigil on a hillside while the town sleeps in oblivion, looking for signs of dawn across the forests.

John Constable, *Trees at Hampstead: The Path to the Church* (1821)

DWELLING

WHEN THE GLACIERS OF THE LAST ICE AGE BEGAN TO RE-
treat some ten thousand years ago, lifting the wintry blanket that
spread over much of the northern hemisphere, it marked the beginning of a new climatic era that geologists call the Neothermal. The
warming trend provoked heavy rainfalls. Forests hitherto suppressed
by the ice age once again covered the land. Melting glaciers, relentless
rainfall, the spread of forests—these concurrent phenomena amounted
to an ecological upheaval of cosmic proportions.

It is hard for us to imagine, several millennia later, how the return
of the forests was experienced as a cataclysm by many of our stone-age
ancestors, who during the most recent period of glaciation had
evolved into a remarkable biological and cultural species—a species of
predators sustained by the great herds that had roamed the open tun-
dras of Europe. With the advent of a neothermal climate their habitat
changed, as did their way of life. As the herds fled the inhospitable
density of the forests, many tribes died of starvation; some followed
the migrating herds further and further north; while some managed to
accommodate themselves to the changing habitat thanks to that genius
for adaptation which had enabled the species to survive other sorts of
upheavals in the past.

From the broad historical perspective, we could say that the major
accommodation to the new climate took the form of the neolithic revolution, or the establishment of agriculture as a way of life. This transformation in the human mode of existence has, to be sure, brought
many blessings to the race, but in the beginning the neolithic revolution amounted to a deep humiliation of the human species—a helpless

surrender to the law of vegetation that had chocked the land with forests, depriving the nomads of their prior freedom of mobility. Agriculture was a means of cultivating and controlling, or better, domesticating, the law of vegetative profusion which marked the new climatic era. In exchange for so many hardships (the toil of agriculture has long been conceived as the affliction of some original sin), the neothermal era gave human families and communities "roots." For the first time humans settled themselves on the land, planted the family tree in one place, and dwelled domestically.

Just as agriculture domesticated the law of vegetation, so did it also domesticate those who lived by it. The *domus* (in Latin, abode) became an *ethos* (in Greek, manner of dwelling). Human history, however we may want to conceive its distinction from prehistory, is predicated in the final analysis on the domestic ethos of a settled humanity. The neolithic way of life has provided the material basis for village and city, nation and empire, in short for history in the grander institutional sense. Whether history has now fallen into Molloy's ditch; whether it is "over" in the spiritual or ideological sense; whether we now find ourselves at the end of Vico's order of institutions or at the beginning of a new order altogether—there is little doubt that we have already witnessed the undoing of the basis of the domestic ethos in Western societies. While mechanized agriculture continues to supply us with food, land-dwelling as a way of life has given way to new forms of errantry. The *domus* loses its limits, its definition, its meaning, and for the first time in cultural memory an increasing proportion of people in Western societies are not sure where they will be buried, or where they should be buried, or even where they desire to be buried.

This uncertainty about one's ultimate place of belonging would have been unthinkable just a few generations ago. Molloy stages his odyssey as a return to his mother—to his place of origin—but the truth is that "Molloy could stay where he happened to be." His ditch is a grave that could be anywhere.

Detachment from the past, which we characterized as the main feature of the post-Christian era, culminates in one way or another with detachment from the earth—"this earth . . . these oaks," to recall Vico's words about the giants who established the first human dwellings. For reasons that remain altogether obscure, Western civilization has decided to promote institutions of dislocation in every dimension of social and cultural existence. The international hegemony of these institutions—metropolis, economy, media, ideology—has led to an aggravated confusion about what it means to dwell on the earth. This confusion, in turn, veils itself in oblivion. If the "end of history" means anything at all, it means that we now dwell in oblivion—in oblivion of the meaning of dwelling. To some extent this oblivion is only natural, for dwelling does not preserve its meaning by making an explicit issue of itself; it embeds itself in habit, ritual, and repetition; but when its meaning has disintegrated or lost its basis, that is to say when it has suffered fundamental traumas, then oblivion becomes a force of destruction rather than of preservation.

Recently ecological movements oriented toward the preservation of the earth have to some extent tried to rouse us from such oblivion by denouncing our destructive manner of being in the world at this moment in history. But even here the basic issues remain largely unclarified or ungrounded. Let us take the case of forests, which have so suddenly become a major focus of ecological activism around the world. Recently we have come to learn a great deal about the ecology of forests. We now know that forests are prodigious ecosystems: environments where various species establish their "niche" and exist in complex, integrated relationships to one another, each contributing its share to the network and each, in turn, depending on the delicate coherence of the network as a whole. The empirical science of ecology examines the mosaic of such systems and elaborates the biological conditions that sustain life within them. Given our increased knowledge of the many interdependencies that constitute such ecosystems, forests have come to assume a powerful symbolic status in the cultural imagination to the degree that they provide a compelling paradigm for the notion of the earth as a single, complex, integrated ecosystem. Ecological concern over forests goes beyond just the forests insofar as forests have now become metonymies for the earth as a whole. What is true for a particular forest's ecosystem is true for the totality of the biosphere. Humanity begins to appear in a new light: as a species caught in the delicate and diverse web of a forestlike planetary environment. More precisely, we are beginning to appear to ourselves as a species of parasite which threatens to destroy the hosting organism as a whole.

By emphasizing the degree to which we belong to the earth's cosmic forest, ecologists tend to redefine humanity's place of dwelling in global terms. The local concept of "here" finds itself projected into an infinite extension of "theres" which make up the totality of the biosphere. All of a sudden our place of dwelling reveals itself as a sprawling network of relations. But this is where ecology, as a *cause* and not a science, risks falling into attitudes that seem naive. The fact that humanity depends on the integrity of the natural world; that human beings belong to the greater network of nature's biodiversity; that we are caught in a forest of interdependencies with the planetary environment; that we are, after all, one species among others—this in itself does not prove that humanity is ontologically continuous with the order of nature.

In the past, this discontinuity was often cast in terms of humanist doctrines that privileged humanity in the order of creation. Whether in its secular or theological versions, humanism is the most naive doctrine of all when it comes to determining the place of human dwelling. One way or another it defines this place as—the city. Be it the city of God or the city of man, it is always a question of an artificial space. For humanism, humanity closes in upon the ideal, self-sustaining autonomy of its civic institutions. Ecologically oriented doctrines tend either to challenge these assumptions by deflating the privileged place of humanity in the order of creation, or else by proposing a form of superhumanism that conceives of humanity as the steward of nature. In either case they fail to think the discontinuity between humanity and nature radically enough.

This discontinuity manifests itself in the phenomenon of language, which does not belong to the order of nature. Language is a differential, a standing-outside of nature, an *ecstasis* that opens a space of intelligibility within nature's closure. Understood not merely as the linguistic capacity of our superior intelligence but as the transcendence of our manner of being, language is the ultimate "place" of human habitation. Before we dwell in this or that locale, or in this or that province, or in this or that city or nation, we dwell in the *logos*.

The Greek word *logos* is usually translated as "language," but more originally it means "relation." *Logos* is that which binds, gathers, or relates. It binds humans to nature in the mode of openness and difference. It is that wherein we dwell and by which we relate ourselves to this or that place. Without *logos* there is no place, only habitat; no *domus,* only niche; no finitude, only the endless reproductive cycle of species-being; no dwelling, only subsisting. In short, *logos* is that which opens the human abode on the earth.

The word "eco-logy" names this abode. In Greek, *oikos* means "house" or "abode"—the Latin *domus*. In this sense *oikos* and *logos* belong together inseparably, for *logos* is the *oikos* of humanity. Thus the word "ecology" names far more than the science that studies ecosystems; it names the universal human manner of being in the world. As a cause that takes us beyond the end of history, ecology cannot remain naive about the deeper meaning of the word that summarizes its vocation. We dwell not in nature but in the relation to nature. We do not inhabit the earth but inhabit our excess of the earth. We dwell not in the forest but in an exteriority with regard to its closure. We do not subsist as much as transcend. To be human means to be always and already outside of the forest's inclusion, so to speak, insofar as the forest remains an index of our exclusion.

From the very outset of this study, which began with antiquity and arrived at Molloy's ditch of historical paralysis, we have seen in how many ways the forest remains a margin of exteriority with respect to civilization. We have even found that the word itself, *foresta,* means literally "outside." The entire history we have recounted so far could be seen as the story of human outsideness. Because we exist first and foremost *outside of ourselves,* forests become something like an ancient and enduring correlate of our transcendence. And because our imagination is a measure of our ecstasis, the history of forests in the Western imagination turns into the story of our self-dispossession.

The task that remains for this concluding chapter is to come to terms with the radical nature of this outsideness and to determine in what way it grounds human dwelling on the earth. In what follows we will approach forests from a new perspective and seek to define more rigorously the *relation* between the human abode and nature as such. We will find that the relation *is* the abode, and that this relation remains one of estrangement from, as well as domestic familiarity with, the earth. This will oblige us to ask what it means to "be at home" on the earth in the mode of estrangement.

Here too forests will provide the essential insights, for in the final analysis the relation between forests and civilization is an instance of the *logos* to which we have been alluding. To express it otherwise, the history we have been tracing in this book culminates, finally, in an effort to awaken from the oblivion that conspires with destruction— destruction not only of forests and nature, but of the human abode that establishes itself in the relation.

THE ELM TREE

Old favourite tree thoust seen times changes lower
But change till now did never come to thee
For time beheld thee as his sacred dower
And nature claimed thee her domestic tree.
(John Clare, "To a Fallen Elm")

Our topic here is forests, *logos,* and human dwelling. The middle term, *logos,* stands for the relation between the two. We translated the term with words like "language," "relation," "gathering," "binding." In the King James Bible, *logos* is translated as "word." When it occurs in the context of Greek philosophical works, *logos* is usually translated as "reason" or "science." In the context of Greek mathematics, in turn, it means numerical "proportion." *Logos* derives from the Indo-European root *leg,* which presumably meant bringing together, or collecting. Thus *legere,* to read, means "to collect letters or meanings"; *ligare,* "to bind together"; *leges,* "those ideas or codes that bind a people together, or that are collected into dicta"; and *lignum,* finally, means "wood," or "that which is collected." The semantic connections between the various forms are a matter of conjecture, to be sure, but everything seems to point to a kinship between the Greek *logos* and Vico's etymology of the Latin *lex,* which has its "roots" in the forest ("First it must have meant a collection of acorns . . . next a collection of vegetables," etc. [*New Science,* § 240]).

If it takes so many English words merely to translate the literal meaning of *logos*—and inadequately at that—then no amount of words can adequately say what *logos* means with regard to the relation between forests and human dwelling. In this case we will let a visual image do the work for us. A picture is worth a thousand words, they say, but sometimes an artwork is worth a single word—the word *logos.* John Constable's *Study of the Trunk of an Elm Tree* is such an artwork. The painting (oil on paper, 306 × 248 mm; see illustration accompanying this section) is of uncertain date. For reasons that have to do with brush-stroke techniques, Graham Reynolds, curator of the Constable Collection in the Victoria and Albert Museum in London, dates it ca. 1821. It is by no means one of Constable's well-known works; rather, it is one of those "studies" that art historians find interesting more for their documentary than artistic value. We will not presume to corroborate or challenge such questions of value here, for if Constable's *Study of the Trunk of an Elm Tree* is worth a single word, that is more than enough for us. Before we turn to the work, however, some preliminary remarks about Constable's aesthetics are in order.

Constable was one of the greatest painters of the sky in the history of art. Striving to infuse his landscape paintings with the inward "sentiment of nature," as he called it, he paid special attention to the "atmosphere" that envelopes nature in veils of mood, tone, and temper. Atmosphere comes from the sky, or from the aerial phenomena that confer a distinctive harmony of light over the landscape. In a famous letter to his friend John Fisher, Constable reflects on the importance of the sky for his aesthetic:

> I have often been advised to consider my Sky—as a *'White sheet drawn behind the objects.'* Certainly if the Sky is *obtrusive*—(as mine are) it is bad, but if they are *evaded* (as mine are not) it is worse, they must and always shall with me make an effectual part of the composition. It will be difficult to name a class of Landscape, in which the sky is not the *'key note'*, the *standard of the 'Scale,'* and the chief *'Organ of sentiment.'* You may conceive then what a *'white sheet'* would do for me, impressed as I am with these notions, and they cannot be Erroneous. The sky is the *'source of light'* in nature—and governs everything. Even our common observations on the weather of every day are suggested by them but it does not occur to us. The difficulty in painting both as to composition and execution is very great, because with all their brilliancy and consequence, they ought not to come forward or be hardly thought about in a picture—any more than extreme distances are.
>
> But these remarks do not apply to *phenomenon* [sic]—or what painters call *accidental Effects of Sky*—because they always attract particularly. (*Correspondence* 6: 76–77)

The letter was written in October 1821, around the time that Constable presumably painted his *Study of the Trunk of an Elm Tree.* What interests us in his remarks is the concept of aerial phenomena. Constable repudiates the "white sheet" technique in landscape painting which reduces the sky to a neutral background against which objects stand in relief. If one believes that "painting is but another word for feeling"—a famous declaration of Constable in the same letter—then one remains bound to the sky as to the source of "music" governing the harmonies of tone, atmosphere, and sentiment in nature. Constable concedes that while the "brilliancy and consequence" of the sky "ought not to come forward or be hardly thought about in a picture," the aerial phenomena that manifest the "source of light" in its accidental effects *must* come forward in all their conspicuous attraction. These phenomena are given an inordinate presence by Constable in his paintings. Vast configurations of clouds hang over the earth with ponderous weight, or drift by with lightness, spreading a definite mood over the landscape as a whole, so much so that sky and earth appear enveloped in a single membrane of atmospheric spirit. The aerial phenomena fill up the space of the "white sheet" and thus bring to presence the otherwise neutral "brilliancy and consequence" of the sky. One could say, therefore, that Constable was not so much a painter of the sky as of the earth's atmosphere, in whose relative opacity the source of light shines forth.

While these aesthetic conceptions seem to conjure up Platonic notions about a suprasensuous realm shining forth in the sensuous radiance of the phenomenon, the issue is more elusive. Constable did not speak in terms of a dichotomy between the sensuous and suprasensuous. He spoke instead of the "chiaroscuro of nature," a term that he liberated from the domain of artistic technique and attributed to nature itself. The chiaroscuro of nature does not refer to separate orders of being—light and dark—which are somehow brought together in the aesthetic phenomenon. It refers instead to the conditions of appearance itself. The phenomenon appears in and through the chiaroscuro of nature. Rather than intimate a realm beyond itself, the phenomenon reveals the "Easy appearance which nature always has" (ibid.)—which is prior to any dichotomy. In other words, there is no pure domain of transcendent light (or white sheet) which allows things to appear; they appear always and only in the relative shades of the chiaroscuro itself.

Perhaps this is why Constable, the lover of the sky, was at bottom a lover of shadows rather than of brilliancy. "I live by shadows," he declared to Fisher, "to me shadows are realities" (ibid.). The statement, so un-Platonic in its import, implies that light attains its reality only in degrees of opacity. It also implies that opacity and illumination are inseparable, or irreducible to a dichotomy, and that beyond the chiaroscuro of nature there is no "reality."

Turning now to Constable's *Study of the Trunk of an Elm Tree,* we may see, quite immediately and dramatically, that the elm tree appears as a primal phenomenon in the chiaroscuro of nature. It stands there in its own ostentation—massive, opaque, conspicuous. The eye first fo-

John Constable, *Study of the Trunk of an Elm Tree* (ca. 1821)

cuses on the elm's rugged bark, which receives more prominence in the painting than any other feature. The bark is impressive not because of its "photographic naturalism," as Reynolds puts it, but because it so powerfully instantiates the chiaroscuro of nature as a whole. Its furrowed surface recapitulates the chiaroscuro of the surrounding scene, above all in the lower central portion of the trunk, which draws the gaze toward its more intense illumination and its more abysmal gaps of darkness.

However conspicuously it is foregrounded in the scene, however, the elm tree does not contrast with its surroundings. On the contrary, it appears to belong quite intimately to its habitat, or to the forest toward which it stretches its branches in an embrace of kinship. It stands detached, but not estranged, from the forest. By virtue of the elm's detachment, the forest in the background appears as the place to which it belongs all the more indubitably. The lower central portion of the tree trunk, more intensely illuminated than the rest, is defined at its outer edges by the dark, bottomless regions of the forest, especially to the right of the trunk, where the forest recedes into deep obscurity. It is toward the forestial abyss that the tree's branches seem to tend, as if to suggest that the elm emerges from its vaginal recess.

But precisely above this dark recess the forest's cover is broken open, allowing the sky's light to stream into the clearing. In the subdued illumination of the clearing, the elm appears in all its massive presence, suggesting to the eye its dependence on the light that invades the forest. Consequently one must wonder if the branches might not in fact tend toward the break in the forest's cover, and not toward the darker recesses of the forest below. The branches seem to close in on a point behind the trunk, forming a similitude with the circular pool of light on the ground. The appearance—an optical illusion—is that the branches make a kind of lens through which the light of the sky falls into the clearing. At the same time there is a strange play with volumes which contradicts normal expectations of perspectival depth—that space recesses at the top of the canvas. Here it recesses in the *middle*. At the top of the canvas, where a traditional landscape would disappear in deep sky, the painting plays off boundless depth and bounded, middle depth in the left and right semicircles of the branches. In short, sky and forest vie with one another in their claims of primacy.

This vying is nothing other than the chiaroscuro of nature revealing its irreducibility in the artwork. Precisely because it so radically probes nature's mode of appearance, this artwork is a "study"—a study, that is, of the essence of the chiaroscuro. If we go on to examine the chiaroscuro effects of the lower half of the picture, dividing it into two planes, we find that the plane defined by the illuminated patch of ground behind the tree intersects the trunk precisely along the line where the trunk's illumination gives way to the darker density at its base. And just where the band of darkness of the surrounding forest intersects the lower central portion of the trunk, the trunk's rugged bark shines forth most strongly. We cannot call this chiaroscuro effect an "opposition." We must call it, as Constable did, the "chiaroscuro of nature"—the very mode of nature's appearance which the artist here chose to "study."

By the same token we cannot speak of an opposition between sky and forest in the background area of the painting which seems to draw the eye and the tree's branches into its receding depths. The narrow channel of open sky falls from left to right directly into the darkest spot of the forest, as if to establish in the meeting point the primordial union of the chiaroscuro. The result is that the clearing appears as much a part of the forest as the darker areas of the underlying enclosure. Likewise the sky in this painting is no "white sheet drawn behind the objects," allowing the tree to appear in relief against its background. It is a "source of light," to be sure, but only because the opacity of the forest environment gives it the "reality" of shadows. Hence the tree, in its presence, reveals the chiaroscuro of nature as the very element of appearance as it reaches out to embrace both the surrounding forest and the open sky that breaks through its cover.

It is of course the artwork that brings the chiaroscuro to bear in this manner. The artist does not, or cannot, represent nature's mode of appearance in so-called objective terms, for nature reveals itself *in this or that manner* to the artist who has within himself the "sentiment of nature." Nature always already appears in its relation to human beings. Constable believed in the natural correspondence between the moods of nature (or its modes of revelation) and the inward states of the human soul, for which reason his landscapes constitute a sort of spiritual testimony or personal confession. Yet his insistence on the spiritual associations between landscape and soul raises a broad theoretical question: How does human presence in the world bring out the being of nature? What does human presence have to do with the way nature appears or comes to presence?

Constable's *Study* would not seem at first glance to offer an answer. Unlike most of his other works, there is no clear indication of human presence in the scene. Nevertheless the enclosed openness in which the tree takes its stand and gives space a boundary points to the irreducible relation of the image as a whole to the human presence that finds itself within its sphere of accessibility. This relation is not that of an object standing over against a subject of representation, even if the artist had to place himself before the tree to paint it, and even if we stand in front of his artwork as aesthetic observers in a gallery. However massive and obtrusive the trunk of the elm tree may appear in the artwork, it is not an object as such. It stands there as the embodiment of something that has come to appearance, that has emerged from the earth, that somehow gives itself in itself before it gives itself over to representation. The tree and its encircling forest, the patch of open sky and its sphere of illumination on the floor of the clearing, appear in Constable's study in what one might call their pregivenness. The phenomenon is always pregiven, the human presence is that to which it is given. Expressed otherwise, the phenomenon takes its stand within a fundamental relation, or correlation, that binds together the human essence and the self-disclosure of the phenomenon. This relation is the *logos. Logos* is the "word" that keeps silent in the artwork by disappearing into the presence of the phenomenon.

We must go further and say that this fundamental correlation underlies the correspondence between soul and landscape which Constable's paintings strive to evoke. Constable's devotion to the light, tone, and atmosphere that pervade a landscape and imbue it with a mood that is like a fusion between human feeling and nature's appearance—this devotion to the emotional modalities of the chiaroscuro indicate the extent to which, for Constable, human presence in the world belongs most intimately to nature's manner of being. "Painting is but another word for feeling," he declared, and feeling is but another word for the relational bond—the *logos*—through which nature comes to presence in the phenomenon.

Another way of speaking about this relational bond is in terms of the marriage of history and nature, where history does not mean the grand events of the past but rather the human appropriation of the earth as a place of dwelling. Constable refused to paint "historical" subjects for which landscape served as a mere background decor for the representation of the grandeur or tragedy of narrative episodes. He painted instead the landscapes of his native region with which he had an intimate historical association and which were already inclusive of his presence. In essence, Constable painted the scene of personal belonging. Hence his disdain for those peregrine artists who painted landscapes with which they had no personal or historical associations—the "Londoners," for example, who, as he wrote to Fisher, "with all their ingenuity as artists know nothing of the feeling of a country life (the essence of Landscape)—any more than a hackney coach horse knows of pasture" (Constable 6: 65).

In this sense Constable's counterpart among English poets was not William Wordsworth, whose name is so frequently associated with his, but John Clare (whose name, to this day, remains all too obscure). This Northamptonshire "peasant poet" was of a different social class but of the same disposition as Constable. He rarely ventured beyond the "safety" of his native horizon and belonged wholly to the land that he wrote about in his lyrics. We will take up the case of John Clare in the following section.

Unlike Wordsworth and Coleridge, Constable was unmoved by the wild landscapes of the Lake District. After an excursion to the region in 1806 he had a fundamental insight that convinced him that he should henceforth paint only the familiar landscapes of his native region. He lost interest in the Lake District not only because it was devoid of personal memories and associations but also because there was no presence of human habitation there. Nature for Constable became real above all in its relation to dwelling. Even in his paintings of the Stour Valley, or what has come to be called "Constable Country," the scenes of nature are rarely devoid of the presence of human settlement: cottages, farms, water mills, churches, hay wagons, locks, and so forth. Nature's vastness does not disappear in Constable's paintings. The skies are still immense as they hang or drift over the land, but thanks to its human appropriation by those who dwell there, the land gathers the endless extension of space and bounds it within the intimacy of *place.*

Constable was more than a landscape artist. He was essentially a painter of places. It is not the local place-name in a painting's title which places a given landscape. It is the way in which the presence of something man-made gathers nature around itself, be it the barge on the Stour, the Salisbury steeple in the meadow, the bridge in Helmingham Park, the broken tower of Hadleigh Castle in the heath, or the windmill near Brighton, to mention just a few such presences. In his career as a landscape artist, Constable strove to capture the "placehood" of place.

What is the placehood of place, and how does it appear in Constable's work? Let us take a typical Constable painting, *Trees at Hamstead: the Path to the Church* (1821: oil on canvas, 914 × 724 mm; see p. 196). It depicts a cluster of towering trees and a great sky of clouds behind and above them. But it is the wondrously understated presence of a wooden fence and a pathway at the extreme bottom-right of the picture that turns the scene of nature into a place. The fence and pathway serve to define its boundaries, to establish it as a place of habitation. The pathway disappears around the line of trees in a circling gesture of delimitation, or of what one could call "emplacement." This circling gesture is subtle enough, but its effect is unmistakable, for at the extreme left of the canvas the church toward which the vanishing pathway leads appears ever so faintly in the distance, thus circumscribing the space in which the trees take their stand. The rising edifice of the church corresponds symbolically to the rising trees encircled by the path that leads toward the church. This church appears tiny in the remote distance, but in truth the entire scene as a whole is part of the church, and vice versa. Nature here has become a temple. It has become sacralized. Human appropriation has bounded this place within the limits of belonging.

Even the sky, for all its immensity, is not a white sheet spread out behind the trees but belongs intrinsically to this place. It too has been brought within the bounds of place by virtue of the fact that humanity here has appropriated the land, and has in turn been appropriated by it. But again, without the presence of the fence or the wandering pathway leading toward the church, this landscape could not properly be called a place, even if the painting retained its place-name. The place-name, "Hamstead," which identifies the landscape empirically, is largely irrelevant to the placehood that the artwork conveys in its composition.

We have already remarked that the *Study of the Trunk of an Elm Tree* seems to lack the human presence that otherwise introduces the element of place in Constable's landscapes. But let us look at the *Study* again. To begin with, this massive tree growing in the midst of a narrow clearing, with its anthropomorphic gesture of embracing the surrounding forest and the sky that breaks through the forest's canopy, this tree, firmly rooted in the ground, seems to gather space around itself with its encompassing branches and make of this site a place of belonging. The sentiment of nature which went into its depiction has given the elm an evocative power of analogy. The gesture of appropriation by which the elm stretches out its branches neither denies the forest nor disappears into its closure, neither denies the sky nor glorifies its clearing. By the fact of its presence the tree simply convokes the chiaroscuro around itself, emplacing the scene of nature. We could say, then, that the artwork as a whole symbolizes the relational bond, or *logos,* by which the realm of nature is disclosed as a place of dwelling.

But let us look more closely at the study, for if we do not look closely enough we will fail to see that precisely in that spot where sky and forest intersect to the right of tree trunk, the faint presence of a house reveals itself. It is difficult to perceive at first, for it remains obscured by the crucial convergence of the chiaroscuro, where nature appears most "clear" and most "obscure" at once. Here, then, is the concealed element of emplacement—a house hidden by the foliage and the reflection of light. Once we have perceived the presence of the house, we view the elm differently. In its appropriating gesture, it now appears determined by the location of the house, for it is toward the house that its branches tend. Indeed, the tree now assumes a powerful correspondence with the *oikos,* the house. Tree and house correspond to one another as if to suggest that their correlation discloses the phenomenal realm itself. This correlation is so "natural" that the wood that went into the making of the house (which we detect in its roof) belongs to the forest in which it opens the place of dwelling.

By way of conclusion we remark that Constable's elm tree appears in the artwork as a phenomenon whose presence is given by an opening at the heart of nature's closure. This opening is more than the forest's clearing. It is the human presence itself, dwelling in the house. All that surrounds the tree, and all that is in turn surrounded by its branches, conspires with the tree's presence in the clearing. The presence is consigned to the correlation that binds the phenomenon to humanity, nature to history, the tree to the house—and vice versa. Nothing assures that this correlation cannot degenerate into the mere subject-object dichotomy of modern metaphysics, which posits a subject of representation which constitutes and organizes its objects of experience. But an artwork of the sort we have been discussing never merely represents objects, just as Constable's sky never merely draws a white sheet against which objects appear in relief. Constable's *Study of the Trunk of an Elm Tree,* and his landscape art as a whole, engages the correlation in its groundless primordiality, giving back to the elm tree its pregivenness as phenomenon, and recalling humanity to its corresponding obligation.

LONDON VERSUS EPPING FOREST

Forests cannot be owned, they can only be wasted by the right to ownership. Forests belong to place—to the placehood of place—and place, in turn, belongs to no one in particular. It is free. Of course nothing can guarantee that a place's freedom, like its forests, will not be violated or disregarded, even devastated. On the contrary, this natural freedom of placehood is the most vulnerable element of all in the domestic relation we have been calling *logos*.

On certain rare occasions this inconspicuous freedom of placehood finds a voice, for example in the poetry of John Clare, whose name we mentioned in connection with Constable. Let us take the time here to listen to it. The need to offer a brief biography of Clare before doing so springs not only from a scandalous undervaluation of this great poet by the English literary canon (one cannot assume any prior knowledge of Clare) but also from the deep roots of Clare's poetry in the place of his birth.

John Clare was born in Helpstone in 1793. He had a minimal school education and became literate largely through his own personal efforts. He never quite mastered the rules of grammar and punctuation, preferring to do without the latter in his poems. He achieved a short-lived notoriety as the "Northhamptonshire peasant poet," but not enough to save him from the troubled times in England's countryside, where Enclosure and the Engrossing policies of rural capitalism were bringing down wages and putting many land laborers out of work. Clare could not maintain economic independence as a poet, nor as a laborer struggling to remain a poet. In 1832 he and his family moved to the neighboring village of Northborough and occupied a cottage with a tiny plot of land. But so attached was Clare to his native horizon, beyond which he had rarely ventured, that this move three miles away from Helpstone led to an aggravated sense of disorientation and uprootedness. His sanity began to give way. When he entered his first asylum five years later, he took with him only the poor possession of his voice.

Clare was indeed poor, poorer than any poet could hope to be. His loss of sanity was only one of the forms of expropriation that his poetry identifies as the fate of poverty. The only thing Clare never lost was his poetic voice. It remains to this day the most authentic and inalienable voice of modern literature. He continued to write poetry up to the very end of his life, composing some of his best poems during the thirty years he spent in various asylums. As one of his physicians observed in 1840: "He has never been able to maintain in conversation, nor even in writing prose, the appearance of sanity for two minutes or two lines together, and yet there is no indication whatever of insanity in any of his poetry" (Clare, 12). This voice was indeed sound and free.

But precisely for that reason Clare was bound from the beginning to go out of his mind.

To begin with, it was the voice of poverty—of poverty as opposed to property. For Clare property meant first and foremost the "tyranny" of private ownership, or Enclosure, which was dividing up the English countryside into individual segments of land fenced or hedged off from one another. Warning signs hung up against trespassers reminded the poor of their increasing degradation and exploitation, of the loss of earlier freedoms (to graze on common lands, for example), and of the wholesale uprooting of their rural habitat in favor of maximized yields. By contrast, poverty meant for Clare the state of defenselessness against the forces of assault and expropriation. It did not mean destitution, at least not intrinsically, which is why the land itself figures as the poorest thing of all in Clare's poetry. The poverty of the land came from its powerlessness to defend itself against the tyranny of owners—its powerlessness to prevent the plough from ravaging its freedom and natural generosity.

The opening verses of Clare's poem "The Mores," composed sometime between 1821 and 1834, introduce us to this voice:

> Far spread the moorey ground a level scene
> Bespread with rush and one eternal green
> That never felt the rage of blundering plough
> Though centurys wreathed springs blossoms on its brow
> Still meeting plains that stretched them far away
> In uncheckt shadows of green brown and grey
> Unbounded freedom ruled the wandering scene
> Nor fence of ownership crept in between
> To hide the prospect of the following eye
> Its only bondage was the circling sky
> One mighty flat undwarfed by bush and tree
> Spread its faint shadow of immensity
> And lost itself which seemed to eke its bounds
> In the blue mist orisons edge surrounds
> Now this sweet vision of my boyish hours
> Free as spring clouds and wild as summer flowers
> Is faded all—a hope that blossomed free
> And hath once been no more shall ever be
> Inclosure came and trampled on the grave

Of labours rights and left the poor a slave
And memorys pride ere want to wealth did bow
Is both the shadow and the substance now.

The poem continues for a total of some eighty verses. Its conclusion reevokes the protest voiced at the beginning:

Each little tyrant with his little sign
Shows where man claims earth glows no more divine
On paths to freedom and to childhood dear
A board sticks up to notice 'no road here'
And on the tree with ivy overhung
The hated sign by vulgar taste is hung
As tho the very birds should learn to know
When they go there they must no further go
This with the poor scared freedom bade good bye
And much they feel it in the smothered sigh
And birds and trees and flowers without a name
All sighed when lawless laws enclosure came
And dreams of plunder in such rebel schemes
Have found too truly that they were but dreams.
(Clare, 90–93)

Clare was not by temperament a poet of protest. Protest in his case was merely a declension of poetic praise, which usually expressed itself in wonder. The poet's attentive observation of the local and minute marvels of nature sustained his concrete poetic descriptions of their unlikely modes of being. The essential poverty of the natural world—its vulnerable and assailable freedom—made its inexhaustible richness all the more wondrous for Clare. What Clare could never understand, until the day he died, was why whatever was poor in this miraculous way necessarily perished or came under siege by the forces of dispossession.

His last poem, written a few months before he died, is about a bird's nest. All his life he had written about nests—"The Moorhens Nest," "The Robins Nest," "The Thrushes Nest," "The Nightingales Nest," "The Yellowhammers Nest," "The Pettichaps Nest," "Wild Bees' Nest," "The Mouse's Nest," "Wild Duck's Nest," "Woodpecker's Nest," "The Green Woodpecker's Nest," "The Puddock's Nest," and so on. Nests for Clare were tiny miracles. They were places of safety, of "ownness," but also of vulnerability and risk. Nests were periodically raided by human beings or, more gravely, destroyed by the blundering plough. Clare took the side of all that was ultimately free and defenceless in this way—the hedgehog hounded in its lair by the hunter's dogs, the badger tormented in the streets of a village, the vixen, the fox, the marten, the animal and plant kingdom in general, all of which knew no safety from human disturbance.

The greatest threat to freedom was the loss of habitat. In "The Lament of Swordy Well," the land itself speaks in the first person of the various upheavals that have rendered it all but unrecognizable. Whereas Swordy Well was once a generous ecosystem that hosted diverse creatures and species, it speaks in the poem as the slave of Enclosure unable to defend its "own" against the claims of private ownership, which have reduced it to a machine of grain production no longer able to welcome bees, flies, rabbits, gypsies, laborers, or any of the "poor" that once visited or inhabited its site. A few stanzas from the poem give us an idea of its fate:

> Ive scarce a nook to call my own
> For things that creep or flye
> The beetle hiding neath a stine
> Does well to hurry bye
> Stock eats my struggles every day
> As bare as any road
> He's sure to be in somethings way
> If eer he stirs abroad [. . .]

> My mossy hills gains greedy hand
> And more then greedy mind
> Levels into a russet land
> Nor leaves a bent behind
> In summers gone I bloomed in pride
> Folks came for miles to prize
> My flowers that bloomed no where beside
> And scarce believed their eyes [. . .]

> I own Im poor like many more
> But then the poor mun live
> And many came for miles before
> For what I had to give
> But since I fell upon the town
> They pass me with a sigh

Ive scarce the room to say sit down
And so they wander bye [. . .]

And save his Lordships woods that past
The day of danger dwell
Of all the fields I am the last
That my own face can tell
Yet what with stone pits delving holes
And strife to buy and sell
My name will quickly be the whole
Thats left of swordy well. (96–99)

This evacuation of the essence of the place—its nearly total alienation and expropriation—eventually leaves only a name behind: Swordy Well. The poet who allied his voice to such poverty shared the fate of Swordy Well in his own life. Toward the end of his life, while he was in an asylum, Clare received a letter from a sympathetic stranger inquiring after his health. His response to the letter, utterly lucid and utterly mad at once, reveals that only the name "John Clare" was left to communicate itself to the outside world:

> March 8 1860
>
> DEAR SIR
>
> I am in a Madhouse and quite forget your Name or who you are. You must excuse me for I have nothing to communicate or tell of and why I am shut up I dont know I have nothing to say so I conclude.
>
> Yours respectfully
> JOHN CLARE

In the final stanza of "The Lament of Swordy Well," cited above, the place that speaks in the poem prays for the preservation of the woods that are still left standing: "And save his Lordships woods that past / The day of danger dwell." It is an ominous ending, for it gives the condition of poverty a broad, almost universal extension to nature as a whole. Preceded by twenty-five stanzas describing the transfiguration of Swordy Well, it confers the most tangible sort of vulnerability on the woods whose endurance it prays for. Speaking as a victim in this day of danger, Swordy Well assumes the status of precedent for what awaits the surrounding woods.

Among the poor who once sought out the hospitality of Swordy Well were the gypsies. Clare knew them well. In his youth he spent time around their camp fires, learned their songs, and listened to their stories (cf. "The Gipseys Camp" [1819–21]). If the peasants were poor, and growing poorer, the gypsies were even poorer still, for they earned no wages and were dependent on free access to places like Swordy Well, which declares in the poem that, before Enclosure, "The gipseys camp was not afraid / I made his dwelling free." This is the sort of quiet freedom for which we might have expected more sympathy from a poet like William Wordsworth, but as Merryn and Raymond Williams suggest, nothing reveals the difference between Clare and other "nature poets" of the period as much as the contrast between Wordsworth's poem "Gipsies" (1807) and Clare's "The Gipsy Camp" (1840–41). In his poem Wordsworth expresses a moralistic outrage at the fact that, for twelve hours, while he has toured the countryside on horseback admiring nature, a band of gypsies has not moved from its camp, apparently indifferent to the rising moon. He rehearses in his poem a conventional, deep-rooted resentment against the gypsy race. The conclusion of the poem speaks eloquently of Wordsworth's prejudice:

> Behold the mighty Moon! this way
> She looks as if at them—but they
> Regard not her:—oh better wrong and strife
> (By nature transient) than this torpid life:
> Life which the very stars reprove
> As on their silent tasks they move!
> Yet witness all that stirs in heaven or earth!
> In scorn I speak not;—they are what their birth
> And breeding suffer them to be;
> Wild outcasts of society! (Wordsworth, 332)

Wordsworth's complaint revolves around the gypsies' passivity. He sees no evidence among them of the great romantic eye that observes the world in rapturous admiration. But what can that romantic eye really see? What can it really perceive about the gypsy's relation to nature? As if those scorned gypsies did not already participate in secrets of nature which the Romantic only rides by atop his horse; as if their "torpor" were not merely a declension of their wandering restlessness; as if the poet's "mighty Moon," which the gypsies do not "regard," were not an image made of paper compared to the fabulous lunacy of the gypsies' night; as if, finally, the gypsies' outcast wisdom did not hold in its possession a knowledge of the forest that reaches back to antiquities, a knowledge that Romantic recollection never dreamed of in its reveries. Wordsworth's impassive gypsies—and somewhere within himself the poet must have sensed this—are already possessed by what the estranged Romantic soul seeks to possess during its forays into nature.

Clare's poem, on the other hand, speaks from within the sphere of the poverty of the outcasts:

> The snow falls deep; the Forest lies alone:
> The boy goes hasty for his load of brakes,
> Then thinks upon the fire and hurries back;
> The Gipsy knocks his hands and tucks them up,
> And seeks his squalid camp, half hid in snow,
> Beneath the oak, which breaks away the wind,
> And bushes close, with snow like hovel warm:
> There stinking mutton roasts upon the coals,
> And the half-roasted dog squats close and rubs,
> Then feels the heat too strong and goes aloof;
> He watches well, but none a bit can spare,
> And vainly waits the morsel thrown away:
> 'Tis thus they live—a picture to the place;
> A quiet, pilfering, unprotected race. (Clare, 165)

The poem takes its place alongside Clare's nest poems, for the gypsy camp is a nest in the forest as gathered and as vulnerable as the pettichap's nest on the side of an open road (cf. "The Pettichap's Nest": "Ive often found their nests in chances way / When I in pathless woods did idly roam / But never did I dream until today / A spot like this would be her chosen home"). The gypsies belong to the poverty of all that remains unprotected in nature's domain, above all the bleak forests that provide such nesting places for the persecuted, be it the gypsies, the fox, or the pregnant robin.

In 1837, at forty-four years of age, Clare took his voice of praise and protest into the forest of Epping. There he voluntarily entered his first insane asylum, where he would remain for four years. Shortly before he fled the asylum and journeyed home on foot he composed the following poem:

The brakes, like young stag's horns, come up in Spring,
And hide the rabbit holes and fox's den;
They crowd about the forest everywhere;
The ling and holly-bush, and woods of beach,
With room enough to walk and search for flowers;
Then look away and see the Kentish heights.
Nature is lofty in her better mood,
She leaves the world and greatness all behind;
Thus London, like a shrub among the hills,
Lies hid and lower than the bushes here.
I could not bear to see the tearing plough
Root up and steal the Forest from the poor,
But leave to freedom all she loves, untamed,
The Forest walk enjoyed and loved by all! (ibid.)

The forest in spring grows thick with brakes that protect the rabbit holes and fox dens, where the vulnerable young have come to life. The holly bush and beech trees flourish, but moderately enough that there is still "room enough to walk and search for flowers," or to look up and see beyond the foliage "the Kentish heights." The forest dispenses an appropriate measure to all, and to none at the expense of the other. This forest belongs to the poor, or to all that lives within the freedom of what knows no ownership except its ownmost freedom to exist. The freedom of all to exist is what defines the forest over against the "greatness" of London.

For that same reason its poverty is extreme. The ploughs steals the forest from the poor. It was because Clare could not bear to see the expropriation of freedom everywhere that he never ceased, even in his madness, to voice the plea to "leave to freedom all she loves, untamed, / The Forest walk enjoyed and loved by all!" This "all" is the poorest genericism in modern poetry. In it lies a call to the Londoners, or the "rich," to learn the essential poverty of freedom—to join the "all." This "all" calls out to London from the forest of freedom.

In an age that rallied around the cry of "freedom," that conceived of freedom as a liberation, or a revolution, or a promise of secular redemption, in short, as a freedom *from*—in such an age, then, Clare located freedom elsewhere: in what already existed in its own right, in what could not be gained but only lost by the drive for gain, in the forest's "all" over against the city's "all," or, quite simply, in the given and not the gotten. Clare knew that he was a poor fool to call for the respect for this kind of freedom. "I am a fool," he wrote with regard to his grief over the felling of a familiar elm tree, "were people *all* to feel as I do the world could not be carried on" (Clare, 219). In other words, were all people poets, the all would hold its own. But Clare knew that he called for what was out of the question. If his voice were heeded the world could not carry on. But then again, it is not the business of poets to help the world carry on its business. Their business is not to lose the voice of freedom, whatever the cost, whatever the loss.

THE WOODS OF WALDEN

We live in a world that traffics in rumors. From prophet to disciple, neighbor to neighbor, nation to nation, the word circulates in whispers or in sermons, binding the living to the dead and the dead to the yet unborn in chains of persuasion. Society depends upon our natural disposition to assume what we are told: that the gods are of such and such a nature, that the "good" lies in this or that direction, that we are on the earth to meet a set of obligations. We feast or starve at the table of laws, being believers. Sometimes we even believe in "freedom." Freedom too is a rumor, as long as one merely believes in it. The pilgrims who set off for America sought in their separation from the European homeland a margin of freedom from the old tyrannies and prejudices of tradition. They arrived on a forested continent, a "well-wooded land," and undertook an experiment in independence. To what did it lead? To more parishes of the predicted and predictable. Concretely speaking, to an even more insidious enslavement to nationhood, property, economy, industry, spectacle, and the monstrous institution of rumor called the press.

By the time Henry David Thoreau took up residence "in the woods, a mile from any neighbor," the collective experiment of American freedom was over. The neighbors were already in their slumber. It was merely "by accident," as he says, that Thoreau went to live at Walden on "Independence Day" in the year 1845. There was, in the accident, no coincidence between the personal and national declarations of Independence, for as Stanley Cavell declares in his commentary on *Walden:*

> America's Revolution never happened. The colonists fought a
> war against England all right, and they won it. But it was not

a war of independence that was won, because we are not free; nor was even secession the outcome, because we have not departed from the conditions England lives under, either in our literature or in our political and economic lives.

(*Senses of Walden,* 7)

Perhaps it is in his knowledge that he could not find in his country's national destiny the meaning of what it means to be American that Thoreau remains most radically American. An American, properly speaking, is an exception. In America freedom lies just beyond the bounds of the institutional order—a mile from any neighbor, in the adjacent woods of Walden, where forests silence the rumors of Concord and allow one to discover America in and for oneself. Even on the American continent those who would discover America must reenact the original gesture of departure and seek out the shores of Walden Pond.

Thoreau goes into the forest not like medieval Christian saints who sought out an extreme condition where a preestablished truth could impose itself more rigorously upon them, but as one who would put to the test the meaning of being on the earth. Life is an experiment of its meaning, and freedom consists in the chance to undertake the experiment for oneself in the "land of opportunity." Like most experiments, Thoreau's excursion to Walden sought to establish the matters of fact:

> I went to the woods because I wished to live deliberately, to front only the essential facts of life, and see if I could not learn what it had to teach, and not, when I came to die, discover that I had not lived. I did not wish to live what was not life, living is so dear, nor did I wish to practise resignation, unless it was quite necessary. I wanted to live deep and suck out all the marrow of life, to live so sturdily and Spartan-like as to put to rout all that was not life, to cut a broad swath and shave close, to drive life into a corner, and reduce it to its lowest terms, and, if it proved to be mean, why then to get the whole and genuine meanness of it, and publish its meanness to the world; or if it were sublime, to know it by experience, and be able to give a true account of it in my next excursion. For most men, it appears to me, are in a strange uncertainty about it, whether it is of the devil or of God, and

have *somewhat hastily* concluded that it is the chief end of man here to "glorify God and enjoy him forever." (II: 16)

The woods do not contain the knowledge that Thoreau seeks by going there; they do, however, uncover the habitual hiding places of the self, leaving it exposed to the facts of life, whatever they be. In his exposure Thoreau presumes to discover his irreducible relation to nature. What he discovers is that this relation remains opaque. We are in relation to nature because we are not within nature. We do not intrinsically belong to the natural order (if we did we would not need to discover the facts of life) but find in our relation the terms of our destiny as excursioners on the earth. Thoreau's allusion to a "next excursion" implies that the experiment at Walden, as well as life in its very essence, are also excursions—excursions into a world where we are at once estranged and alive, or better, alive in our estrangement. Those who have never gone into the woods to "live deliberately," or who merely drift on the stream of institutional history, never get to the bottom of what life is (and *Walden* affirms that life *does* have a bottom). Caught in the network of social relations, they are doomed to a "strange uncertainty" about life, for, never having essayed their own lives in a test of reality, they hear only vague and contradictory rumors about it, like a foreign country.

Thoreau's excursion to the woods of Walden, then, seeks to reduce life to the essentiality of its facts, in other words to reduce life to the fact of death. A fact of life is not so much something to live with but to die with. It is a self-knowledge that is either in you or not in you when you "come to die," depending upon your choice, while alive, to live or not to live what is life. Unlike a fact of science, it is nontransferable and nonreiterative. It escapes the circuit of rumor. You cannot purchase or inherit it from another, for, in the economy of living, a fact of life is the measure of one's solvency in death. No one else can live for you your capacity to die, and life does not assume the status of a fact until you discover within yourself this innermost capacity. In this sense a fact of life amounts to a personal fatality: "If you stand right fronting and face to face with a fact, you will see the sun glimmer on both its surfaces, as if it were a cimeter, and feel its sweet edge dividing you through the heart and marrow, and so you will happily conclude your mortal career. Be it life or death, we crave only reality" (II: 18).

Walden is a written testimony of the craving for reality. It is written in a personal style that makes an identification between reader and author ultimately impossible. The woods that isolate Thoreau from his neighbors also surround the dense, enigmatic prose through which this "mortal career" speaks. The writer's words linger in shadows, then burst into a blinding illumination; before the reader's eyes clear, they are elsewhere again. This voice evades us, as we are alternately lured and confused. ("It is a ridiculous demand which England and America make, that you shall speak so that they can understand you. . . . I fear chiefly lest my expression not be *extravagant* enough, may not wander far enough beyond the narrow limits of my daily experience, so as to be adequate to the truth of which I have been convinced" [XVIII: 6]).

Is Thoreau a sage, an ornery bastard, a "rugged individualist," or merely a neurotic? All we know for sure is that he is not a parson or a press agent. *Walden* does not merely add to the rumors about life but gives a precise account of how its author went about verifying for himself what is real and not real about his sojourn on the earth. To arrive at this boundary of finitude where a decision about what is real and not real about life becomes possible requires a personal estrangement that *Walden,* as a work of American literature, can only encourage, not effect, in a reader.

In other words, *Walden* becomes just another rumor the moment we take Thoreau at his word when he declares that Walden pond is approximately one hundred and seven feet deep. The bottom of Walden Pond is the ground that we are free either to sound for ourselves or to leave bottomless. I, the author of *Walden,* sounded it. Will you do likewise? The rigors of freedom. In a passage that is at once literal and allegorical, and which recapitulates his experiment of life in the woods, Thoreau describes how he went about sounding the depth of his pond in the winter of 1846. He had a particular interest in the fact, for by that time Walden Pond had become his life:

> As I was desirous to recover the long lost bottom of Walden Pond, I surveyed it carefully, long before the ice broke up, early in '46, with compass and chain and sounding line. There have been many stories told about the bottom, or rather no bottom of this pond, which certainly had no foundations for themselves. It is remarkable how long men will believe in the bottomlessness of a pond without taking the trouble to sound it. I have visited two such Bottomless Ponds in one walk in this neighborhood. Many have believed that

Walden reached quite through to the other side of the globe. Some who have lain flat on the ice for a long time, looking down through the illusive medium, perchance with watery eyes into the bargain, and driven to hasty conclusions by the fear of catching cold in their breasts, have seen vast holes "into which a load of hay might be driven," if there were anybody to drive it, the undoubted source of the Styx and entrance to the Infernal Regions from these parts. Others have gone down from the village with a "fifty-six" and a wagonload of inch rope, but yet have failed to find any bottom; for while the "fifty-six" was resting by the way, they were paying out the rope in the vain attempt to fathom their truly immeasurable capacity for marvelousness. But I can assure my readers that Walden has a reasonably tight bottom at a not unreasonable, though at an unusual, depth. I fathomed it easily with a cod-line and a stone weighing about a pound and a half, and could tell accurately when the stone left the bottom, by having to pull so much harder before the water got underneath to help me. The greatest depth was exactly one hundred and two feet; to which may be added the five feet it has risen since, making one hundred and seven. This is a remarkable depth for so small an area; yet not one inch of it can be spared by the imagination. What if all ponds were shallow? Would it not react on the minds of men? I am thankful that this pond was made deep and pure for a symbol. While some men believe in the infinite some ponds will be thought to be bottomless. (XVI: 6)

A bottomless pond has no depth. A life without ground has no reality. Imagination discovers its real freedom in the measured finitude of that which is the case, not one inch of which can be spared. Those who have come to "hasty conclusions" about Walden Pond are those who have also "*somewhat hastily* concluded" we are on the earth to glorify heaven. The sounding of the pond, or the pondering of life in its depth, goes to the very basis of the earth as the ground of life.

Saint Augustine had declared in his *Confessions* that "my weight is my love." He called this doctrine the *pondus amoris,* or weight of love. A stone (weighing, say, a pound and a half) tends downward toward the earth, for the weight of its love propels it toward its own proper element or domicile. Fire, on the other hand, being less heavy than either earth, water, or air, rises upward toward the higher cosmic spheres:

> A body tends to go of its own weight to its own place, not necessarily downward toward the bottom, but to its own place. Fire tends to rise upward; a stone falls downward. Things are moved by their own weights and go to their proper places. If you put oil underneath water it will rise above the level of the water; if you pour water on top of oil, it will sink below the oil; things are moved by their own weights and go to their proper places. When at all out of their place, they become restless; put them back in order and they will be at rest. My weight is my love; wherever I am carried, it is my love that carries me there. By your gift we are set on fire and are carried upward; we are red hot and we go.
> (*Confessions* 13.8 [322])

Thoreau, on the other hand, finds his *pondus amoris* in the stone with which he sounds Walden. And in the cosmic levitation of the elements, the earth is heavier than water.

How deeply do we live? How fundamentally do we live? Lying on the other side of the great stream of the Atlantic Ocean, America once held out the promise of a land on which to base a new *ethos,* or mode of dwelling on the earth. No such luck. The oceans that separate also unite, and Thoreau's nation as a whole now swims in the streams of opinion, delusion, and the old ways. Thoreau is the American exception who must search for the ground of life under the alluvion that engulfs even his own country:

> Let us spend one day as deliberately as Nature. . . . Let us settle ourselves, and work and wedge our feet downward through the mud and slush of opinion, and prejudice, and tradition, and delusion, and appearance, that alluvion which covers the globe, through Paris and London, through New York and Boston and Concord, through church and state, through poetry and philosophy and religion, till we come to a hard bottom and rocks in place, which we call *reality,* and say, This is, and no mistake; and then begin, having a *point d'appui,* below freshet and frost and fire, a place where you might found a wall or a state, or set a lamp-post safely, or perhaps a gauge, not a Nilometer but a Realometer, that fu-

ture ages might know how deep a freshet of shams and appearances had gathered from time to time. (II: 23)

The hard bottom of reality is a foundation upon which to build a wall, or, perhaps, a house. Thoreau built such a house for himself at Walden according to the essential measure of life—a small wooden cabin made of the forest's offerings. Early on in *Walden* he indicates that the only other house he had owned before was a boat. "But the boat, after passing from hand to hand, had gone down the stream of time" (II: 8). Most houses are boats of this sort, passed down from one generation to another, or bought and sold in the promiscuous marketplace of real estate. Of course to call such houses "real estate" is a misnomer in the allegorical economy of *Walden,* since what they lack is precisely a foundation in reality. Such houseboats house only our own groundlessness. They house our debts to the bank, to the forefathers, and to the still unborn. They perpetuate our evasion of reality in labor and commit to the stream of time our insolvency in death.

The Walden house was of a different sort. It was a dwelling on the earth, a frame whose limits made of the forest its larger extension. "This frame," writes Thoreau, "so slightly clad, was a sort of crystallization around me" (II: 8). The Walden house was a structure of exteriority rather than interiority. "I was not so much within doors as behind a door where I sat, even in the rainiest weather" (II: 8). Thoreau's house was the foundation for his life at Walden, spent for the most part listening to the sounds of the forests, observing the ways of its animals, familiarizing himself with the facts of the vicinity, conversing with visitors, reading and writing. It was not a houseboat to the degree that it converted the interior and exterior spaces into one another. In one of the most striking passages of *Walden* Thoreau describes such conversion:

> Housework was a pleasant pastime. When my floor was dirty, I rose early, and, setting all my furniture out of doors on the grass, bed and bedstead making but one budget, dashed water on the floor, and sprinkled white sand from the pond on it, and then with a broom scrubbed it clean and white; and by the time the villagers had broken their fast the morning sun had dried my house sufficiently to allow me to move in again, and my meditations were almost uninterrupted. It was pleasant to see my whole household effects out upon the grass, making a little pile like a gypsy's pack, and

my three-legged table, from which I did not remove the books and pen and ink, standing amid the pines and hickories. They seemed glad to get out themselves, as if unwilling to be brought in. I was sometimes tempted to stretch an awning over them and take my seat there. It was worth the while to see the sun shine on these things, and hear the wind blow on them; so much more interesting most familiar objects look out of doors than in the house. A bird sits on the next bough, life-everlasting grows under the table, and blackberry vines run around its legs; pine cones, chestnut burs, and strawberry leaves are strewn about. It looked as if this was the way these forms came to be transferred to our furniture, to tables, chairs, and bedsteads—because they once stood in their midst. (IV: 3)

The dislocation of the household from its interior to its exterior, this externalization of the place of dwelling in the forest itself, where the familiar display of furniture reveals its relation to the surrounding environment, summarizes the innermost vocation of *Walden* as a work of American literature. Like the excursion of the author's furniture from his house to the open clearing, *Walden* wants to reopen the *ethos* of America to the nature of its promise, or to the promise of its nature. Economy, industry, production—on what are the projects of the nation founded that they continue to enclose its citizens in the "strange uncertainty" about life? All that is to be learned about what is real and not real lies in the exteriority of our inner lives.

Nature is the setting of this exteriority, if only because it is that to which we remain external. It is only in our relation to what we are not that what we are may finally become the ground of our dwelling. Nature is where we go to get lost, so that we may find again that which in us is irrevocable: "Not till we are completely lost, or turned round,—for a man needs only to be turned round once with his eyes shut in this world to be lost,—do we appreciate the vastness and strangeness of Nature. . . . Not till we are lost, in other words, not till we have lost the world, do we begin to find ourselves, and realize where we are and the infinite extent of our relation" (VIII: 2).

The lesson of *Walden* lies in this pedagogy of estrangement. As it recalls us to our estrangement, nature also teaches us that it cannot assume responsibility for human existence. We "turn round" to nature to find ourselves in the midst of something absolute which we do not possess and which in turn refuses to possess us. In this manner we appropriate nature as the place of dwelling. Nature receives our visitations but also reminds us that we must find a way to complete our excursion by taking our leave. Nature, in short, teaches us economy. The management of our house—or the *nomos* of our *oikos*—lies in our overcoming of nature itself. "Nature is hard to overcome, but she must be overcome," writes Thoreau (XI: 12). This utterance is given its full weight by Cavell:

> Our nature is to be overcome. (Society does not have to be
> overcome, but disobeyed; but what that means comes later.)
> At the same time, nature is the final teacher powerful enough
> to show us overcoming. She is, the new Romantic might say,
> my antagonist, whose instruction I must win. The times of
> the day and the seasons of the year are not referred to by my
> instincts; nature is not my habitat, but my exemplar, my
> dream of habitation. In the newest testament, nature may
> prompt and bless my redemption; but it does not accomplish
> it on my behalf. What I have to work out is still my salva-
> tion. . . . (*Senses of Walden,* 43–44)

What nature cannot provide is an image for the longing that pervades human finitude. It is this longing that seeks an abode on the earth, but the only thing that can house it are the words in which it confesses its longing for closure. This is why the excursion to Walden has its conclusion in the writing of *Walden,* a testimony of leave-taking.

The contemporary American "nature poet" A. R. Ammons is someone who knows what it means to write a book like *Walden.* One of the few Americans to have rediscovered America after Thoreau, Ammons has spent a lifetime in nature searching for a conclusion to his mortal career. In one of his poems he speaks of what obliges him to speak at all:

> I went to the summit and stood in the high nakedness:
> the wind tore about this
> way and that in confusion and its speech could not
> get through to me nor could I address it:
> still I said as if to the alien in myself
>   I do not speak to the wind now:
> for having been brought this far by nature I have been
> brought out of nature

and nothing here shows me the image of myself:
for the word *tree* I have been shown a tree
and for the word *rock* I have been shown a rock,
for stream, for cloud, for star
this place has provided firm implication and answering
   but where here is the image for *longing:*
so I touched the rocks, their interesting crusts:
I flaked the bark of stunt-fir:
I looked into space and into the sun
and nothing answered my word *longing:*
   goodbye, I said, goodbye, nature so grand and
reticent, your tongues are healed up into their own
element
and as you have shut up you have shut me out: I am
as foreign here as if I had landed, a visitor:
so I went back down and gathered mud
and with my hands made an image for *longing:*
   I took the image to the summit: first
I set it here, on the top rock, but it completed
nothing: then I set it there among the tiny firs
but it would not fit:
so I returned to the city and built a house to set
the image in
and men came into my house and said
   that is an image for *longing*
and nothing will ever be the same again.
   ("To Harold Bloom")

    A house is a place to set an image in. This image is made of mud,
of the earth, but it is the image of something which the earth cannot
contain. It is the image of . . . a word. Not a linguistic word but the
logos of human transcendence. It is not for nothing that *logos* in Greek
means relation, gathering, binding, before it means language. In Ammons's poem the *logos* is that which longs. In its longing it reaches out
or speaks our human nature to the world, but nature does not respond
to the call. We humans do not speak the language of nature's self-
inclusion, but one of extraneous excess. Our *logos* is the outside of
things—a boundary of finitude at which we are lost but which, in return, enables us to utter words at all. The words "tree" and "rock" are
utterable because *logos,* in its longing, projects us beyond the contain-

ment of trees, rocks, wind, and forests. In excess of the earth, we dwell in longing as in a house turned inside out. Whether or not the words we utter have a mundane reference (tree or rock), the fact of uttering them means that we have already left nature's closure behind. This movement beyond things themselves to the dimension of their "meaning" is the *logos*. We long for meaning's closure, but only in our longing does the human world make any "sense." Sense is the openness of the *oikos*—the ecology of longing itself.

It is this self-produced image of longing that the poet houses in the poem. As an image of ourselves, it sits in his house—or in the poem—as the measure of our excess. Nature itself cannot accommodate it, but men and women can enter his house and say, "that is an image for longing." To be human means to be bound together on the basis of this fact. People speak to one another, recognize their kinship, only because each inhabits the longing whose image the poet has housed in the poem. There is no "rugged individualism" in this sort of Americanism. Human speech is in every case a confession of longing and finitude, no matter what it says or does not say or even cannot say. We speak our death to one another. We forge for one another in speech an image made of earth and mud: the *logos*. This *logos*, in turn, once it finds the bottom of Walden Pond, binds humans together in finitude.

What can it mean, then, the phrase "return to nature"? Thoreau goes into nature to be brought out of nature. He enters the woods of Walden in order to learn how to be transitory there. Just as he never presumed to leave his furniture out of doors indefinitely, so too he never presumed that this sojourn in the woods of Walden could serve as a permanent model for dwelling. There are no permanent models. The purpose of the excursion was to defamiliarize his life so as to return to the irreducible loss at the heart of it:

> I long ago lost a hound, a bay horse, and a turtledove, and am still on their trail. Many are the travelers I have spoken to concerning them, describing their tracks and what calls they answered to. I have met one or two who have met the hound, and the tramp of the horse, and even seen the dove disappear behind a cloud, and they seemed as anxious to recover them as if they had lost them themselves. (I: 24)

We do not need to know exactly what these lost creatures might signify in their specific symbolism. What matters is that, in their absence, they establish loss as a "fact of life" in Thoreau's sense. Loss is what we begin with. It is the state in which Thoreau goes to Walden as well as the fact of life which he discovers there. We may define the loss mythologically, as a fall from the garden of Eden, and Eden, in turn, we may identify with this or that dream of loss plenitude. One way or another longing is the loss of life, and loss the life of longing. Speak about a hound, a bay horse, and a turtle dove to others, and they will know what you mean; remind them of loss, and they too will become anxious to recover what you alone have lost. Loss is the rock bottom foundation of the communal.

Walden is nothing less than its reminder. To live loss as a matter of fact means to live poetically, knowing that we are not the possessors of the world we inhabit precisely because we have not yet found the hound. Where else but in nature do we learn to overcome nature and thereby become our humanity—our finite, open-ended transcendence? Thoreau speaks of "living deliberately," of living what is life and not what is not life. This requires that "you stand right fronting and face to face with a fact," and so "conclude your mortal career." The conclusion of a mortal career does not come at the end of that career but already claims it as a whole in advance. Such a conclusion is not of the order of the "hasty conclusions" of those who imagine that Walden Pond is bottomless or who assume in their uncertainty that our chief aim on earth is to glorify some other world. It is the knowledge that one has already lost whatever there is to lose and that life is therefore given, or for-given, gratuitously.

As it concludes a mortal career, a fact of life awakens to the fact there is something rather than nothing, that nature *is* without a human reason for being, and that we dwell in the givenness of loss. This knowledge, this self-knowledge alone, is freedom.

But was it not precisely a poetic freedom of this sort that America promised those who willingly lost themselves across the seas of departure? Was America not discovered precisely in the expectation of for-giveness? For some reason it was the fate of America not to become itself, not to build its house upon the foundation of a loss for which no recovery was possible. Its fate, rather, was to sacrifice its freedom to nationhood, to reiterate and exasperate the rage for possession, and to fall into the watery mire of what is not life. Instead of a nation of poets, it became a nation of debtors, property owners, shopkeepers, spectators, gossipers, traffickers in rumor, prejudice, and information—capitalists who in their strange uncertainty about life pursue the delusions of recovery in their appropriation of everything. In its continuous flight from the conclusions of a mortal career, America became not the *caput mundi* of poetic freedom but the *caput mortuum* of modernity— capitalism turned into the death's head. America will forever be what it did not become, and *Walden* will remain its empty house.

FALLINGWATER

In a forest in Pennsylvania, barely visible through the leaves in any other season than winter, lies a house built on the ledge of a waterfall. Its fame as a masterpiece of architectural design seems strangely at odds with the feature for which it is famous, namely its discretion. It does not exactly "blend in" with the forest, for it reposes on a series of horizontal planes that conspicuously intersect the vertical rise of the trees; yet the surrounding forest seems to gather around the lateral extension of the house and to become more itself in its presence, as if the house had somehow elevated the earth to the height of the leaves in order to dramatize its reality as the ground that supports both forest and house. The thin, multiple strata of reinforced concrete which articulate the structure of the house correspond to the geology of time visible in the rock of the river bed and the jagged ledge over which the water falls in a steady vertical descent. The discretion of Frank Lloyd Wright's Fallingwater comes from the fact that the house not only comes to rest in its environment but also embodies an extension of the foundation upon which it rests.

It is hard to believe that Wright did not have *Walden* in mind when he designed Fallingwater in the thirties. The site's forested landscape would naturally have evoked the woods of Walden in the mind of an American like Wright, but what is most reminiscent of *Walden* is the way the house exploits the dynamic relation between flowing water and solid foundations. Thoreau did not want to drift on the streams of convention. He did not want to live in a houseboat but in a house built on the foundation of reality, on the earth. The overwhelming impression created by Fallingwater, despite its utopic character, is precisely of such reality. In short, the house is a masterpiece of stability: a solidity that stabilizes the various elements of the environment by virtue of its repose on the earth.

Such a house makes of its dwelling place the space of freedom. The repose of buildings on horizontal planes was, for Wright, an architectural ambition as well as the very substance of freedom: "I see this extended horizontal line as the true earth-line of human life, indic-

Frank Lloyd Wright, *Fallingwater*

ative of freedom. Always." There is much to ponder in this statement from Wright's autobiography, especially its last word. In the same text we read: "The broad expanded plane is the horizontal plane infinitely extended. In that lies such freedom for man on this earth as he may call his" (Wright, 61). The search for freedom in horizontality, and not in the celestial nostalgias of the vertical rise, makes of Wright an American in the exceptional, Thoreauvian sense. Whatever freedom we may call ours is to be found on the earth, whose surface is round only from a perspective beyond the earth. For those *on* the earth its surface extends horizontally, that is to say, constitutes a horizon. A house is that which gathers the horizon around itself. Wright: "I had an idea (it still seems to be my own) that the planes parallel to the earth in buildings identify themselves with the ground, do most to make the buildings belong to the ground" (ibid.). When buildings belong to the ground in this way they are at once shelters as well as openings into nature. The concept of shelter is redefined by Wright in terms of openness rather than closure, precisely because we derive our shelter from the earth, not from the house that shuts it out. Shelter comes from the house's emplacement:

> An idea (probably deeply rooted in instinct) that *shelter* should be the essential look of any dwelling, put the low spreading roof, flat or hipped or low-gabled with generously projecting eaves, over the whole. I began to see a building primarily not as a cave but as broad shelter in the open, related to vista; vista without and vista within. You may see in these various feelings all taking the same direction that I was born an American, child of the ground and of space. . . . (ibid.)

The only true shelter on earth is the earth itself. The earth is able to offer shelter because, paradoxically, it has a natural tendency to draw back into its absolute closure. If it is to provide this shelter, the earth must be drawn out of its closure by the house, or better, its closure must come forth intact around the house. The forest, for example, is a closed environment, yet there is no shelter in the forest for human beings without an abode to call forth its protection. The abode does not create a shelter that was not there already; it does not shelter by closing itself off but rather by summoning the closure around itself. It does this by placing itself on the earth in its openness. A house is an architectonic of exteriority defined not so much by its walls but by its windows, its doors, its porch, its porous openness to the earth.

Fallingwater is in this sense a metahouse. Its utopian exemplar makes a statement about what it means to be a house. Frank Lloyd Wright taught by example that shelter is grounded on the principle of architectural openness, not closure. Time and again he insists that freedom and democracy must ground themselves on the natural openness of dwelling:

> When *unfolding* architecture as distinguished from *enfolding* architecture comes to America there will be truth of feature related to truth of being: individuality realized as a noble at-

tribute of *being*. *That* is the character the architecture of democracy will take, and probably that architecture will be an expression of the highest form of aristocracy the world has conceived when we analyze it. (256)

This is what we might call Wright's concrete version of "fundamental ontology." The truh of feature and the truth of being are related to one another by what we have called, in other contexts, *logos*. This relation in turn serves to ground democracy, for at bottom democracy is for Wright the "truthful" manner of being in the world. This is why it must have its basis in architecture. We do not live in ideas, values, political systems, or ideologies; we live, essentially, in houses. Democracy is a particular kind of shelter grounded on the earth.

Wright reminds us that the earth tends to fold into itself, or to withdraw into its own closure, and that the earth cannot become a shelter unless it is *unfolded,* or disclosed, by human appropriation. It has become clear by now that appropriation does not mean acquisitive possession but the disclosure of freedom in the space of dwelling. Freedom rests on the decision to be or not to be what we already are, namely dwellers on the earth. For Wright the political decision of freedom is decided by a nation's architecture. If architecture remains the fundamental agency of democratic freedom it is because it figures as the "mother art" by which a people may make itself at home on the land that founds the nation itself. Architecture has within its power the decision whether the people will be free or not, whether they will be at home in the "broad openness of shelter" or alienated in boxes that close off the *logos* and consign it to oblivion. People are free only when they are housed; and they are housed only when their abode *unfolds* rather than *enfolds* itself. Thus when Wright spoke of an "unfolding architecture" as related to the "truth of being," he was challenging his nation to assume responsibility for freedom at the ground level. Such responsibility begins with the realization that freedom lies in "this extended horizontal line as the true earth-line of human life, indicative of freedom. Always."

A government that guarantees your rights does not by that measure guarantee your freedom, for your freedom is protected first and foremost by a house that gathers the earth's shelter around itself. Only the "mother art" can establish the basis for such freedom. One of the ways in which Wright conceived of freedom was as a liberation from the tyranny of the International Style in architecture:

Organic architecture believes in the destruction of what the so-called International Style has maintained as the box. We had a feeling that since the nature of modern life was marked by its profession of freedom, there should be a free expression in building. The box was merely an inhibition and a constraint. All architecture had been the box—a decorated box, or a box with its lid exaggerated, or a box with pilasters, but always a box. . . . What could happen horizontally could also happen to the vertical. The essential nature of the box could be eliminated. Walls could be screens independent of each other; the open plan appeared naturally; the relationship of inhabitants to the outside became more intimate; landscape and building became one, more harmonious; and instead of a separate thing set up independently of landscape and site, the building with landscape and site became inevitably one. So the life of the individual was broadened and enriched by the new concept of architecture, by light and freedom of space. (83–84)

Let us pause here a moment and speak about a letter that Jimmy Carter recently sent to hundreds of thousands, if not millions, of American families (a dispatch that in itself confirms that an abode and an address are wholly different phenomena). The letter explains why Jimmy and Rosalynn decided to support the work of "Habitat for Humanity," an organization devoted to helping "hundreds of thousands of families right here in America [which] live in the most deplorable housing conditions imaginable: roach- and rat-infested ghetto flats; dilapidated rural shacks; decaying crumbling old apartments." In order to personalize and render pathetic the plight of such dispossessed families, Carter describes the living conditions of one particular family in Cartersville, Georgia—the Bohannons. He evokes a scene of Sara, Lonnie, and their two children Tony and Carolyn "struggling to get by in two corrugated metal storage sheds (the kind where you and I might keep a lawn mower)! . . . They had no running water, no toilet, and not much hope. . . . But Sara and Lonnie were very proud, and refused to accept any form of charity." Through revolving-loan funds and the commitment of over 100,000 volunteers, Habitat for Humanity has enabled the Bohannons to buy a low-cost, interest-free home. It hopes to do likewise for many more thousands of families across the country, with the help of all of us who presumably own lawn mowers.

We do not know what sort of "habitat" the Bohannons left behind, for the letter does not say whether their shack gave out onto the earth, onto a forest, a stream, a field, or merely an urban slum. We can be sure, however, that their new "home" is essentially a box. "Oh, it's nothing fancy, at least by the standards of most of us," writes Carter of their new living conditions, "but it does have bedrooms . . . and plumbing . . . and safe wiring." What can we make of this happy ending? What sort of concept of home is operative here? Can safe wiring and running water of themselves redeem the alienation of living in a box?

How now? Are we to house everyone in homes designed by Frank Lloyd Wright? What more can "affordable housing" projects do for the dispossessed than offer them a box? In approaching such questions let us first be wary of declaring, in the mode of politicians, that there are no easy answers. Fallingwater is not so much a house as a statement about the essence of a house. Wright conceived of housing as the basis of American democracy, not as the privilege of the rich. That is why he spent so much of his time developing models for the so-called Usonian homes—low-cost single-family houses as well as multiple-unit complexes. These models embody the extreme concept of "affordable housing," yet they show us a way out of the box. In the wondrous simplicity of the Usonian home one lives in the unfolding of space, in the exteriority of its "broad open shelter," in the freedom of space as such. If "architecture is poetry," as Wright insisted, why this illegible prose of the urban? Why is housing still governed by intolerable models when poets have shown, down to the last tangible detail, how to build even the most modest dwelling in accordance with the meaning of dwelling?

Frank Lloyd Wright was no solitary dreamer spinning out poems in the woods, a mile from any neighbor. He was a builder of homes, a designer of buildings, a planner of cities who showed us, step by step, how to bring the broad open shelter of freedom to the modern metropolis. He was the poet of technology as well as the concrete architect of the abstract visions of a visionary like Thoreau. His work and blueprints demonstrated concretely, in ways that encouraged imitation and continuation, how to build a world on the rock-bottom foundation of freedom in accordance with the meaning of dwelling. His career as a whole confirms that poetic vision can translate into a practice that starts on the solid ground, at the very basis of things. This career is evidence of realization; evidence that a testimony like *Walden* need not remain the private language of a solitary poet but can become the basis for a public creed.

It suffices to compare a model of the Usonian home to what today falls under the rubric of "affordable housing" to wonder why the nation as a whole invariably and systematically ignores its poets. The consequences of such neglect are immeasurable, for when a nation loses its poets it loses access to the meaning of dwelling. When it loses the meaning of dwelling, it loses the means to build. By the same vicious logic, when it loses the means to build, dwelling itself loses its meaning. No amount of running water or safe wiring can of itself turn a house into a home, for when a nation ignores its poets it becomes a nation of the homeless.

ANDREA ZANZOTTO

Provided human society does not lose its memory in the meantime, the last decades of the twentieth century will one day be remembered as among the most critical in history—a time when humanity as a whole was violently projected into a new, utterly divergent, millennium. The scale of the transformations we are witnessing today has no precedent either in natural or cultural history. The global uprooting of both nature and humanity makes each and every one of us a refugee of sorts. How long we will remain refugees on the earth no one can say, but the fact of homelessness has by now become obvious even to most privileged or protected members of the human family.

What is not at all obvious to us, on the other hand, are the potential saving forces that may one day rise up against the tide of nihilism. It may well be that, in the future, these decades will be remembered above all for the improbable existence of a handful of poets who brought the old household gods into hiding. From our present perspective nothing seems more superfluous to the contemporary turbulence of history than poets, yet our present perspective may turn out to be the most superfluous thing of all. In other words, it may turn out that one of the redeeming facts of our time is that a poet like A. R. Ammons existed, that his voice spoke from beyond the edge of present-day nihilism, and that his poems gave asylum to the mysterious genetic link that binds human historicity to nature. This much is certain: at a time when the gods have no choice but to flee from the falling city of man, it is only the poets who can take them into their safekeeping.

It is possible and even likely, then, that our time will be remembered not only for its ecstatic destruction of all that was culturally and historically authentic, but also for the saving efforts of its few—very few—vigilant poets. Among these very few is an Italian poet whose initials circumscribe our alphabet—Andrea Zanzotto. His name was invoked in the preface to this book, and now, at the end of the history we have been tracing, the time has come to invoke it again. Andrea Zanzotto.

Zanzotto has an unremarkable biography. He was born in 1921 north of Treviso, in a small town called Pieve di Soligo, at the foot of the pre-Alpine mountains of Veneto region. Somewhat like John Clare, he has rarely journeyed beyond his native horizon. He does not trust the "many promises" of journeys. He remarks, and rightly so, that a true journey is realized only rarely, and by very few people at that. Thus Zanzotto "stays in the provinces," to use Heidegger's phrase, working as a school teacher in the town of his birth. He has written poems in his provincial dialect, yet most of his poetic corpus is in Italian. He has achieved considerable recognition both in Italy and the United States (a selection of his poetry was translated into English in 1975; scholarly books, dissertations, and articles have followed), but it will probably take another decade or two before his achievement is fully acknowledged.

The Italian critic Gianfranco Contini once said of him that he hides away in his hometown as in a catacomb. Zanzotto concedes the truth of the analogy. He lives in hiding deliberately. As he understands it, his provincial isolation gives him a margin of detachment from the metropolitan centers of history, from which margins he can look "behind the appearances" of history to the occult forces that motivate, shape, or deform it. Furthermore, such isolation protects him from the "negative radioactivity" that emanates from those centers. Zanzotto finds Contini's analogy of living in the catacombs particularly apt, for, as he observes, catacombs are not only places of refuge for the persecuted, they are also places where new religions are born. And perhaps nothing is more needed at this juncture in history than the advent of a new religion, however ancient its origins may be.

It is not the poet's task, nor is it within his power, to give birth to a new religion. At most he may keep open the space or possibility for some new revelation. How this might come about—why, when, where, above all *whether*—remains imponderable, but there is little doubt that, in the present age, it could happen only in some catacombal space.

To descend into the catacombs means, for Zanzotto, to look behind the appearances of both nature and history to the genetic source of both. Since it is a source that disappears behind the appearances—Zanzotto in fact calls it the *ricchissimo nihil,* the rich no-thing—it requires a particular kind of vision of appearances to see behind the appearances. In other words, we never get "beyond" appearances in some Platonic sense. Nature and history, in their enigmatic bond, appear to Zanzotto above all in the surrounding landscape of Pieve di Soligo. He hides away in his hometown because it is only on the basis of his genetic affiliations with his native landscape that he can begin to probe the mysteries that lie *Dietro il paesaggio,* or "Behind the Landscape," as the title of his first collection of poems has it.

By staying in his hometown the poet also chooses to remain enmeshed in the diverse and heterogenous fabric of language. His own local dialect is a distinct idiom within a regional dialect that varies perceptibly from town to town in the Veneto. Alongside this spoken dialect is the national Italian language, to which Zanzotto has a different relationship altogether. French and German are also a palpable presence in his northern province. Still another dimension of the linguistic heritage is the ritualized Latin of the mass. And in recent years Pieve di Soligo has been subjected to the invasive pressures of English, which has barbarously insinuated itself even into the remotest provinces ("snack bar," "supermarket," "blue jeans"—such words even find their way into some of the poems). For Zanzotto this linguistic diversity or proliferation of codes leads to the ancient but still bewildering question about the bonds—arbitrary or natural—that link language to reality. What does a word really say? What is its origination? What of the thing it names? In short, how are language and the realities it refers to given in the first place? A question, ultimately, about the *logos.*

The landscape around Pieve di Soligo raises questions similar to those posed by the diversity of linguistic codes. The traditional interlacing of nature and culture in the landscape—a rich, historicized texture that is vanishing before Zanzotto's eyes at the hands of those destructive millenial forces alluded to above—this interlacing points to the enigmatic, underlying relation between the two. If nature and culture arise from a common origin, what is it? What is it behind the landscape which generates both the forms of nature and the forms of culture? Will this generating source also be destroyed along with what it has slowly generated over the centuries? Another question about the *logos*.

The reason we are turning to Zanzotto at the end of the history we have been tracing in this book is because, in his poetry as a whole, the most pervasive and privileged emblem for the originating source of both nature and culture is the forest. More precisely, it is those remnants of the *selva antica,* or ancient forest, of the Montello mountain near Pieve de Soligo where, in 1918, the Italians won a decisive victory over the Austro-Hungarians. Strewn about the Montello mountain, amid the old and new growth forests, are ossuaries of the Great War. This already makes of the forest a place of intersection between history and nature. In the *selva antica* Zanzotto seeks and finds vestiges of nature's capacity for untold diversity and speciation, that is to say he finds countless *signs* that point to the creative source of all that is in being. Yet at the heart of this abundance he also finds traces of destruction, suggesting that destruction too derives its motivation from the same source. In such a manner, then, the forest appears in Zanzotto's poetry as the quintessential phenomenon originating from the origin of both nature and culture, so much so that we could say that Zanzotto figures as the poet of the forest's genesis. His forest, in turn, figures as a synecdoche for the totality of what comes into, and goes out of, being.

The originating source itself remains unspeakable, for it already claims human language in advance. It lies behind the landscape, to be sure, yet not like a face that hides behind a mask. It is nothing other than the landscape in its unaccountable presence. As it withdraws behind the appearances, it leaves in its place a landscape, that is to say a forest of phenomena to which language and history intrinsically belong.

It is this forest, wholly circumscribed by natural as well as cultural history, that the present age is ravaging. The reasons for such devastation remain obscure, yet, as suggested above, they would seem to share with the creative forces a common origin. One way or another the quest for this origin—its questionability, so to speak—leads Zanzotto back to the facticity of the *logos,* which we have defined in terms

of humanity's irreducible relation to nature. It is this relation, ultimately, that gives the world. Within its abyss—and it is an abyss, insofar as the relation is groundless—the world first comes to appearance. Without *logos* there is neither nature nor history, which amounts
to saying that there is no "landscape" (which always implies the two).
In other words, it is the relation between nature and history which
accords to each its specific dimension of being. Nature without history
has no being. Whatever scientists may tell us about the galactic antiquity of the universe, nature has no being—it *is* not—outside of the
sphere of the *logos*. The latter is what allows the origin to originate in
the first place. This, and this above all, is the irreducible fact for which
history must now assume full responsibility, yet it is precisely in this
respect that our present irresponsibility remains extreme.

A poet like Zanzotto assumes such responsibility in the most radical way possible, namely by probing the genetic secret of the *logos* in
the poetic word, not in order to master or decode it—that, in any case,
would be impossible—but rather to keep open the dimension of its
unfathomability. His poetry takes the *logos* into its custody, as it were;
it speaks from out of the relation's groundless facticity; or better, it is
spoken by that which makes speech possible in the first place. Such
poetry is difficult to read, to be sure, precisely because it is catacombal—forestial.

It is not our intention to engage in a critical analysis of the poetry
itself, an endeavor whose results could only be dubious at this moment
in time. We have not yet learned how to engage in critical analysis
without drowning the silence of such poetry in the language of reflection. Perhaps in the future we will find a way to go beyond the language of reflection. In such a future the fact that there was once an
Andrea Zanzotto may turn out to be one of the more significant historical events of our time, for we cannot know in advance what will
one day come out of the catacombs of poetry—a new god, a new ecology, a new *selva antica*. Meanwhile let us listen to one of Zanzotto's
early poems, from the collection *Dietro il paessagio:*

GATHERING

The appearance of the wild
soldiers still lingers
on the doors, and evening
hoists hostile banners over fortresses,
summoning piazzas to the assembly.

A burnt star destroyed this earth
deep in wells and lairs
the shadow of summer hurls itself
from alleyways and terraces
and broken theaters.

In the design of pavements
in the cracks of barracks
in the seclusion of gymnasiums
a disease is glowing,
the glass seed of the frost degenerates,
wine and gold decay on the tables.

But, mean glory of the world,
misshapen memories of other seasons,
the forest remains.

THE ECOLOGY OF FINITUDE

WE BEGAN THIS BOOK WITH AN EPIGRAPH FROM VICO'S
New Science: "This was the order of human institutions: first the forests, after that the huts, then the villages, next the cities, and finally
the academies." Each stage of the order represents a manner of dwelling. The order gets underway when the giants take up residence in the
clearing; establish an abode for their estrangement; appropriate the
ground of the fallen acorns through the law of gathering, or the *lex*.
The inaugural wonder of the giants—their dread beneath the sky—
binds them to the earth to which they consign their dead. Burial of the
dead domesticates the place of dwelling as *logos* makes an *oikos* of the
openness, terror, and inscrutability of finitude.

As the order of institutions follows its course, or as huts give way
to villages and then to cities and finally to cosmopolitan academies,
the forests move further and further away from the center of the clearings. At the center one eventually forgets that one is dwelling in a
clearing. The center becomes utopic. The wider the circle of the clearing, the more the center is nowhere and the more the *logos* becomes
reflective, abstract, universalistic, in essence ironic. Yet however wide
the circle may get through the inertia of civic expansion, it presumably
retains an edge of opacity where history meets the earth, where the
human abode reaches its limits, and where the *logos* preserves its native

grounding. This edge is generally called a province. Only the province assures the containment of the center.

When one ceases to dwell in a province, or when the province gets overtaken by the center, one finds oneself within the dispersed utopia of cities and academies. The provincial dweller knows that if you pull a rock from out of the ground and turn it upside down, you are likely to find on its underside a covert world of soil, roots, worms, and insects. A nonprovincial dweller either never suspects or else tends to forget such a thing, for the stones that make up his city have already been abstracted from the ground, wiped clean, and made to order. A province, in other words, is a place where stones have two sides.

The most one-sided stones of all are perhaps those that make up the walls of the academy. The moment thinking takes refuge within these walls and leaves the provinces of the mind, the nation, or the empire, it can no longer remain radical. At most it can become a form of "metaphysics" that searches for cosmic foundations within the clearings of Enlightenment. The most fundamental kind of thinking is invariably provincial, in one form or another. Hence the famous anecdote about Heraclitus, reported by Aristotle: "The story is told of something Heraclitus said to some strangers who wanted to come visit him. Having arrived, they saw him warming himself at a stove. Surprised, they stood there in consternation—above all because he encouraged them, the astounded ones, and called for them to come in with the words, 'For here too the gods are present' " (*De parte animalium* I. 5.645a.17). The visitors never imagined that the philosopher from Ephesus would be a provincial, even less that the gods of destiny could be present in an ordinary household. After all, the home of the gods is in the celestial spheres, or at the very least on lofty mountain peaks. Yet Heraclitus reminds his visitors that the gods are present wherever human estrangement has made an abode for itself on the earth.

The anecdote, however, is not clear about exactly why these visitors were astounded by the sight of Heraclitus warming himself by a domestic stove. Perhaps they were provincials who had traveled to Ephesus to behold the marvels of the metropolis, among them a famous philosopher. Provincials are so easily astounded—which is why they are often so quick to abandon the provinces—but nothing could astound them quite as much as the sight of the thinker communing with gods familiar to them from their own hearths.

We ourselves have already lost the capacity to be astounded by such an anecdote, for we hardly have any conception of what a province is anymore. As one of the traditional definitions of God puts it, the center is now everywhere and the circumference nowhere. (The god thus defined was not a domestic but a civic god, without doubt.) This gradual loss of an edge of opacity, where the human abode finds its limits on the earth, is part of the global story of civic expansionism. In the West its first and last victim has been the forest. As we have tried to suggest in so many versions throughout this study, forests mark the provincial edge of Western civilization, in the literal as well as imaginative domains. Although they were brought early on within the jurisdiction of public institutions (royal preserves, forest management, ecology, and so forth), they have nevertheless retained to this day their ancient associations in the cultural imagination. Their antecedence and outsideness with regard to the institutional order has not really changed in our minds. What has changed recently is our anxiety about the loss of an edge of exteriority.

The global problem of deforestation provokes unlikely reactions of concern these days among city dwellers, not only because of the enormity of the scale but also because in the depths of cultural memory forests remain the correlate of human transcendence. We call it the loss of nature, or the loss of wildlife habitat, or the loss of biodiversity, but underlying the ecological concern is perhaps a much deeper apprehension about the disappearance of boundaries, without which the human abode loses its grounding. Somewhere we still sense—who knows for how much longer?—that we make ourselves at home only in our estrangement, or in the *logos* of the finite. In the cultural memory of the West forests "correspond" to the exteriority of the *logos*. The outlaws, the heroes, the wanderers, the lovers, the saints, the persecuted, the outcasts, the bewildered, the ecstatic—these are among those who have sought out the forest's asylum in the history we have followed throughout this book. Without such outside domains, there is no inside in which to dwell.

Those who stay at home, who dwell strictly within the cleared space of the institutional order, are left homeless without the containment of the province. More essentially, they are left homeless the moment they are left without a provincial envoy who departs from the homeland and returns from afar with the message of estrangement. Such an envoy is not someone who leaves the province for the capitals of the world, returning with reports about the wonders of the metropolis, but rather the poet who departs in the opposite direction—beyond the bounds of the province and into the forest's underworld. This underworld is the earth in its enigmatic fatality.

Georg Trakl, an Austrian poet who died in the year 1914, speaks of a soul that is called to "go under," or to follow its natural estrangement on the earth. When it responds to the call, this soul goes into the forest. In the poem "On the Mönchberg," the wandering soul hears a voice as it crosses over a bridge:

> Where the crumbling pathway descends into the shadow of
> autumn elms,
> Far from the leafy huts, the sleeping shepherds,
> The dark shape that came from the coolness still follows the
> wanderer
>
> Over the footbridge of bone, and the boy's hyacinth voice
> Softly reciting the forest's forgotten legend,
> And more gently, a sick thing now, the brother's wild
> lament.
>
> Thus a little green touches the knee of the stranger,
> And his head that turned to stone;
> Nearer, the blue spring murmurs the women's lament.
> (Trakl, 57)

The boy with the hyacinth voice is one who has "died early." In his early death he retains an ancient memory of the forest legend. At the moment when the wanderer crosses the "footbridge of bone," the legend is heard again in the boy's voice, rising from the realm of the dead. This legend has countless versions in the Western imagination (we have traced only some of them in this book). It is by now forgotten, for in the "leafy huts" the shepherds are asleep. We dwell in an oblivion that only poets can rouse us from, when every now and then they hear the boy's hyacinth voice again. But as the forests disappear, so does the legend in the antiquities of memory. And then what is left for poets to hear?

The Irish poet Desmond O'Grady has recently declared, "I am not dead yet." Paradoxically, this would imply that death is still "alive," however improbably, and that every now and then the ecology of finitude still comes forth in the poet's word. In the Northeast, to be sure, A. R. Ammons still walks in the woods a mile from any neighbor. At the foothills of the Alps the Italian provincial Andrea Zanzotto knows where there are remnants of the *selva antica*, or ancient forest, of the

Montello mountain, reminding us in his *Galateo in bosco,* or "Manner Book of the Woods," that we exist in the mode of exclusion from that which has either disappeared or is disappearing before our very eyes. Every now and then the poet's word still brings *logos* to language, yet we lose the ability to reappropriate it. Why? Perhaps because such language does not "communicate" anything. It merely recalls the fact that the *logos* binds our dwelling to our death; that language is predicated upon our capacity to die; that every authentic act of predication is not a statement of the order "S is P," but an avowal that our finitude *is* the *logos* that binds S and P together. As human beings who dwell above all in estrangement, we do not merely "speak meaning" to the world but "speak our death" to the world.

Precisely because finitude is given over to us in language, we lose the instinctive knowledge of dying. Nature knows how to die, but human beings know mostly how to kill as a way of failing to become their ecology. Because we alone inhabit the *logos,* we alone must learn the lesson of dying time and time again. Yet we alone fail in the learning. And in the final analysis only this much seems certain: that when we do not speak our death to the world we speak death to the world. And when we speak death to the world, the forest's legend falls silent.

FOR EACH SECTION OF EVERY CHAPTER THERE IS A SEPARATE BIBLIO-
graphical entry. To keep the bibliography to a strict minimum I have included
here only those secondary works that were directly relevant, useful or inspiring to me during the course of my research. Some of my interpretations in
this book may have been proposed by other critics before, but unless otherwise indicated I arrived at them on my own.

1. FIRST THE FORESTS

George Marsh's nineteenth-century classic *Man and Nature* contains one
of the most eloquent and comprehensive reports I know about forests and the
prehistoric landscape of the West from ecological and geographical perspectives (see 128–329). Lewis Mumford rightly called this book "the fountain-
head of the conservation movement" (Caufield, 52). Other empirical accounts
that were useful to me include Karl W. Butzer's *Environment and Archaeology
from an Ecological Perspective* (62–78); William Russell's *Man, Nature and History*
(35–46); and David Attenborough's *The First Eden: The Mediterranean World
and Man* (1–60).

The Virgil passage comes from Fitzgerald's translation of the *Aeneid*.
Verse numbers refer to this edition.

Vico's Giants. For those who may want to read Vico's *New Science* for the
first time I offer the following suggestion: to read it backward, beginning with
the conclusion. I am convinced that Vico has remained relatively unappre-
ciated until recently because of the obscure and largely illegible introduction
to his *New Science,* entitled the "Idea of the Work." The title is misleading, for
this introduction is comprehensible only to those who already have a good
idea of what the *New Science* is all about. It is such a bewildering starting point
that many curious readers never get beyond it, even readers who would have
had much to gain from the *New Science:* Montesquieu, for example, or
Goethe, Herder, Hamann, and so many others (even Rousseau perhaps) who

may have actually tried to read the work but many of whom probably got lost in the baroque shadows of its introduction.

An indispensable companion book to the *New Science,* in my opinion, is Fustel de Coulanges's *The Ancient City.* Apart from its own autonomous value, this French masterpiece reconstructs the domestic religions of antiquity, knowledge of which Vico all too often takes for granted in his reader. (Fustel de Coulanges is discussed in relation to Vico in the second section of chapter 4 of this study.)

For English readers unfamiliar with Vico, valuable introductions to his life and thought include Peter Burke's *Vico;* Bergin and Fisch's introduction to their translation of Vico's *Autobiography* (1–107); Benedetto Croce's now classic *The Philosophy of Giambattista Vico;* and the two collections edited by Giorgio Tagliacozzo: *Giambattista Vico's Science of Humanity* and *Vico and Contemporary Thought.*

The critic who most rigorously comes to terms with Vico's genetic psychology is, in my opinion, Donald Verene (*Vico's Science of Imagination*). In this regard I have also learned from Giuseppe Mazzotta's essay on Vico's creative philology, "Vico's Encyclopedia." Hayden White offers a fine analysis of the "tropological" nature of Poetic Wisdom in his essay "The Tropics of History: The Deep Structure of the *New Science*" in *Tropics of Discourse* (197–217).

Finally, the suggestion that forests lie at the origin of the concept of the circle and wheel comes from Roland Bechmann's *Des arbres et des hommes,* where we read: "For the wheel no doubt came out of the forest: it is the tree which, growing in concentric rings, introduced into nature the circular form that man later so greatly exploited once he had discovered the properties of the circle's center and combined the axle with the wheel" (258; my translation).

The Demon of Gilgamesh. Kramer's translation of the Sumerian "Gilgamesh and the Land of the Living" is included in Pritchard's *Ancient Near Eastern Texts Relating to the Old Testament* (47–50). Italicized words occur in the original.

My discussion of the historical background of the epic is indebted to my conversations with Maureen Gallery Kovacs, who has recently published a new translation of the Akkadian version of the Gilgamesh cycle. Her edition contains a valuable introduction and "Chronology of the Gilgamesh Epic." Kramer's *The Sumerians: Their History, Culture and Character* is a classic study on the history of Sumerian civilization. More recently see also Kramer's *History Begins at Sumer.*

For the historical as well as literary background of Gilgamesh's forest journey as such, I have consulted Aaron Shaffer's essay "Gilgamesh, The Cedar Forest and Mesopotamian History," which focuses mostly on the motif of sororate marriages in the Old Babylonian period (Gilgamesh tricks Huwawa by offering the demon his sister in marriage), but which also points to the provocative parallels between the Gilgamesh story and the *Rex nemorensis* myth that inspired Frazer's *The Golden Bough.* These parallels have to do with a sacred grove, its paranoid guardian, and the plucking of the bough. Shaffer also informs us that "[t]he cedar forest motif is retained in Mesopotamian historical literature in the form of the ritual claim of kings, from the old Akkadian period on, to have gone to the cedar mountain and to have cut cedars there" (307n). He also relates the motif to Isaiah 37:24, where Sennacherib boasts of cutting the cedars (ibid.).

William Irwin Thompson offers a critique of the governing ideology of the Gilgamesh epic in his *The Time Falling Bodies Take to Light,* where he remarks, among other things, that this epic remains "the very foundation of Western literature, for what we are witnessing here is to set the pattern for all Hebrew and Greek literature to come" (198). Whether or not the epic had any direct influence on the Homeric epics (an ongoing debate among scholars), the remark still holds true.

On the question of civilization and the denial of death, one of the undeniably good books is Ernest Becker's *The Denial of Death.*

The Virgin Goddess. Four books above all, one more remarkable than the other, have been useful to me in my discussion of the great Mother goddess. Rachel Levy's *The Gate of Horn* is a classic that traces the universal symbols of the goddess (the bull's horns, for example) throughout various ancient cultures. The opening chapters of Vincent Scully's *The Earth, the Temple and the Gods* are eloquent and informative on the subject of the goddess's prehistory in Greece. William Irwin Thompson's *The Time Falling Bodies Take to Light* tells the story of the patriarchal revolutions that not only dispossessed the goddess of her ancient supremacy but also sought to appropriate her traditional powers and functions in new religious contexts. Monica Sjöö and Barbara Mor's *The Great Cosmic Mother* is a remarkable work of historical, cultural, and symbolic analysis—perhaps the most complete and inspiring work on this topic. My remarks about Gilgamesh's slaying of Inanna's bull are in some ways derivative of their interpretation of the Sumerian hero (see 246).

On the topic of labyrinths, forests, and the space of the sacred, I have been inspired by Angus Fletcher's discussion in *The Prophetic Moment* (14–34), and by Penelope Doob's *The Idea of the Labyrinth* (especially 11–16, 78–79).

For the history of Artemis in Greek historical times I have relied mostly on Walter Burkert's *Greek Religion* (149–52). Burkert tends to reject the idea of a universal Mother goddess in Greek prehistory, but the evidence of Artemis's prehistory as an earth goddess seems undeniable. On the history of the Ephesian Artemis I have relied also on Herbert Muller's *The Loom of History* (139–73). It is in that work that Artemis's connection with Mary was first brought to my attention. For a report on the recent findings with regard to the famous Ephesian statue of Artemis, see Attenborough (105–7).

The English translation of the Anaximander fragment comes from the English edition of Heidegger's *Early Greek Thinking* (13), which contains a ponderous commentary by Heidegger on the fragment.

In his Freiburg lecture course of 1940, Heidegger analyzed with great depth and clarity the passage I discuss from book 2 of Aristotle's *Physics.* Heidegger's commentary, which was very useful to me, appears in English as "On the Being and Conception of *physis* in Aristotle's Physics B, 1."

For the linguistic origins of the Greek word *hyle* I relied on Liddell & Scott, *A Greek-English Lexicon;* the word's archaic link to the Latin *silva* is suggested by Lewis & Short, *A Latin Dictionary.* For the etymological root of the words *materia* and *mater*, see the entry for "mater" in *The American Heritage Dictionary of Indo-European Roots*, edited by Watkins (39).

Finally, the verses of Dylan Thomas cited in this section come from his poem "The force that through the green fuse drives the flower" in *Dylan Thomas: Collected Poems* (10).

Dionysos. My notion of a covert but essential kinship between Dionysos and Artemis was originally no more than an intuition, hence I was glad to find in Burkert's *Greek Religion* substantial evidence of cultic connections between the two deities. As for my notion of Dionysos as the god of dissolution and originary indeterminateness, it derives essentially from Nietzsche. The Nietzschean conception is expanded in significant ways by Marcel Detienne's *Dionysos à ciel ouvert*, which furthers Walter Otto's insight that Dionysos is by nature the god who arrives from afar. Detienne emphasizes the motif of Dionysos as a stranger—"étranger de l'intérieure," as he puts it—and as the god of multiplicity and equivocity. Related studies that were also useful for me include Maria Daraki's *Dionysos;* and Mihai Spariosu's *Dionysos Reborn.*

Martha Nussbaum includes a fine discussion of Dionysos's role in *The Bacchae* in her "Introduction" to C. K. Williams's new English version, *The Bacchae of Euripides* (from which I cite). Nussbaum's remarks about the god's affinity with the animal world are especially relevant to my theme (xvi–xx). On the subject of Dionysos's relation to animals see also Walter Otto's *Dionysus* (110, 134, 166, 176, 193).

On the general topic of Dionysos as the god of tragedy I appeal for the most part to Nietzsche's thesis in *The Birth of Tragedy.* For more recent investigations I have found interesting, Oddone Longo's "The Theater of the *Polis*" (12–19), and John J. Winkler's "The Ephebes' Song: *Tragoidia* and *Polis*" (20–62), both included in the collection *Nothing To Do With Dionysos?* (see Winkler). My interpretation of the role of Socrates in the evolution of Greek culture is essentially Nietzschean, although my interpretation of Plato's *Symposium* is autonomous.

In the background of part of my discussion of Nietzsche's *Zarathustra* is Heidegger's *What is Called Thinking?* (especially 88–110). For perspectives different from my own on Zarathustra's relation to his animals, see Heidegger's *Nietzsche* (2:45–48) and David L. Miller's essay "Nietzsche's Horse and Other Tracings of the Gods" in *Nietzsche in Italy* (159–70). Heidegger discusses Nietzsche's "On the Vision and the Riddle" in *Nietzsche* (2:37–44), but from a perspective that is only indirectly related to my own.

The English translation of the Hymn to Dionysos comes from Apostolos N. Athanassakis's *The Homeric Hymns* (65).

The Sorrows of Rhea Silvia. My reflections on the founding myths of Rome are much inspired by Michel Serres's *Rome: Le livre des fondations*, which provides an extended literary, cultural, and philosophical meditation on book I of Livy's *History of Rome.*

I have also consulted Jacques Poucet's scholarly discussion of the relation between history and legend in the founding myths of Rome (*Les origines de Rome*, 35–70). Poucet also traces the history and background of the Evander story (128–35). For background to both the Silvius and Romulus stories I have consulted Ettore Pais's *Storia di Roma* (219–24, 299–320).

On the myth of Arcadia in Roman literature I have been instructed above all by Bruno Snell's chapter in his book *The Discovery of the Mind* (281–309), which opens with the famous sentence: "Arcadia was discovered in the year 42 or 41 B.C.," and also by Charles Segal's *Poetry and Myth in Ancient Pastoral* and David Halperin's *Before Pastoral*. Translations from book 6 of the *Aeneid* come from the Mandelbaum translation. Verse numbers refer to this edition.

My remarks about the *res nullius* and the *nemus/nemo* connection derive from Bechmann (*Des arbres*, 25–26).

For a fine discussion of the Stygian forest that surrounds the entrance of the underworld, see Penelope Doob's *The Idea of the Labyrinth* (238–40).

Finally, my somewhat cryptic allusions to the afterlife of Rome in the modern era are corroborated from another perspective by William Appleman Williams in his *Empire as a Way of Life*.

From Mythic Origins to Deforestation. On the topic of the deforestation of the Mediterranean in antiquity I have relied above all on J. V. Thirgood's *Man and the Mediterranean Forest* (19–45); Attenborough's *The First Eden* (116–19); and Bruce Brown and Lane Morgan's *The Miracle Planet* (220–24). The latter book reports the results of the recent scientific analyses of the ancient pollen samples around the city of Ephesus (222).

2. SHADOWS OF LAW

One of the best accounts I know about forests in the medieval Christian imagination is Jacques Le Goff's essay "Le désert-forêt dans L'Occident médiéval" in *L'imaginare médiéval* (59–75). It compares and contrasts the deserts of Judaism and forests of Christianity as parallel spaces of transcendence; it also contains a fine analysis of how the forest figures as a wild but benevolent asylum for the lovers Tristan and Isolde in Béroul's *Tristan* (70–72). A less inspired treatment of the theme is Paolo Golinelli's essay "Tra realtà e metafora: il bosco nell'immaginario letterario medievale" in *Il bosco nel medioevo* (see Andreolli in *Works Cited*). I have learned a great deal from Richard Bernheimer's *Wild Men of the Middle Ages*, a valuable study when it comes to the forest's relation to the civic space during the medieval period (especially 1–48). On the forest as a place of errancy in medieval romance, see Doob's *The Idea of the Labyrinth* (177–81).

For an empirical account of forests in medieval Europe, I should mention the following studies: *Il bosco nel medioevo* (dealing mostly with Italy, but more in general see 15–34, 83–96); Bechmann's *Des arbes* (especially 99–136); and Charles Higounet's "Les forêts de l'Europe occidentale du V au XI siècle" (343–98).

On the topic of the forest's moral allegorization in Christianity, consider, for example, the following utterance by Saint Augustine in reference to his life of sin and perdition prior to his conversion to Christianity: "In this enormous forest [*immensa silva*] so full of snares and dangers, many are the temptations which I have cut off and thrust away from my heart" (*Confessions* 10. 35 [246]).

On the theological association of forests with prime matter (Chalcidius translated the Greek *hyle* as *silva*), see Eugenio Garin's *Studi sul platonismo medievale* (58–62). Finally, Jules Michelet's *La sorcière* has been a source of inspiration for my reflections on the Christian ideological revolution with regard to forests and nature in general.

My concept of comedy is influenced in part by Giorgio Agamben's study "Comedìa: la svolta comica di Dante e la concezione della colpa." I have also written on this topic elsewhere (see R. Harrison, "Comedy and Modernity: Dante's Hell").

The Knight's Adventure. On the topic of wild men and knights I have learned the most from Bernheimer's *Wild Men of the Middle Ages.* I have also consulted Penelope Doob's chapter on "The Unholy and Holy Wild Man" in *Nebuchadnezzar's Children* (134–207).

The coauthored essay by Jacques Le Goff and Vidal Nacquet, "Lévi-Strauss en Brocéliande" (in Le Goff, *L'imaginare,* 151–87), offers a detailed analysis of the scene in Chrétien de Troyes's *Yvain* in which the knight loses his mind. On the basis of this scene, the authors paint a fascinating picture of the medieval rural landscape, delineating with documentary precision the topographical relation between court, rural surroundings, and wilderness. Seth Lerer's elegant essay "Artifice and Artistry in *Sir Orfeo,*" which deals with similar questions about the relation between court and wilderness, king and wild man, nature and artistry, in the Middle English poem *Sir Orfeo,* was also helpful for my meditation in this section.

Forest Law. On the origins and history of the word *foresta* I have relied on Lewis & Short, *A Latin Dictionary;* Bechmann's *Des arbres* (25–26); and Le Goff's discussion in "Le dèsert-forêt" (65–66).

A classic study of the royal forests of England is J. C. Cox's *The Royal Forests of England.* E. P. Thompson's *Whigs and Hunters* contains a fine report on the history of forest laws in England (27–113). I have also consulted the first chapter of Cyril Hart's *Royal Forest,* which contains a brief summary of the early history of the Forest Law in England (1–20).

There is very little secondary literature dealing with John Manwood's *Treatise of the Laws of the Forest,* but Richard Marienstras discusses it in terms related to my own in his remarkable book on Shakespeare, *Le proche et le lointain* (30–63). Marienstras analyzes the treatise in order to relate it to his readings of moral savagery in Shakespeare's plays. He makes insightful remarks about the parallels between Manwood's concept of the forest as sanctuary for wildlife and the sanctuary offered by the Church to outlaws or fugitives who enter its precincts (see especially 36–44). About Manwood's treatise in its historical context, Marienstras remarks: "In the Middle Ages the struggle of the barons against the king had as its goal to restrain the royal privileges, deemed exorbitant. One had to protect men against the royal forest. Here [in Manwood] the proposition is the opposite: one must protect the forest against men, so that it might endure and continue to serve as a refuge for animals" (35; my translation).

Outlaws. One of the most helpful secondary sources during my research for this section was Maurice Keen's *Outlaws of Medieval Legend.* On the Norman invasion of England I have consulted David C. Douglas's *William the Conqueror.*

I am grateful to Seth Lerer for valuable comments on an earlier draft of this section. In reference to *The Peterborough Chronicle,* which contains the poem with the line about William loving the stags "as much as if he were their father," Lerer sent me the following written communication:

> What is fascinating to me about these entries in the *Chronicle* is the way in which the *Anglo-Saxon* chronicler (writing in late Old English) emphasizes the alien, Continental aspects of William's reign. The first line of the poem in the *Chronicle* is "Castelas he let wyrcean": he had castles built. The Anglo-Saxons did not build monumentally in stone (they built in timber or flint). Castles, both linguistically and architecturally, are foreign to the English, and by beginning the poem with this statement, the poet makes clear the immediate impress of Norman life on English soil. The point that needs stressing is that this Chronicle is the work of an English community, in essence, under invasion: it is the sole surviving prose record *in English* after 1080 (the Chronicle goes to 1154; there is no continuous prose historical document originally written in English until the late 13th century). It therefore constitutes a critique, as well as a record, of William's actions, and its remarks on the forest, on hunting, and on building projects constitute a kind of cultural obituary for the Anglo-Saxon landscape in the guise of a formal obituary for the Conqueror. With these contexts in mind, I think that the poem's line about William loving the stags as if he were their father takes on an ironic and critical resonance. The line about him loving the stags like a father implies of course that he *did not* love his people like a father.

Dante's Line of Error. Translations from Dante's *Divine Comedy* are my own. Secondary sources that were directly useful to my reading of Dante include John Freccero's essay "The Prologue Scene" (1–28), which juxtaposes the forest in *Inferno* 1 with the earthly paradise in *Purgatorio;* his essay "The Firm Foot on a Journey Without a Guide" (29–54), which contains relevant observations about the "error" of Dante's presumption to pursue the path of intellectual transcendence without bringing the will into alignment with the intellect; and Giuseppe Mazzotta's *Dante: Poet of the Desert,* which to my mind offers one of the best discussions of the poetic theology I find operative in the forest and desert allegories of the *Comedy* (especially 227–74).

Shadows of Love. The novella of Boccaccio which I discuss in this section has not generated any secondary literature that was particularly useful to me, but my understanding of Boccaccio in general has been influenced by Giuseppe Mazzotta, whose seminars on the *Decameron* at Cornell (1981) and whose book *The World at Play in Boccaccio's "Decameron"* have helped to persuade me that Boccaccio is by far the most interesting author of the Italian literary canon.

The Human Age. Translations from Ariosto's *Orlando* are my own. On the rise of Italian humanism I have learned the most from Eugenio Garin's *Umanesimo italiano;* and *Ritratti di umanisti.* In the background of my discussion of humanism in general lies Heidegger's "Letter on Humanism" and his discussion of the motto "Man is the measure of all things" in his *Nietzsche* (4:85–101).

On the changing natural landscape around this time I have consulted Lewis Mumford's *The City in History* and Keith Thomas's *Man and the Natural World,* the latter of which deals primarily with England. My discussion of the Venetian Republic's contribution to the deforestation of the Mediterranean during the fifteenth and sixteenth centuries relies mostly on the information provided by J. V. Thirgood in *Man and the Mediterranean Forest* (46–54) and Attenborough in *The First Eden* (166–73). I have also consulted Peter Pierson's *Philip II of Spain* for instruction on parallel developments in Spain.

Mazzotta's essay on Petrarch's *canzone* "Chiare, fresche e dolci acque" ("Petrarch's Song 126") was helpful for my discussion of the poem in this section. I have analyzed Petrarch's *canzone* in another context and from another perspective in *The Body of Beatrice* (102–5).

As for secondary sources to Ariosto, I have learned from Albert Ascoli's book *Aristo's Bitter Harmony* (on Orlando's madness, see 304–31); and Robert Durling's *The Figure of the Poet in Renaissance Epic.* Durling's seminar on Ariosto at Cornell in 1981 has no doubt inspired some of my remarks in this section.

Macbeth's Conclusion. On the changing landscape of England at this time and the degradation of the English forests, see Keith Thomas's *Man and the Natural World.* I am grateful to Seth Lerer for his suggestions about how I might push my reading of *Macbeth* further than I had in an earlier draft of this conclusion.

3. ENLIGHTENMENT

The Ways of Method. In general, although not in particular, my approach to Descartes in this section is influenced by Heidegger, especially the fourth volume of his *Nietzsche,* which contains an extended analysis of Descartes's founding of modern metaphysics (4:96–149). I have also consulted Jean-Luc Nancy's *Ego Sum,* a book that adds to Heidegger's ontological reading a more literary reading of the *Discourse on Method.* For an interpretation different than my own of the "fable" aspect of Descartes's *Discourse,* see Nancy's discussion (97–127).

On the topic of algebraic geometry as the basis of Descartes's method for pursuing infallible scientific truth, I learned a great deal from Michel Serres's *Le système de Leibniz* (2:450–55).

In *Death of the Soul: From Descartes to the Computer* (3–10), William Barrett interprets the Copernican revolution in terms indirectly related to my own. My suggestion that the Copernican revolution was essentially a revolution in irony is beholden, however, to Pirandello, who speaks of Copernicus as the greatest "humorist" of the modern age. In his essay on "Umorismo," Pirandello remarks that after Copernicus the world can only be taken in jest.

Krautheimer's book on the transfiguration of Rome by Pope Alexander VII and its analogical relation to Descartes's forest scene in the *Discourse on Method* were brought to my attention by my friend Thomas Sheehan, whose reading of an earlier draft of this section was very helpful.

What Is Enlightenment? A Question for Foresters. My approach to Enlightenment has obvious affinities with the critical views put forth by Horkeimer and Adorno in their book *Dialectic of Enlightenment*. However, the affinities are even greater with Italo Calvino, whose novel *The Baron in the Trees* (set in the eighteenth century) contains a poetic critique of Enlightenment's humanist ideology. Calvino's Baron, named Cosimo, spends his life in the trees. He attains notoriety among the French *philosophes* (Voltaire, Diderot, etc.) for certain "politically correct" treatises that he writes on topics such as republican constitutions and social contracts. Cosimo writes one treatise, however, which for some reason was ignored by the intellectuals of the time. Given its title, it is no mystery why it did not attract any enlightened attention: *Constitutional Project for a Republican City with a Declaration of the Rights of Men, Women, Children, Domestic and Wild Animals, Including Birds, Fishes and Insects, and All Vegetation, whether Trees, Vegetables, or Grass.* Cosimo's brother, the narrator of *The Baron in the Trees*, remarks: "It was a very fine work, which could have been a useful guide to any government; but which no one took any notice of, and it remained a dead letter" (205).

Cosimo's treatise was ignored because the age was concerned solely with the declaration of the rights of man—the rights of human subjects, not nature's objects or species. Today we are witnessing the consequences of those one-sided declarations of the right of a single species to disregard the natural rights of every other species. In this sense Cosimo's treatise was ahead of its time—ahead of our own time, for that matter—but if one wants to get an idea of what it may have proposed in terms of a declaration of rights for objects as well as subjects, one might read the recent book by Michel Serres, *Le contrat naturel,* a manifesto for a "natural contract" beyond the mere "social contracts" of Enlightenment.

The English translations from Le Roy's entry in the *Encyclopèdie* are my own. Let me remark here, however, that Le Roy's idea that religion consecrated forests in the past in order to preserve them for the sake of the "public interest" is not original. Almost half a century earlier, the Italian naturalist Giovanni Maria Lancisi (1654–1720) had made the same suggestion: "These are the major reasons I adduce as clear proof of the utility forests have for us. So that such forests would not be cut or burned down, our ancestors consecrated them to some Deity, so that they would be protected by religion, where mere human laws were not sufficient to defend them" ("Taglio delle selve," 707; my translation).

On the rise of the natural sciences during the Age of Enlightenment I have learned from Ernst Cassirer's *The Philosophy of Enlightenment* (37–92) and Michel Foucault's *The Order of Things* (especially 128–32, 157–64). The latter book especially is a source of inspiration for anyone dealing with the Age of Reason. On the rise of forest management as a rigorous mathematical science I have relied mostly on the essay by Henry Lowood quoted in my discussion, but I have also consulted the chapter in Thomas Cox's *This Well-Wooded Land* which deals with the institution of policies of forest management in the United States at the turn of the century (191–214).

An excellent study on the history of forest management in France from the eighteenth to the twentieth centuries is Andrée Corvol's *L'homme aux bois.* Her argument is provocative to the extent that it claims that contemporary ecological activism as well as government policies seeking to protect forests from the peasants who have cultivated them for centuries represents nothing less than metropolitan ignorance with regard to the traditional practices and empirical realities of forest management. She argues persuasively that the peasantry is the natural caretaker of the forests.

The most lucid, informative, and thoughtful report I have read on the current debate about the spotted owl and the old-growth forests of the Pacific Northwest is Catherine Caufield's "The Ancient Forest."

Finally I am grateful to Henry Lowood not only for making his article available to me prior to its publication but also for the informative conversations we have had on this topic.

Rousseau. My analysis of Rousseau is essentially autonomous, but I should mention Jean Starobinski's discussion of the relation between poetic vision and history in *Jean-Jacques Rousseau: La transparence et l'obstacle* (25–26). The appendix of this book also contains a fine essay, somewhat related to my theme, entitled "Rousseau et la recherche des origines" (319–29). I also found in Arthur M. Melzer's *The Natural Goodness of Man: On the System of Rousseau's Thought* a lucid commentary on what he calls "the introspective and psychological arguments" of Rousseau (29–48). I have also consulted John Stephenson Spink's analysis of the lexical history and operative concept of the word "sentiment" in Rousseau's discourse (see "Rousseau et la morale du sentiment," 239–50). Finally I am grateful to Pierre Saint-Amand for bringing to my attention the passage from Rousseau's *Projet de constitution pour la Corse* which deals with the Corsican forests. Translations of passages from that treatise are my own.

Conrad's Brooding Gloom. In the background of my discussion of Conrad's relation to the twentieth century is Ian Watt's *Conrad in the Nineteenth Century.* Watt makes the point that Kurtz and his European compatriots in Africa lack the moral quality which the African natives possess, namely restraint (226–28). Dorothy Van Ghent, in her fine analysis of the tragic irony of Jim's fate, made me realize how dense and deliberate is the symbolism of Jim's hill overlooking the forests of Patusan (*The English Novel: Form and Function*, 236–39). On Conrad's impressionistic symbolism as a writer—his power to engage the reader actively in the psychological intrigue of character and circumstance—I have learned above all from Albert J. Guerard's *Conrad the Novelist* (in relation to *Lord Jim* see especially 125–34). Fredric Jameson interprets Conrad's technique of describing the modern city impressionistically, from a detached distance, as a way of repressing political consciousness with regard to the brutal historic realities of Western capitalism and colonialism. Jameson refers to a passage in *Lord Jim,* but for some reason he does not refer to the strikingly analogous description of London in the opening scene in *Heart of Darkness* (perhaps because there is nothing "unconscious" about Conrad's confrontation with those same realities in the earlier work; see Jameson, 210ff).

Wastelands. At various junctures in *What is Called Thinking?* Heidegger discusses Nietzsche's statement: "The wasteland grows. Woe to him who harbors wastelands within." Some of Heidegger's remarks call for citation here:

> It means, the devastation is growing wider. . . .Devastation is more unearthly than destruction. Destruction only sweeps aside all that has grown up or been built up so far; but devastation blocks all future growth and prevents all building. . . .The African Sahara is only one kind of wasteland. The devastation of the earth can easily go hand in hand with a guaranteed supreme standard of living for man, and just as easily with the organized establishment of a uniform state of happiness for all men. Devastation can be the same as both, and can haunt us everywhere in the most unearthly way—by keeping itself hidden. Devastation does not just mean a slow sinking into the sands. Devastation is the high-velocity expulsion of Mnemosyne. (29–30)

My point in this section is that the figurative and the literal meanings of "wasteland" are mirrored by one another—or that desertification in the literal sense is the "objective correlative" of the various figurative wastelands of modernist literature. In this sense I take to a manifest extreme what Stanley Cavell, in his essay "Ending the Waiting Game: A Reading of Beckett's *Endgame,*" calls "the *hidden literality*" of the words spoken by Beckett's characters in *Endgame* (Cavell, *Must We Mean What We Say?,* 118).

For T. S. Eliot's theory of the objective correlative, see his essay "Hamlet and His problems" in *T. S. Eliot's Selected Essays* (121–26).

4. FORESTS OF NOSTALGIA

On the logic, pathos, and psychology of nostalgia as such, I should mention two books with diametrically opposed views: Ralph Harper's *Nostalgia* and Susan Stewart's *On Longing.* The former argues that nostalgia is a fundamental condition of presence, while the latter sees it as a textuality of absence. Both views, I believe, are operative in one way or another in this fourth chapter.

Forest and World in Wordsworth's Poem. My discussion of Wordsworth is largely autonomous, but the following studies have helped me to orient myself: Leslie Brisman's *Romantic Origins* (276–361); Geoffrey Hartman's *Wordsworth's Poetry, 1787–1814;* David Ferry's *Wordsworth;* the chapter on Wordsworth in Harold Bloom's *The Visionary Company* (120–91); and Paul de Man's "Wordsworth and Hölderlin" (47–66) and "Symbolic Landscape in Wordsworth and Yeats" (125–44), both in *The Rhetoric of Romanticism.* On the topic of Wordsworth' relation to the modern city I have consulted the chapter on Wordsworth in William Sharpe's *Unreal Cities* (16–38).

The Brothers Grimm. I am indebted in this section above all to Jack Zipes' excellent book *The Brothers Grimm: From Enchanted Forests to the Modern World.* But I have also learned a great deal from John Ellis's more critical *One Fairy Story too Many: The Brothers Grimm and Their Tales,* which accuses the Brothers Grimm of deliberate deceit in their accounts of the origin of the tales and of how they went about collecting them. Ellis's accusation extends to those German scholars who, even after the evidence became clear, were reluctant to acknowledge that the "Germanic" origins of the tales were for the most part a fairy tale of the brothers' invention.

The connection I establish between the Brothers Grimm and Vico is original. No one, as far as I can tell, has yet suggested it. For Savigny's influence on the Grimms, see Zipes (31–35, 51).

Forests of Symbols. My information about tree sanctuaries in ancient Greece comes mostly from Walter Burkert's *Greek Religion* 28–29. But on the subject of sacred groves and tree worship in ancient religions around the world, the best discussion is still to be found in Sir James Frazer's *The Golden Bough* (106–29), which has provided a source of inspiration for many other meditations in my book. Another excellent book on this topic is Jacques Brosse's *La mythologie des arbres.*

On the origins and religious symbolism of the archaic Greek temple, I have been inspired above all by Vincent Scully's *The Earth, The Temple and the Gods.* Scully does not specifically link the Greek temple to forests, to be sure, nor does any other scholar known to me. But it was his book that first stirred my suspicion that there might indeed exist an obscure symbolic correspondence between them.

My discussion of Baudelaire's theory of correspondences is in many ways inspired by Walter Benjamin's essay "On Some Motifs in Baudelaire," in which Benjamin remarks, among other things, that "the *correspondences* are the data of remembrance—not historical data, but the data of prehistory" (182). I have also learned from Paul de Man's essay "Anthropomorphism and Trope in the Lyric," in *The Rhetoric of Romanticism* (especially 243–52).

On the topic of symbolism I would also mention Angus Fletcher's *Allegory: The Theory of a Symbolic Mode,* which inspired me to think more radically about the difference between hierarchical differentiation and indeterminate correspondence (especially 1–24, 112–13). My thinking on this topic was further stimulated by Reiner Schürmann's remarkable Heideggerian analysis of symbolism in his essay "La différence symbolique."

The English translation of Baudelaire's "Correspondences" is my own, as is the translation of the passage from Mallarmé about the "horror of the forest" and the vocation of symbolist literature. The Mallarmé passage is discussed from a more strictly literary perspective by Leo Bersani in *The Death of Stéphane Mallarmé* (4–5).

For an extended discussion of Musil's notion of the "still undefined relations of things" from another perspective than my own, see Thomas Harrison's *Essayism*.

Waiting for Dionysos. The English translations of Leopardi's poems and prose are my own, as is the translation of Rimbaud's "Marine." Leopardi's love of *il vago* is discussed from a different, idiosyncratic perspective by Italo Calvino in the third "Memo" of his *Six Memos for the Next Millennium* (57–64).

5. DWELLING

Background sources for my remarks about climatic epochs and the neolithic revolution include Karl Butzer's *Environment and Archaeology* (on ice ages see 13–28, 101–25; on forests, 62–78); Grahame Clark's *World Prehistory* (on environmental change, 10–17; on the neolithic revolution, 39–47); Robert J. Wenke's *Patterns in Prehistory* (on domestication, agriculture, and sedentary communities, 155–97); and Stuart Piggott & Grahame Clark's *Prehistoric Societies*.

The Elm Tree. The etymology of the word *logos* given in the first paragraph of this section comes from *The American Heritage Dictionary of Indo-European Roots* (see entry for *leg*, 35).

In his *Constable and His Influence in Landscape Painting* (243), C. J. Holmes dated Constable's "Study of the Trunk of the Elm Tree" *ca.* 1815, but Graham Reynolds's analysis of Constable's brushstroke techniques in the painting led him to date it *ca.* 1821 (*Catalogue of the Constable Collection*, 146).

On the topic of Constable's aerial aesthetics I have learned from Kurt Badt's study *John Constable's Clouds*. On Constable's theory of the "chiaroscuro of nature," I have learned from Basil Taylor, from whom I also derive the comment that Constable's landscape paintings constitute a spiritual confession of sorts. In his introduction to *Constable: Paintings, Drawing and Watercolors*, Taylor writes: "The three aspects of chiaroscuro—as a natural phenomenon, as a pictorial device and as a metaphor for the range of human emotions— were at last, in such works as *Hedleigh Castle*, to be so instinctively combined by Constable that for him landscape became, to an unprecedented degree, an instrument of self-confession" (27). On the question of Constable's excursion to the Lake District and his subsequent conversion, I have relied on Michael Rosenthal's account in his *Constable* (47–96); Graham Reynolds (14–16); and Basil Taylor (23–24).

Finally it is interesting to note that Constable understates the presence of a house in other of his studies of the same period. This in fact helped persuade Reynolds that the "Study of the Trunk of the Elm Tree" was executed around 1821: "The treatment of the foliage and the glimpse of the house beyond recall similar features in Nos. 222 and 226 ["Study of Sky and Trees, With a Red House, at Hamstead," and "Study of Sky and Trees at Hamstead"], and the sketch is accordingly listed here under the year 1821" (*Catalogue*, 146).

London versus Epping Forest. Secondary sources that have been helpful for my essay on Clare include Merryn and Raymond Williams's introduction and critical commentary in their edition of *John Clare: Selected Poetry and Prose* (1–20, 201–22); John Barrell's *The Idea of Landscape and the Sense of Place, 1730–1840: An Approach to the Poetry of John Clare;* and Elizabeth Helsinger's excellent essay "Clare and the Place of the Peasant Poet." The latter provides, among other things, a thorough background of the Enclosure and Engrossing policies of rural capitalism—a background against which Clare's refusal of punctuation in his poetry takes on a provocative meaning indeed.

See the extraordinary essay of Angus Fletcher, "Style and the Extreme Situation," whose analysis of Clare's letter to Hipkins from Saint Andrew's Asylum goes to the heart of what Fletcher calls Clare's "paradoxical conniption of oddness" (294).

The contrast between Wordsworth's poem "Gipsies" and Clare's "The Gipsy Camp" is proposed by Merryn and Raymond Williams in their critical commentary (210–13).

The Woods of Walden. The numerals that follow citations from *Walden* refer to sections (Roman) and paragraphs (Arabic) in the work.

My meditation on *Walden* is inspired by Stanley Cavell's *The Senses of Walden,* which is one of the most remarkable works of literary criticism I know.

Barbara Johnson's reflections on Thoreau's use of figurative speech were helpful for my own thinking about the same issue (see *A World of Difference,* 49–56). Johnson's discussion of Thoreau's stylistic obscurity is enlightening, yet it leaves a contradiction unresolved. On the one hand Johnson argues that Thoreau's symbols of hound, horse, and dove have no literal referents but refer to their own impossibility of achieving any such reference. But on the other hand she declares that we are to understand Thoreau's excursion to Walden as the author's having "*literally* crossed over into the very parable he is writing, where *reality itself* has become . . . both ground and figure at once" (56). I prefer the latter notion of promiscuity between the literal and the figurative to the former notion of an aporetic divorce. (It is surely a more *dangerous* one.)

My thoughts about A. R. Ammons were inspired by our years of close friendship in Ithaca, between 1980 and 1985. Ammons's relation to the American tradition is a topic that has been dealt with in depth by Harold Bloom in his essay, "Emerson and Ammons: A Coda"; his introduction to *A. R. Ammons* (1–31); and his essay "The Breaking of the Vessels," in the same volume (151–68). In this regard see also Helen Vendler's essay, "Ammons," in the same volume edited by Bloom (73–80).

Fallingwater. In the background of my discussion of Frank Lloyd Wright and the question of dwelling is Heidegger's "Letter on Humanism," especially his remark: "The talk about the house of Being is no transfer of the image 'house' to Being. But one day we will, by thinking the essence of Being in a way appropriate to its matter, more readily be able to think what 'house' and 'to dwell' are" (236–37).

Also in the background of my discussion is an attempt to collapse a distinction that Stanley Cavell makes at the end of his essay "Thinking of Emerson," where he writes:

> The substantive disagreement with Heidegger, shared by Emerson and Thoreau, is that the achievement of the human requires not inhabitation and settlement but abandonment, leaving. Then everything depends upon your realization of abandonment. For the significance of leaving lies in its discovery that you have settled something, that you have felt enthusiastically what there is to abandon yourself to, that you can treat the others there are as those to whom the inhabitation of the world can now be left. (138)

In my understanding, Heidegger's idea of dwelling is akin to what Cavell means by "abandonment" and to what Wright means by an "unfolding" as opposed to an "enfolding" architecture. Heidegger's early word for what is implied by Cavell's notion of "inhabitation" is "inauthenticity." In essence, the problem lies with the word "inhabitation." I have tried to suggest in so many ways throughout this chapter that we do not "inhabit" the earth in the closed sense; rather, that we *dwell*. I like the word "dwell" because its etymology contains the notion of abandonment. In Old English *dwellan* means precisely "to lead or go astray," as in a forest. In other words, we inhabit our estrangement, our "abandonment," even when we stay put in one particular place—as long, that is, as we do not close ourselves off to the alien element that inhabits our finitude.

Andrea Zanzotto. I am grateful to Beverly Allen for having given me the opportunity to meet Zanzotto and visit the Montello forests with him. Her book, *Andrea Zanzotto: The Language of Beauty's Apprentice,* is one of the few book-length studies of Zanzotto in English, though it does not treat his later work. Another book is John P. Welle's *The Poetry of Andrea Zanzotto,* which focuses mostly on Zanzotto's *Il galateo in bosco.* Essays that were helpful for my meditation in this section include Thomas J. Harrison's "Andrea Zanzotto: From the Language of the World to the World of Language," and Tyrus Miller's "In Darkness, in Snow: Figures beyond Language in the Poetry of Andrea Zanzotto." I have written on Zanzotto previously, in my article "The Italian Silence." The translation of "Gathering" comes from *The Selected Poetry of Andrea Zanzotto,* though I have revised it significantly.

[WORKS CITED]

Aeschylus. *The Orestia*. Translated by R. Lattimore. Chicago: University of Chicago Press, 1953.

Agamben, Giorgio. "Comedìa: La svolta comica di Dante e la concezione della colpa." *Paragone* 346 (December 1978): 3–27.

Allen, Beverly. *Andrea Zanzotto: The Language of Beauty's Apprentice*. Berkeley and Los Angeles: University of California Press, 1988.

Ammons, A. R. "To Harold Bloom." In *Sphere*. New York: W. W. Norton, 1974.

Andreolli, Bruno, ed. *Il bosco nel medioevo*. Bologna: CLUEB, 1988.

Ariosto, Ludovico. *Orlando furioso*. Edited by E. Bigi. 2 vols. Milan: Rusconi, 1982.

Aristotle. *Physics*. In *The Complete Works of Aristotle*. Vol. 1. Edited by Jonathan Barnes. Princeton: Princeton University Press, 1984.

Ascoli, A. R. *Ariosto's Bitter Harmony*. Princeton: Princeton University Press, 1987.

Attenborough, David. *The First Eden: The Mediterranean World and Man*. Boston: Little, Brown and Co., 1987.

Augustine, Saint. *Confessions*. Translated by Rex Warner. New York: Mentor, 1963.

Badt, Kurt. *John Constable's Clouds*. London: Routledge and Kegan Paul, 1950.

Barrell, John. *The Idea of Landscape and the Sense of Place, 1730–1840: An Approach to the Poetry of John Clare*. Cambridge: Harvard University Press, 1983.

Barrett, William. *Death of the Soul: From Descartes to the Computer*. Garden City: Anchor Press, 1985.

Baudelaire, Charles. *Art in Paris 1845–1862: Salons and Other Exhibitions*. Translated and edited by Jonathan Mayne. London: Phaidon, 1965.

————. *Les fleurs du mal*. Paris: Editions de Cluny, 1941.

————. *The Painter of Modern Life and Other Essays*. Translated by Jonathan Mayne. New York: Phaidon, 1964.

Bechmann, Roland. *Des arbres et des hommes*. Paris: Flammarion, 1984.

Becker, Ernest. *The Denial of Death*. New York: Free Press, 1973.

Beckett, Samuel. *Endgame*. New York: Chelsea House Pubs., 1988.

————. *Molloy*. New York: Grove Press, 1955.

Benjamin, Walter. "On Some Motifs in Baudelaire." In *Illuminations,* edited by Hannah Arendt, 155–200. New York: Schocken Books, 1959.

Bernheimer, Richard. *Wild Men of the Middle Ages*. Cambridge: Harvard University Press, 1952.

Bersani, Leo. *The Death of Stéphane Mallarmé*. Cambridge: Cambridge University Press, 1982.

Bloom, Harold, ed. *A. R. Ammons*. New York: Chelsea House Pubs., 1981.

————. "Emerson and Ammons: A Coda." *Diacritics* 3, no. 4 (Winter 1973): 45–46.

————. *The Visionary Company: A Reading of English Romantic Poetry*. Ithaca: Cornell University Press, 1961.

Boccaccio, Giovanni. *The Decameron*. Translated by G. H. McWilliam. London: Penguin Books, 1972.

Brisman, Leslie. *Romantic Origins*. Ithaca: Cornell University Press, 1978.

Brosse, Jacques. *La mythologie des arbres*. Paris: Plon, 1989.

Brown, Bruce, and Lane Morgan. *The Miracle Planet*. New York: Gallery Books, 1990.

Burke, Peter. *Vico*. Oxford: Oxford University Press, 1985.

Burkert, Walter. *Ancient Mystery Cults*. Cambridge: Harvard University Press, 1987.

————. *Greek Religion*. Translated by John Raffan. Cambridge: Harvard University Press, 1985.

Butzer, Karl W. *Environment and Archaeology from an Ecological Perspective*. Chicago: Aldine-Atherton Pub., 1971.

Calvino, Italo. *The Baron in the Trees*. Translated by Archibald Colquhoun. New York: Harcourt Brace Jovanovich, 1959.

————. *Six Memos for the Next Millennium*. Translated by Patrick Creagh. Cambridge: Harvard University Press, 1988.

Cassirer, Ernst. *The Philosophy of Enlightenment*. Translated by F. C. Koellin and J. P. Pettegrove. Boston: Beacon Press, 1951.

Caufield, Catherine. "The Ancient Forest." *The New Yorker* (14 May 1990): 46–84.

Cavell, Stanley. "Ending the Waiting Game: A Reading of Beckett's *Endgame*." In *Must We Mean What We Say?,* 115–62. New York: Charles Scribner's Sons, 1969.

———. *The Senses of Walden*. San Francisco: North Point Press, 1981.

———. "Thinking of Emerson." In *The Senses of Walden*, 121–38.

Chrétien de Troyes. *Yvain*. In *Arthurian Romances*, translated by W. W. Comfort, New York: E. P. Dutton, 1976.

Clare, John. *Selected Poetry and Prose*. Edited by Merryn and Raymond Williams. London: Methuen, 1986.

Clarke, John Grahame. *World Prehistory*. Cambridge: Cambridge University Press, 1977.

Conrad, Joseph. *Heart of Darkness*. London: Penguin Books, 1983.

———. *Lord Jim*. Edited by Thomas Moser. New York: W. W. Norton, 1968.

Constable, John. *John Constable's Correspondence*. Edited by R. B. Beckett. 6 vols. Ipswitch: Suffolk Records Society, 1962–70.

Corvol, Andrée. *L'homme aux bois*. Paris: Fayard, 1987.

Cox, J. C. *The Royal Forests of England*. London: Methuen, 1905.

Cox, Thomas, et al. *This Well-Wooded Land*. Lincoln: University of Nebraska Press, 1985.

Croce, Benedetto. *The Philosophy of Giambattista Vico*. Translated by R. G. Collingwood. New York: Macmillan Co., 1913.

Dante. *La Divina Commedia secondo l'antica vulgata*. Edited by G. Petrocchi. 4 vols. Milan: Mondadori, 1966–67.

Daraki, Maria. *Dionysos*. Paris: Arthaud, 1985.

De Man, Paul. *The Rhetoric of Romanticism*. New York: Columbia University Press, 1984.

———. "The Rhetoric of Temporality." In *Interpretation: Theory and Practise*, edited by Charles S. Singleton, 190–210. Baltimore: John Hopkins University Press, 1969.

Descartes, René. *Discourse on Method*. Translated by Donald A. Cress. Indianapolis: Hackett Publishing Co., 1980.

Detienne, Marcel. *Dionysos à ciel ouvert*. Paris: Hachette, 1986.

Diderot, Denis. "Encyclopédie." In *Encyclopédie*, edited by Denis Diderot and Jean Le Rond D'Alembert.

Doob, Penelope R. *The Idea of the Labyrinth from Classical Antiquity through the Middle Ages*. Ithaca: Cornell University Press, 1990.

———. *Nebuchadnezzar's Children*. New Haven: Yale University Press, 1974.

Douglas, David C. *William the Conqueror: The Norman Impact Upon England*. Berkeley and Los Angeles: University of California Press, 1964.

Durling, Robert. *The Figure of the Poet in Renaissance Epic*. Cambridge: Harvard University Press, 1967.

Eliot, T. S. *T. S. Eliot's Selected Essays*. New York: Harcourt, Brace and Co., 1950.

Ellis, John. *One Fairy Story Too Many: The Brothers Grimm and Their Tales*. Chicago: University of Chicago Press, 1983.

Euripides. *The Bacchae of Euripides*. Translated by C. K. Williams. New York: Noonday Books, 1990.

———. *Hippolytus*. In *The Complete Greek Tragedies,* edited by David Grene and Richard Lattimore, vol. 3. Chicago: University of Chicago Press, 1958–59.

———. *Iphigenia in Tauris*. In *The Complete Greek Tragedies,* edited by David Grene and Richard Lattimore, vol. 4. Chicago: University of Chicago Press, 1958–59.

Evans, Sir Arthur. "Mycenaean Tree and Pillar Cult." *Journal of Hellenistic Studies* 21 (1901): 1–103.

Evelyn, John. *Sylva: Or a Discourse of Forest-Trees and the Propagation of Timber.* London, 1664.

Ferry, David. *Wordsworth.* New York: Dell Publishing Co., 1959.

Fletcher, Angus. *Allegory: The Theory of a Symbolic Mode.* Ithaca: Cornell University Press, 1964.

———. *The Prophetic Moment: An Essay on Spenser.* Chicago: University of Chicago Press, 1971.

———. "Style and the Extreme Situation." In *Textual Analysis,* edited by Mary Ann Caws. New York: Modern Language Association of America, 1986.

Foucault, Michel. *The Order of Things.* New York: Vintage Books, 1973.

Fraser, Sir James. *The Golden Bough.* Edited by Theodor Gaster. New York: New American Library, 1959.

Freccero, John. *Dante's Poetics of Conversion.* Edited by Rachel Jacoff. Cambridge: Harvard University Press, 1986.

Fustel de Coulanges, Numa Denis. *The Ancient City.* Baltimore: Johns Hopkins University Press, 1980.

Garin, Eugenio. *Ritratti di umanisti.* Florence: Sansoni, 1967.

———. *Studi sul platonismo medievale.* Florence: Le Monnier, 1958.

———. *Umanesimo italiano.* Florence: Sansoni, 1961.

———. *Umanisti, artisti, scienziati.* Rome: Riuniti, 1989.

Grimm, Jacob and Wilhelm Grimm. *The Complete Fairy Tales of the Brothers Grimm.* Translated by Jack Zipes. New York: Bantam Books, 1987.

Guerard, Albert J. *Conrad the Novelist.* Cambridge: Harvard University Press, 1958.

Halperin, David. *Before Pastoral: Theocritus and the Ancient Tradition of Bucolic Poetry.* Princeton: Princeton University Press, 1981.

Harper, Ralph. *Nostalgia.* Cleveland: Press of Western Reserve University, 1966.

Harrison, Robert. *The Body of Beatrice.* Baltimore: Johns Hopkins University Press, 1989.

———. "Comedy and Modernity: Dante's Hell." *MLN* 103, no. 1 (1987): 219–29.

———. "The Italian Silence." *Critical Inquiry* 13 (1986): 81–99.

Harrison, Thomas. "Andrea Zanzotto: From the Language of the World to the World of Language." *Poesis* 5, no. 3 (1984): 68–85.

———. *Essayism: Conrad, Musil and Pirandello*. Baltimore: Johns Hopkins University Press, 1991.

Hart, Cyril. *Royal Forest*. Oxford: Clarendon Press, 1966.

Hartman, Geoffrey. *Wordsworth Poetry, 1787–1814*. New Haven: Yale University Press, 1964.

Heidegger, Martin. *Early Greek Thinking*. San Francisco: Harper and Row, 1975.

———. "Letter on Humanism." In *Basic Writings*, edited by David F. Krell. New York: Harper and Row, 1977.

———. *Nietzsche*. Edited by David F. Krell. 4 vols. New York: Harper and Row, 1979–84.

———. "On the Being and Conception of *physis* in Aristotle's Physics B, 1." Translated by Thomas Sheehan. *Man and World* 9, no. 3 (August 1976): 219–70.

———. *What is Called Thinking?* Translated by J. Glenn Gray. New York: Harper and Row, 1968.

Helsinger, Elizabeth. "Clare and the Place of the Peasant Poet." *Critical Inquiry* 13 (1987): 509–31.

Higounet, Charles. "Les forêts de l'Europe occidentale du V au XI siècle." In *Agricoltura e mondo rurale in Occidente nell'alto medioevo*. Spoleto: XIIIa Settimana di studio del centro italiano di studi sull'altro medioevo, 1966.

Holmes, C. J. *Constable and His Influence in Landscape Painting*. Westminster: Archibald Constable and Co., 1902.

Homer. *The Homeric Hymns*. Translated by Apostolos N. Athanassakis. Baltimore: Johns Hopkins University Press, 1976.

———. *The Iliad of Homer*. Translated by Richard Lattimore. Chicago: University of Chicago Press, 1951.

———. *The Odyssey of Homer*. Translated by Allen Mandelbaum. Berkeley and Los Angeles: University of California Press, 1990.

Horkeimer, Max and Theodor Adorno. *Dialectic of Enlightenment*. Translated by John Cumming. New York: Continuum Publishing Co., 1982.

Jameson, Fredric. *The Political Unconscious: Narrative as a Socially Symbolic Act*. Ithaca: Cornell University Press, 1981.

Johnson, Barbara. *A World of Difference*. Baltimore: Johns Hopkins University Press, 1987.

Kant, Immanuel. "An Answer to the Question: What is Enlightenment?" In *Perpetual Peace and Other Essays*, translated by Ted Humphrey, 41–48. Indianapolis: Hackett Publishing Co., 1983.

Keen, Maurice. *Outlaws of Medieval Legend*. Rev. ed. London: Routledge and Kegan Paul, 1977.

Kovacs, Maureen, ed. and trans. *The Epic of Gilgamesh*. Stanford: Stanford University Press, 1989.

Kramer, Samuel Noah. *History Begins at Sumer*. 3d rev. ed. Philadelphia: University of Pennsylvania Press, 1981.

———. *The Sumerians: Their History, Culture and Character*. Chicago: University of Chicago Press, 1963.

Krautheimer, Richard. *Roma Alessandrina*. New York: Vassar College, 1982.

Lancisi, Giovanni Maria. "Il taglio delle selve." In *Antologia della prosa scientifica italiana del seicento*, edited by Enrico Falqui, vol. 2. Florence: Vallecchi, 1943.

Le Goff, Jacques. *L'imaginaire médiéval*. Paris: Gallimard, 1985.

Leopardi, Giacomo. *Canti*. Milan: Rissoli, 1949.

———. *Zibaldone di pensieri*. Edited by Anna Maria Moroni. 2 vols. Milan: Mondadori, 1937.

Lerer, Seth. "Artifice and Artistry in *Sir Orfeo*." *Speculum* 60, no. 1 (1985): 92–109.

Le Roy. "Forêt." In *Encyclopédie*, edited by Denis Diderot and Jean Le Rond D'Alembert.

Levy, Rachel G. *The Gate of Horn*. London: Faber & Faber, 1948. Republished as *Religious Conceptions of the Stone Age and Their Influence Upon European Thought*. New York: Harper and Row, 1963.

Lewis, Charlton T. and Charles Short. *A Latin Dictionary*. Oxford: Clarendon Press, 1969.

Lichtenberg, Georg Christof. *The Lichtenberg Reader*. Translated and edited by Frauz H. Mautner and Henry Hatfield. Boston: Beacon Press, 1959.

Liddel, Henry G., and Robert Scott. *A Greek-English Lexicon*. New York: Harper and Brothers, 1897.

Littré, Emile. *Dictionnaire de la langue française*. Paris: Jean-Jacques Pauvert, 1956.

Livy. *The Early History of Rome*. Translated by Aubrey de Sélincourt. London: Penguin Books, 1960.

Lowood, Henry. "The Calculating Forester: Quantification, Cameral Science, And the Emergence of Scientific Forestry Management in Germany." In *The Quantifying Spirit of the Eighteenth Century*, 315–342. Berkeley and Los Angeles: University of California Press, 1991.

Mallarmé, Stéphane. "Crises de vers." In *Oeuvres complètes*. Paris: Gallimard, Pléiades, 1945.

Manwood, John. *Manwood's Treatise of the Forest Laws*. Edited by William Nelson. 4th ed. corrected and enlarged. London: E. Nutt, 1717.

Marienstras, Richard. *Le proche et le lointain*. Paris: Minuit, 1981.

Marsh, George. *Man and Nature: Or Physical Geography*. New York: Charles Scribner, 1865.

Marx, Karl. "Proceedings of the Sixth Rhine Province Assembly. Third Article: Debates on the Law of Thefts of Wood." In *Karl Marx, Frederick Engels: Collected Works,* vol. 1. London: Lawrence and Wishart, 1975.

Mazzotta, Giuseppe. *Dante: Poet of the Desert.* Princeton: Princeton University Press, 1981.

———. "Petrarch's Song 126." In *Textual Analysis: Some Readers Reading,* edited by Mary Ann Caws, 121–31. New York: Modern Language Association of America, 1986.

———. "Vico's Encyclopedia." *Yale Journal of Criticism* 1 (Spring 1988): 65–79.

———. *The World at Play in Boccaccio's "Decameron."* Princeton: Princeton University Press, 1986.

Melzer, Arthur M. *The Natural Goodness of Man: On the System of Rousseau's Thought.* Chicago: University of Chicago Press, 1990.

Michelet, Jules. *La sorcière.* Paris: A. Lacroix, Verboeckhoevn, 1867.

Miller, David L. "Nietzsche's Horse and Other Tracings of the Gods." In *Nietzsche in Italy,* edited by Thomas Harrison. Stanford: Anma Libri, 1987.

Miller, Tyrus. "In Darkness, in Snow: Figures beyond Language in the Poetry of Andrea Zanzotto." *Stanford Italian Review* 9, no. 1: 211–28.

Muller, Herbert. *The Loom of History.* New York: Harper and Brothers, 1958.

Mumford, Lewis. *The City in History.* New York: Harcourt & Brace, 1961.

Musil, Robert. *Young Törless.* Translated by Eithne Wilkins and Ernst Kaiser. New York: Pantheon Books, 1955.

Nancy, Jean-Luc. *Ego Sum.* Paris: Flammarion, 1979.

Nietzsche, Friedrich. *The Birth of Tragedy.* Translated by Walter Kaufmann. New York: Vintage Books, 1967.

———. *The Gay Science.* Translated by Walter Kaufmann. New York: Vintage Books, 1974.

———. *On the Genealogy of Morals.* Translated by Walter Kaufmann. New York: Vintage Books, 1969.

———. *Thus Spoke Zarathustra.* In *The Portable Nietzsche.* Translated by Walter Kaufmann. New York: Viking Press, 1968.

Nussbaum, Martha. "Introduction." *The Bacchae of Euripides.* Translated by C. K. Williams, vii–xliv. New York: Noonday Books, 1990.

Otto, Walter F. *Dionysus: Myth and Cult.* Translated by Robert B. Palmer. Bloomington: Indiana University Press, 1965.

Ovid. *Metamorphoses.* Translated by Frank J. Miller. Vol. 1. Loeb Classical Library. Cambridge: Harvard University Press, 1984.

Pais, Ettore. *Storia di Roma: Dalle origini all'inizio delle guerre puniche.* 5 vols. Rome: Optima, 1926.

Petrarch, Francesco. *Petrarch's Lyric Poems.* Translated and edited by Robert M. Durling. Cambridge: Harvard University Press, 1976.

Pierson, Peter. *Phillip II of Spain*. London: Thames and Hudson, 1975.

Piggott, Stuart, and Grahame Clarke. *Prehistoric Societies*. New York: Alfred A. Knopf, 1965.

Pirandello, Luigi. *Umorismo*. Milan: Mondadori, 1986.

Plato. *Critias*. In *The Complete Dialogues*. Translated and edited by B. Jowett. 2 vols. New York: Random House, 1937.

———. *Symposium*. Translated by Walter Hamilton. New York: Penguin Books, 1951.

Poucet, Jacques. *Les origines de Rome: Tradition et histoire*. Brussels: Facultés Universitaires Saint-Louis, 1985.

Pound, Ezra. *The Cantos of Ezra Pound*. New York: New Directions Publishing Co., 1983.

Pritchard, James Bennett, ed. *Ancient Near Eastern Texts Relating to the Old Testament*. Princeton: Princeton University Press, 1969.

Reynolds, Graham. *Catalogue of the Constable Collection in the Victoria and Albert Museum*. London: H. M. Stationery Office, 1960. 2d ed., 1973.

Rimbaud, Arthur. *Oeuvres complètes*. Paris: Editions Pléiades, 1963.

Rosenthal, Michael. *Constable*. London: Thames and Hudson, 1987.

Rositzke, Harry A., ed. and trans. *The Peterborough Chronicle*. New York: Columbia University Press, 1951.

Rousseau, Jean-Jacques. *Confessions*. Translated by J. M. Cohen. New York: Penguin Books, 1953.

———. *Discourse on the Origin and Basis of Inequality Among Men*. In *The Essential Rousseau*, translated by Lowell Blaire. New York: Mentor, 1974.

———. *Projet de constitution pour la Corse*. In *Oeuvres complètes*, vol. 3. Paris: Gallimard, Pleiade, 1964.

Russell, William M. S. *Man, Nature and History*. Garden City: Natural History Press, 1969.

Sartre, Jean-Paul. *Existentialism and Humanism*. Translated by Philip Mairet. Brooklyn: Haskell House. 1977.

———. *Nausea*. Translated by Lloyd Alexander. New York: New Directions Publishing Co., 1964.

Schürmann, Reiner. "La différence symbolique." *Cahiers Internationaux de Symbolisme* 21 (1975): 51–77.

Scully, Vincent. *The Earth, The Temple and the Gods*. New Haven: Yale University Press, 1979.

Segal, Charles. *Poetry and Myth in Ancient Pastoral*. Princeton: Princeton University Press, 1981.

Serres, Michel. *Le contrat naturel*. Paris: François Bourin, 1990.

———. *Rome: Le livre des fondations*. Paris; Grasset, 1983.

———. *Le système de Leibniz*. 2 vols. Paris: Presses Universitaires Francaises, 1968.

Shaffer, Aaron. "Gilgamesh, The Cedar Forest and Mesopotamian History." *Journal of the American Oriental Society* 103, no. 1 (1983): 307–13.

Shakespeare, William. *King Lear*. Edited by A. Harbage. New York: Penguin Books, 1970.

———. *Macbeth*. Edited by Kenneth Muir. London: Methuen, 1951.

Sharpe, William. *Unreal Cities*. Baltimore: Johns Hopkins University Press, 1990.

Shelley, Percy Bysshe. *Prose and Poetry*. Oxford: Clarendon Press, 1948.

Sjöö, Monica, and Barbara Mor. *The Great Cosmic Mother: Rediscovering the Religion of the Earth*. San Francisco: Harper and Row, 1987.

Slavin, Arthur. *The Way of the West*. Vol. 1. Lexington, Mass.: Xerox College Publishing, 1972.

Snell, Bruno. *The Discovery of the Mind: The Greek Origins of European Thought*. Translated by G. Rosenmeyer. Cambridge: Harvard University Press, 1953.

Spariosu, Mihai. *Dionysus Reborn*. Ithaca: Cornell University Press, 1989.

Spink, John Stephenson. "Rousseau et la morale du sentiment." In *Rousseau After 200 Years: Proceedings of the Cambridge Bicentennial Colloquium*, edited by R. A. Leigh, 239–50. Cambridge: Cambridge University Press, 1982.

Starobinski, Jean. *Jean-Jacques Rousseau: La transparence et l'obstacle*. Paris: Gallimard, 1971.

Stewart, Susan. *On Longing*. Baltimore: Johns Hopkins University Press, 1984.

Tacitus. *Germania*. Translated by H. Mattingly, revised by S. A. Handford. London: Penguin Books, 1970.

Tagliacozzo, Giorgio, ed. *Giambattista Vico's Science of Humanity*. Baltimore: Johns Hopkins University Press, 1976.

———. *Vico and Contemporary Thought*. Atlantic Highlands, NJ: Humanities Press, 1979.

Taylor, Basil. *Constable: Paintings, Drawings and Watercolors*. London: Phaidon Press, 1973.

Thirgood, J. V. *Man and the Mediterranean Forest: A History of Resource Depletion*. London: Academic Press, 1981.

Thomas, Dylan. *Complete Poems*. New York: New Direction Books, 1971.

Thomas, Keith. *Man and the Natural World*. New York: Pantheon Books, 1983.

Thompson, E. P. *Whigs and Hunters: The Origin of the Black Art*. New York: Pantheon Books, 1975.

Thompson, William Irwin. *The Time Falling Bodies Take to Light: Mythology, Sexuality and the Origins of Culture*. New York: St. Martin's Press, 1981.

Thoreau, Henry David. *The Variorum Walden*. Edited by Walter Harding. New York: Twayne Pub., 1962.

Thucydides. *The Peloponnesian War*. Translated by Rex Warner. Baltimore: Penguin Books, 1954.

Trakl, Georg. *Selected Poems.* Edited by Christopher Middleton. London: Grossman Pub., 1968.

Van Ghent, Dorothy. *The English Novel: Form and Function.* New York: Rinehart & Co., 1953.

Vendler, Helen. "Ammons." In *A. R. Ammons,* ed. Harold Bloom, 73–80. New York: Chelser House Pubs., 1981.

Verene, Donald. *Vico's Science of Imagination.* Ithaca: Cornell University Press, 1981.

Vico, Giambattista. *Autobiography.* Translated by T. G. Bergin and M. H. Fisch. Ithaca: Cornell University Press, 1944.

———. *The New Science.* Translated by T. G. Bergin and M. H. Fisch. Ithaca: Cornell University Press, 1968. Numerals in brackets refer to section numbers.

Virgil. *Aeneid.* Translated by Robert Fitzgerald. New York: Vintage Books, 1983.

———. *Aeneid.* Translated by Allen Mandelbaum. New York: Bantam Books, 1972.

Walker, John. *John Constable.* New York: Harry N. Abrams, 1978.

Watkins, Calvert, ed. *The American Heritage Dictionary of Indo-European Roots.* Boston: Houghton Mifflin Co., 1985.

Watt, Ian. *Conrad in the Nineteenth Century.* Berkeley and Los Angeles: University of California Press, 1979.

Welle, John P. *The Poetry of Andrea Zanzotto: A Critical Study of "Il galateo in bosco."* Rome: Bulzoni Editore, 1987.

Wenke, Robert J. *Patterns in Prehistory.* 2d ed. New York: Oxford University Press, 1984.

White, Hayden. *The Tropics of Discourse: Essays in Cultural Criticism.* Baltimore: Johns Hopkins University Press, 1978.

Williams, William Appleman. *Empire as a Way of Life.* New York: Oxford University Press, 1980.

Winkler, John J., ed. *Nothing To Do With Dionysos?* Princeton: Princeton University Press, 1990.

Wordsworth, William. *William Wordsworth.* Edited by Stephen Gill. Oxford: Oxford University Press, 1984.

Wright, Frank Lloyd. *An American Architecture.* Edited by Edgar Kaufmann. New York: Horizon Press, 1955.

Zanzotto, Andrea. *Il galateo in bosco.* Milan: Mondadori, 1978.

———. *Selected Poetry of Andrea Zanzotto.* Edited and translated by Ruth Feldman and Brian Swann. Princeton: Princeton University Press, 1975.

Zipes, Jack. *The Brothers Grimm: From Enchanted Forests to the Modern World.* New York: Routledge, Chapman and Hall, 1988.

INDEX

Absurdity: in comedy, 79; in existentialism, 145, 146–47
Academies, 11, 38, 245, 246
Achilles, 9
Acid rain, 177
Actaeon: and Artemis, 24–26; metamorphosis of, 29, 30, 33; Pentheus compared to, 34, 37
Adorno, Theodor, 259
Aeneas, 1–2, 47, 49–51, 52
Agamben, Giorgio, 256
Agamemnon, 21, 54
Agathon, 39, 40
Agave, 34–35, 37
Agriculture, 197–98
Alba Longa, 47, 48, 49
Alcibiades, 39
Alexander VII (pope), 113
Allen, Beverly, 265
America. *See* United States of America
Ammons, A. R., 228–29, 238, 248
Amor fati, 40–41, 46
Amulius, 48
Anaximander, 27
Animals (wildlife): Artemis and, 23; in Brothers Grimm, 170; Dionysos and, 32; Endangered Species Act, 123–24; extermination during human age, 92; in Le Roy's definition of forest, 121; in

Manwood's definition of forest, 72–73; Zarathustra and, 45–46
Antiphon, 27, 28
Antiquity, 53–54. *See also* Greece, ancient; Rome
Arcadia, 50, 178
Architecture, 234–37
Ariosto, 93, 95, 97, 99
Aristotle, 27–28
Artemis: Dionysos compared to, 30, 31–32, 33; as great Mother goddess, 20–26, 29–30; temple at Ephesus, 57
Ascoli, Robert, 258
Asylum: for animals, 73; for English outlaws, 76–77; in medieval European world, 61, 62–63; in Roman world, 49–50
Attenborough, David, 55, 251, 255
Augustine, Saint, 224–25, 255
Auspices, 5, 10, 11

Bacchae, The (Euripides), 33, 36, 38
Badt, Kurt, 263
Barbarism of reflection, 101, 136–37
Barrell, John, 264
Barrett, William, 258
Baudelaire, Charles, 179–83, 186, 187, 195
Bechmann, Roland, 252, 255, 256

68; in Shakespeare, 100; and
  tragedy, 104
Confessions (Augustine), 224–25
Confessions (Rousseau), 128–30
Conrad, Joseph, 133–44
Consent, 90
Constable, John, 196, 202–11
Contini, Gianfranco, 239
Convivio (Dante), 84
Copernican revolution, 109–10, 259
Correspondence, doctrine of, 179,
  180, 187, 262
"Correspondences" (Baudelaire),
  179–81, 183, 187
Corvol, Andrée, 260
Cosmetics, 181–82
Covert realism, 97
Cox, J. C., 256
Cox, Thomas, 260
Critical reason, 12, 13, 38
Croce, Benedetto, 252
Cybele, 9, 19
Cyclops, 9–10

Dante, 81–87, 110, 111
Daraki, Maria, 254
Death of God, 41, 109, 144
Decameron (Boccaccio), 87–91
Deforestation: of ancient world,
  55–58; city dwellers' reaction to,
  247; in Dante's purgatory, 84; of
  England, 71; and greenhouse ef-
  fect, 148; during human age, 92,
  100; and rationalism, 114
Deities: forest sanctuaries, 178;
  Heraclitus on, 246; as poetic
  characters, 9. *See also* God
De Man, Paul, 262
Descartes, René, 107–13, 118, 123,
  144
Desertification, 148–49, 261
Deserts, 112, 185
Desire, 91, 95, 97
Detienne, Marcel, 254
Deuteronomy, 62
Diana nemorensis, 23
Diderot, Denis, 115

Dionysos, 30–40; bridging of hu-
  manity and animals, 45; Diony-
  sian rapture, 193–94; and house
  of Cadmus, 2; Nietzsche and,
  46, 254
Discourse on Method (Descartes),
  107, 109, 110, 111–13, 123, 144
*Discourse on the Origin and Basis of
  Inequality Among Men* (Rousseau), 127–28
Divination, 6, 11; auspices, 5, 10, 11
Divine Comedy (Dante), 81–87
Divinity: and providence, 5. *See
  also* Deities; God
Doob, Penelope, 253, 255, 256
Dorians, 20
Douglas, David C., 257
Durling, Robert, 258
Dwelling, 197–243; and burial, 245;
  and dislocation in Western society, 198; Heidegger on, 264–65;
  and *logos*, 200–202; nature as,
  227, 228; and nature in Con-
  stable, 209, 211; and oblivion,
  199; Thoreau's, 226, 230;
  Wright's houses as, 232, 234–35,
  237–38. *See also* Houses

Ecology, 149, 199–200, 200–201
Eliot, T. S., 149, 194, 261
Ellis, John, 262
Endgame (Beckett), 150, 151
England: Anglo-Saxon versus Nor-
  man, 257; deforestation of, 71;
  Epping Forest, 218–20; forest
  law, 69, 70, 75–76; New Forest,
  75; outlaws, 75–81
Enkidu, 15, 18, 65
Encyclopédie, 115, 118, 121, 125
Endangered Species Act, 123–24
Enlightenment, 107–52; definition
  of, 114–15, 116; and Descartes,
  107, 111; forest types in, 107,
  125; and Rousseau, 125, 126–27,
  131; and utility, 120; Vico's ac-
  count of, 5
Entropy, law of, 54, 57–58

Ephesus, 20, 21, 57
Epping Forest, 218–20
Eternal return, 43–45
Euripides, 33, 36, 38
Europe: medieval attitude toward forests, 61–64
Eustace the Monk, 77
Evander, 1–2, 49–50
Evans, Sir Arthur, 178
Evelyn, John, 100
Existentialism, 144–45

Fallingwater, 232–33, 237
Families: family clearings, 7, 9; in Greek tragedy, 35–36; in *Macbeth*, 103, 104; Vico on, 6–7
Ferry, David, 262
Figurative speech, 264
Finitude, 245–49
Fire, 10
Firearms, 99
Fisch, Max H., 252
Fisher, John, 203
Fitzwarin, Fulk, 77, 80
Fletcher, Angus, 253, 262, 264
Flora, 9
Forest law, 69–75, 76, 117
Forest mathematics, 108, 123, 176
Foresty (forest management), 108, 116–24
Forests: an antecedent of human world, 1; and Artemis, 23, 25, 29, 30; in Beckett, 150, 151–52; in Brothers Grimm, 164, 165, 168–69; and cities in Roman law, 49; cities' metamorphosis into, 100, 101; civilization defined against, 2; civilization exterior to, 201; and civilization in Christian era, 103–4; in Conrad, 140, 141–42; and death of God, 41; in *Decameron*, 88; 89–90; Descartes on, 107, 110–11, 123; in Dionysian poetry, 194–95; and Dionysos, 31, 37–38; in *Di-*

vine Comedy, 81–82, 84–87; dwelling related to, 202; and ecology, 199; English outlaws in, 76–77, 79–80; enigmas of, x; and Enlightenment, 107, 120, 122, 125; Fallingwater and, 232; forest law, 69–75, 76, 117; forest mathematics, 108, 123, 176; and forestry, 108, 116–24; genealogy obscured by, 6; and Germany, 164, 175–77; in Gilgamesh epic, 14, 17; and great Mother goddess, 19; and humanism, 145; humanity opposed to, 13; and *hyle*, 28; and ice ages, ix, 197; and law of entropy, 57–58; in Leopardi, 190; Le Roy's definition of, 115–16, 121; and lyric nostalgia in Petrarch, 93, 98; in *Macbeth*, 103–4; Manwood's definition of, 71–73, 100, 115; medieval European attitude toward, 61–64; and memory, 156; and metamorphosis, 33, 66–67; and method, 113; origin of word, 69–70; in *Orlando Furioso*, 93, 95, 99–100; and placehood of place, 211–12; rain forests, 108; and Rome, 47, 48, 49, 50, 51; in Rousseau, 126, 128, 130, 132; as scene for comedy, 80; and sexuality, 89–90; in Shakespeare's comedies, 100; and shelter for humans, 234; sky concealed by, 6; symbolism of, 177–86; and temples, 178, 262; and time, 8; and unconscious, 87; United States policy on, 123–24; Vico's giants in, 3, 4; Vico's views on, 11, 13; and Western civilization, ix, xi, 247; William the Conqueror and, 75; in Wordsworth, 157–58, 162–63; in Zanzotto, 241; and Zarathustra, 45. *See also* Deforestation
Form: and matter, 27–28; and re-

straint, 34; in Socratic philosophy, 38
Foucault, Michel, 260
France, 116–17, 126
Frazer, Sir James, 23, 252, 262
Freccero, John, 257
Freedom: in America, 220, 221, 231; bestial, 3; in Clare, 214, 215, 219, 220; and loss, 231; of place, 211–12; in Wright houses, 232–33, 235, 237
Free verse, 192, 193
Friedrich, Caspar David, 154
Fustel de Coulanges, Numa Denis, 165, 252
Future, the, 5, 8, 14, 125, 127

Gamelyn, 77, 80
Garin, Eugenio, 256, 258
Gathering, 35, 245
"Gathering" (Zanzotto), 242–43
Genealogy, 6–7
Germany: forest management, 122–23; forests and national unity, 164, 175–77
Giants: in Vico's account of human institutions, 3–13, 245; as wild men, 65
Gilgamesh, 14–18; and Enkidu, 65; as slayer of Inanna's bull, 20
"Gipsey's Camp, The" (Clare), 217, 218
"Gipsies, The" (Wordsworth), 217
God: death of, 41, 109, 144; Descartes's, 109; in existentialism, 144. See also Deities
Golden Bough, 23
Golinelli, Paolo, 255
Gothic cathedrals, 178, 179
Great Mother goddess, 19–30
Greece, ancient: and great Mother goddess, 20; temples and forest sanctuaries, 178, 262; philosophy, 26–27; Rome compared to, 53–55
Greek tragedy, 35–36, 104

Greenhouse effect, 148, 149
Grimm, Brothers. *See* Brothers Grimm
Groves, sacred, 178
Guerard, Albert J., 261

Halperin, David, 255
Harper, Ralph, 261
Harrison, Thomas J., 263, 264
Hart, Cyril, 256
Hartman, Geoffrey, 262
Heart of Darkness (Conrad), 133–34, 136–144
Heidegger, Martin, 253, 254, 258, 261, 264–65
Helsinger, Elizabeth, 264
Heraclitus, 246
Herewald, 77, 79, 80
Heske, Franz, 122
Higounet, Charles, 255
Hippolytus, 23
Historical school of law, 166–67
Historicity: and nature in poetry, 238, 240, 242; in Wordsworth, 159–61, 163
Historiography, 164–65
Holmes, C. J., 263
Homelessness, 238, 247
Homer: and Cyclops, 10; on Dionysos, 30–31; on great Mother goddess, 21; as poetic character, 9; on Troy's destruction, 54
Homme sauvage. See Wild men
Horkheimer, Max, 259
"House in the Forest, A" (Brothers Grimm), 170
Houses: Heidegger on, 264–65; Thoreau's, 226; Usonian homes, 237, 238; Vico's giants' huts, 11, 245; Wright's, 232–34, 235, 237–38
Human age, 91–100
Humanism: on dwelling, 200; of *Encyclopédie*, 121; existentialism as, 144; and forests, 145, 147;

gion, 5; in Wright's architecture, 235; in Zanzotto's poetry, 240, 241–42, 249
"London Versus Epping Forest" (Clare), 219
Loneliness, 90
Longing, 229–30, 231
Longo, Oddone, 254
Lord Jim (Conrad), 134, 138
Loss, 231
Love, 90–91
Lowood, Henry, 122, 260
Lucus, 9–10, 11, 13, 53, 58, 182

Macbeth, 102–4
Machiavelli, 94, 97
Maenads, 31, 33–34
Mallarmé, Stéphane, 183
Manwood, John, 70–74, 100, 115, 120–21, 123–24
Marienstras, Richard, 256
"Marine" (Rimbaud), 193
Marriage. *See* Matrimony
Marsh, George, 251
Marx, Karl, 176–77
Mary, Virgin, 21
Materialism, 26–30, 183
Mathematics, 107–8, 110, 111, 122–23, 176
Matrimony: and linear time, 8; and loneliness, 90; and sexuality, 89, 91; Vico's account of, 3, 6
Matter: and chaos, 34, 61; and form, 27–28
Mazzotta, Giuseppe, 252, 256, 258
Meaning, 230
Melzer, Arthur M., 260
Memory: in external things, 186; and forests, 156; and the future, 13–14; and languange, 188; Leopardi on, 187–91
Mesopotomia: Gilgamesh epic, 14–18; great Mother goddess in, 20
Metamorphosis: in Actaeon myth, 26, 29; of cities into forests, 100, 101; and Dionysus, 32–33, 45; of knights, 67

Method, 107–14, 123
Michelet, Jules, 165, 166, 256
Middle Ages: attitudes toward forests, 61–64; forest law, 69–75; wild men in, 65
Miller, David L., 254
Miller, Tyrus, 265
Molloy (Beckett), 151–52, 198
Mor, Barbara, 253
"Mores, The" (Clare), 213–14
Morgan, Lane, 255
Moses, 62
Mother goddess. *See* Great Mother goddess
Muller, Herbert, 253
Mumford, Lewis, 258
Musil, Robert, 183–84
Mycenae, 53–54
Mythos, 26, 29

Nacquet, Vidal, 256
Nancy, Jean-Luc, 258
Natural law, 101–2, 104
Natural man, 127–28, 132
Nature: in Baudelaire, 179–81, 183; chiaroscuro of, 204–5, 206–7, 210, 211; in Constable, 209; in Descartes, 107–8; discontinuity between humanity and, 200–201; and dwelling, 209, 227–28; and history in poetry, 238, 240–41, 242; and human law, 101–2, 104; mastery of, 87, 92, 108, 118; *physis*, 27–28; returning to, 230; in Rousseau, 127–28, 129–30; as temple, 179–81, 183, 210; and transcendence, 231; in Wordsworth, 158–64. *See also* Forests
Naturpoesie, 168, 169, 173
Nausea (Sartre), 145–48
Neothermal era, 197, 198
Neptune, 9
New Forest, 75
New Science (Vico): account of human institutions, 3, 11, 245; as admonition to Enlightenment, 13; difficulties of, 251–52; on

New Science (continued)
law's relation to language, 166;
Michelet influenced by, 165; and
patriarchy, 19; poetic characters
in, 9; and Poetic Wisdom, 8
Niebuhr, Barthold, 9
Nietzsche, Friedrich: and amor fati,
40–41, 46; on death of God, 41,
109; on Dionysos, 254; on Euripides and Dionysos, 38; on
metamorphosis, 32–33; on overman, 124; theory of repression,
68; on wasteland, 149
North Africa: deforestation of,
56–57
Nostalgia, 155–95; ambivalence of,
156; of Baudelaire, 180, 186; of
Brothers Grimm, 168, 175; for
Dionysian rapture, 194; in poetry, 195
Numitor, 48
Nussbaum, Martha, 254

Oblivion, 199
"Ode to the West Wind" (Shelley),
194, 195
Odysseus, 9, 10, 54
O'Grady, Desmond, 248
"On the Mönchberg" (Trakl), 248
Orlando Furioso (Ariosto), 93–100
Otto, Walter, 30, 32, 254
Outlaws: English outlaws, 75–81;
in medieval forests, 61, 63
Overman, the, 42, 45, 124
Ovid, 24–26

Paganism, 61–62, 64
Pais, Ettore, 255
Parole, 188–89, 190
Pascal, Blaise, 109
Patriarchy, 19, 20
Pentheus, 32, 33–37
Peterborough Chronicle, 75, 76, 257
Petrarch: and humanism, 107; and
lyricism, 93, 98, 99

Petrarchism, 98, 99
Philosophy: Dante and, 84; Des-
cartes on, 112; Nietzsche as end
of, 40; origins of, 26–27; Socra-
tic, 27–38
Physis, 27–28
Piazza del Popolo (Rome), 113
Pierson, Peter, 258
Piggott, Stuart, 263
Pirandello, Luigi, 259
Placehood of place, 209, 211–12
Plato, 27, 39, 55
Pleasure principle: in Wordsworth,
159
Poetic characters, 8–9
Poetic Wisdom, 165–66
Poetry: and freedom, 220; free
verse, 192, 193; Leopardi on,
188; Naturpoesie, 168, 169, 173;
of nostalgia, 195; and religion,
239; as saving force, 238–39; as
spiritual ecology, 149; and
Wordsworth, 157
Pomona, 8
Poucet, Jacques, 254
Pound, Ezra, 150–51
Profit, 120
Projet de constitution pour la Corse
(Rousseau), 125–27
Providence, 5, 8
Provinces, 246–47
Public interest, 116, 118, 120

Rain forests, 108
Reason: critical, 12, 13, 38; in Descartes, 107; and Enlightenment,
114; in existentialism, 144
Redemption, 86, 87
Religion: and catacombs, 239; forests consecrated by, 115, 116;
and linear time, 8; Vico's account of, 3, 5–6. See also Christianity
Remus, 48, 49
Renaud de Montaubon, 61

Restoration: in Brothers Grimm,
173–75
Restraint: European lack of, 260;
and forms, 34; as primordial virtue, 137
Reynolds, Graham, 202, 205, 263
Rhea Silvia, 48
"Rhyme of King William, The," 76
Riehl, Wilhelm H., 176
Rights of man, 259
Rimbaud, Arthur, 193–94, 195
Robin Hood, 77, 79–80
Romanticism: historiography, 164–
65; in Wordsworth, 163–64,
217–18
Rome, 46–52; Alexander VII's
transformation of, 113; Greece
compared to, 53–55; and mod-
ern Europe compared by Con-
rad, 142–43; reclaimed by for-
ests, 13; Romulus's founding of,
9; sylvan origin of, 1–2
Romulus: in founding of Rome,
47–48, 49; as poetic character, 9
Rosenthal, Michael, 263
Rousseau, Jean-Jacques, 125–33;
and nostalgia, 155, 156; and
Wordsworth, 156, 157, 158, 161
Royal hunting privilege, 69, 72, 74–
75
Russell, William, 251

Sacred groves, 178
Saint-Amand, Pierre, 260
Sartre, Jean-Paul, 144–48
Saturn, 50–51
Savigny, Friedrich Karl von, 166,
167, 262
Schürmann, Reiner, 262
Science, 10–11, 259–60
Scott, Robert, 253
Scully, Vincent, 253, 262
Segal, Charles, 255
Serres, Michel, 111, 254, 258, 259
Sexuality, 89–90
Shadow of the law: in *Divine*

Comedy, 81, 87; and law, 63; in
Macbeth, 105; outlaws in, 77,
79–80, 81
Shaffer, Aaron, 252
Sharpe, William, 262
Sheehan, Thomas, 259
Shelley, Percy, 194, 195
Shelter, 234, 235
Short, Charles, 253, 256
Signs: divination of, 6; in forests,
241; Jove's use of, 5
Sjöö, Monica, 253
Sky: in Constable's paintings, 203–
4; forests' concealment of, 6; and
great Mother goddess, 19; and
science, 11; and technology, 10;
Vico's giants' awareness of, 4
Slavin, Arthur, 54
Snell, Bruno, 255
Socrates, 27, 38–40
Spariosu, Mihai, 254
Spink, John Stephenson, 260
Spotted owl, 124
Starobinski, Jean, 260
Stewart, Susan, 261
Study of the Trunk of an Elm Tree
(Constable), 202–8, 210–11
Sublime, the, 180–81
Superman (Nietzsche). *See* Over-
man, the
Sylvanus, 49
Sylvian family, 47–48
Sylvius, 47
Symbolism of forests, 177–86
Symposium (Plato), 39–40

Tacitus, 2, 177–78
Tagliacozzo, Giorgio, 252
Taylor, Basil, 263
Technology, 10
Temples, 178–80, 210, 262
Thirgood, J. V., 255, 258
Thomas, Dylan, 29, 254
Thomas, Keith, 258
Thompson, E. P., 256

Winkler, John J., 254
Wolf, Friedrich August, 9
Wordsworth, William, 156–64,
    195, 209, 217–18
"World Is Too Much with Us,
    The" (Wordsworth), 159–60,
    161–62, 163
Wright, Frank Lloyd, 232

Yahweh, 19
Ygrain (Chrétien de Troyes), 65–68
Young Törless (Musil), 183–86

Zanzotto, Andrea, 239–43, 248–49
Zarathustra, 40–46
Zeus, 5
Zipes, Jack, 167–68, 262

[ILLUSTRATION CREDITS]

Antonio Vaccaro, engraving of God, Metaphysics, and Homer, from the frontispiece to *The New Science of Giambattista Vico*.

Artemis of Ephesus (ca. second century A.D.). Selcuk Museum, Ephesus, Turkey. Photo: © E. Birch, SPECTRUM COLOUR LIBRARY.

William Blake, *Dante and Virgil Penetrating the Forest*. Courtesy of the Department of Rare Books, Cornell University Library.

Woodpile, Karlstejn, Czechoslovakia, © Michael Kenna 1989.

Caspar David Friedrich, *Winter Landscape with Church* (1811). Courtesy of the Museum für Kunst und Kulturgeschichte der Stadt Dortmund, Germany.

John Constable, *Trees at Hampstead: The Path to Church*. By courtesy of the Board of Trustees of the Victoria & Albert Museum. (Neg. no. Q1751).

John Constable, *Study of the Trunk of an Elm Tree*. By courtesy of the Board of Trustees of the Victoria & Albert Museum. (Neg. no. GD3514).

Frank Lloyd Wright, *Fallingwater*. Photo by Christopher Little.